Computing Essentials

Making IT work for you

INTRODUCTORY 2015

• The O'Leary Series

Computing Concepts

- *Computing Essentials 2013* Introductory & Complete Editions
- *Computing Essentials 2014* Introductory & Complete Editions
- *Computing Essentials 2015* Introductory & Complete Editions

Microsoft Office Applications

- *Microsoft® Office 2010: A Case Approach*
- *Microsoft® Office Word 2010: A Case Approach* Introductory & Complete Editions
- *Microsoft® Office Excel 2010: A Case Approach* Introductory & Complete Editions
- *Microsoft® Office Access 2010: A Case Approach* Introductory & Complete Editions
- *Microsoft® Office PowerPoint 2010: A Case Approach* Introductory & Complete Editions
- *Microsoft® Windows 7: A Case Approach*
- *Microsoft® Office 2013: A Case Approach*
- *Microsoft® Office Word 2013: A Case Approach* Introductory Edition
- *Microsoft® Office Excel 2013: A Case Approach* Introductory Edition
- *Microsoft® Office Access 2013: A Case Approach* Introductory Edition
- *Microsoft® Office PowerPoint 2013: A Case Approach* Introductory Edition

Computing Essentials

Making IT work for you

INTRODUCTORY 2015

Timothy J. O'Leary
Professor Emeritus
Arizona State University

Linda I. O'Leary

Daniel A. O'Leary
PhD Candidate
University of California at Santa Cruz

Mc
Graw
Hill
Education

COMPUTING ESSENTIALS 2015 INTRODUCTORY EDITION
Published by McGraw-Hill Education, 2 Penn Plaza, New York, NY 10121. Copyright © 2015 by McGraw-Hill Education. All rights reserved. Printed in the United States of America. No part of this publication may be reproduced or distributed in any form or by any means, or stored in a database or retrieval system, without the prior written consent of McGraw-Hill Education, including, but not limited to, in any network or other electronic storage or transmission, or broadcast for distance learning.

Some ancillaries, including electronic and print components, may not be available to customers outside the United States.

This book is printed on acid-free paper.

1 2 3 4 5 6 7 8 9 0 RMN/RMN 1 0 9 8 7 6 5 4

ISBN   978-1-259-22315-0
MHID   1-259-22315-9
ISSN   2159-6336

Senior Vice President, Products & Markets: *Kurt L. Strand*
Vice President, Content Production & Technology Services: *Kimberly Meriwether David*
Director: *Scott Davidson*
Senior Brand Manager: *Wyatt Morris*
Executive Director of Development: *Ann Torbert*
Development Editor II: *Alan Palmer*
Digital Development Editor II: *Kevin White*
Senior Marketing Manager: *Tiffany Russell*
Director, Content Production: *Terri Schiesl*
Content Project Manager: *Brent dela Cruz*
Senior Buyer: *Michael R. McCormick*
Design: *Srdjan Savanovic*
Cover Image: © *Alex White/Veer*
Senior Content Licensing Specialist: *Jeremy Cheshareck*
Typeface: *10/12 Palatino*
Compositor: *Laserwords Private Limited*
Printer: *R. R. Donnelley*

All credits appearing on page or at the end of the book are considered to be an extension of the copyright page.

www.mhhe.com

Dedication

We dedicate this edition to Nicole and Katie—our inspiration.

Brief Contents

Contents

PRIVACY, SECURITY, AND ETHICS *222*

New to Computing Essentials 2015

Every chapter's "Why should I read this chapter" has been dramatically revised to engage students. Every Making IT Work for You, Ethics, and Environment has been carefully revaluated, enhanced, and/or replaced and new Privacy information has been added to each chapter. Additionally, this in-chapter content has been carefully coordinated with an end-of-chapter section titled Discussion that provides thought-provoking questions designed for in-class discussion or homework assignments. More specific new coverage includes the following.

Chapter 1   Revision of the traditional five-part information system to include the Internet
             Expanded coverage of Windows 8, Office 2013, and mobile devices including smartphones
             New coverage of technology's potential impact on privacy

Chapter 2   Expanded coverage of Web 3.0 and social networking
             Revised Making IT Work for You: Online Entertainment
             New privacy discussion related to social networking and privacy controls within Facebook

Chapter 3   Expanded coverage of Office 2013, specialized applications, and apps
             New privacy discussion related to the ability of some mobile phone apps to track a smartphone's precise location without the owner's knowledge

Chapter 4   Expanded coverage of Microsoft's Windows 8, Windows 8 utilities, and Apple's operating systems including OS X Mavericks
             Revised Making IT Work for You: Windows Task Manager for Windows 8
             New privacy discussion relating to protecting sensitive information on a lost or stolen smartphone

Chapter 5   Expanded coverage of ultrabooks, mini tablets, and Thunderbolt
             New section of mobile devices including expanded coverage of smartphones
             New privacy discussion on cryptoprocessors, a specialty processor devoted exclusively to protecting your privacy

Chapter 6   New coverage of 3-D printers, UPC codes, MaxiCode, and QR codes
             Expanded coverage of display resolutions, touch-sensitive displays, flat-panel monitors, and ergonomic issues specifically related to portable computers including tablets and smartphones

Chapter 7   New coverage of hybrid solid-state storage systems and cloud storage issues related to maintenance, hardware upgrades, file-sharing collaboration, access speed, and file security
             Revision of Making IT Work for You: Cloud Storage
             New privacy discussion of how to securely remove sensitive information from the hard disk before selling or recycling a computer

Chapter 8   Expanded coverage of 4G networks
             New coverage on fiber-optic connection services
             New privacy discussion about relentless attacks on government and private networks to gain unauthorized access and the resulting risk to sensitive personal information

Chapter 9   Expanded coverage of social networking risks including "tagging" by friends without an individual's knowledge or consent
             New content on identity theft, data collection at social networking sites, big data, and the unauthorized creation of detailed personal profiles

The 20th century brought us the dawn of the digital information age and unprecedented changes in information technology. In fact, the rate of change is clearly increasing. As we begin the 21st century, computer literacy is undoubtedly becoming a prerequisite in whatever career you choose.

The goal of *Computing Essentials* is to provide you with the basis for understanding the concepts necessary for success. *Computing Essentials* also endeavors to instill an appreciation for the effect of information technology on people, privacy, ethics, and our environment and to give you a basis for building the necessary skill set to succeed in the 21st century.

Times are changing, technology is changing, and this text is changing too. As students of today, you are different from those of yesterday. You put much effort toward the things that interest you and the things that are relevant to you. Your efforts directed at learning application programs and exploring the web seem, at times, limitless. On the other hand, it is sometimes difficult to engage in other equally important topics such as personal privacy and technological advances.

At the beginning of each chapter, we carefully layout why and how the chapter's content is relevant to your life today and critical to your future. Within each chapter, we present practical tips related to key concepts through the demonstration of interesting applications that are relevant to your lives. Topics presented focus first on outputs rather than processes. Then, we discuss the concepts and processes.

Motivation and relevance are the keys. This text has several features specifically designed to engage and demonstrate the relevance of technology in your lives. These elements are combined with a thorough coverage of the concepts and sound pedagogical devices.

Visual Learning

VISUAL CHAPTER OPENERS

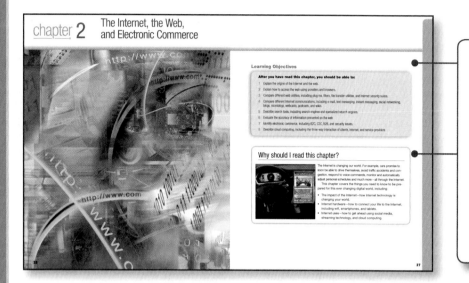

Each chapter begins with a list of chapter learning objectives and provides a brief introduction to what will be covered in the chapter. Additionally, the newly revised Why Should I Read This? feature presents a visually engaging and concise presentation of the chapter's relevance to the reader's current and future life in the digital world.

VISUAL SUMMARIES

Visual summaries appear at the end of every chapter and summarize major concepts covered throughout the chapter. Like the chapter openers, these summaries use graphics to reinforce key concepts in an engaging and meaningful way.

MAKING IT WORK FOR YOU

Special-interest topics are presented in the Making IT Work for You section found within nearly every chapter. These topics include Installing a Free Antivirus Program, Online Entertainment, Google Docs, Skype, and Cloud Storage.

Reinforcing Key Concepts

CONCEPT CHECKS

Located at points throughout each chapter, the Concept Check cues you to note which topics have been covered and to self-test your understanding of the material presented.

☑ **concept check**

Define data. List four common types of files.

Define connectivity and the wireless revolution.

What is a network? Describe the Internet, web, and cloud computing.

KEY TERMS

KEY TERMS

Throughout the text, the most important terms are presented in bold and are defined within the text. You will also find a list of key terms at the end of each chapter and in the glossary at the end of the book.

3-D printers (152)
active display area (148)
additive manufacturing (152)
aspect ratio (148)
bar code (144)
bar code reader (144)
bar code scanner (144)
Bluetooth (153)
card reader (144)
carpal tunnel syndrome (158)
cathode-ray tube (CRT) (150)
clarity (147)
cloud printer (153)
combination key (141)
contrast ratio (148)
cordless mouse (142)
dance pad (143)
digital camera (146)
digital whiteboard (150)
display screen (147)
dot pitch (148)
dots per inch (dpi) (151)
duplex printing (152)
e-book reader (148)
e-books (148)
e-ink (148)
e-reader (148)
electronic books (148)
ergonomics (157)
flat-panel monitor (148)
flatbed scanner (144)
game controller (142)
gamepads (143)
gloves (157)
Google Cloud Print (153)
grayscale (151)
handwriting recognition software (143)
hard copy (151)

headgear (157)
headsets (153)
high-definition television (HDTV) (150)
immersive experience (157)
inkjet printer (152)
input (140)
input device (140)
interactive whiteboard (150)
Internet telephone (154)
Internet telephony (154)
joystick (143)
keyboard (140)
laptop keyboard (141)
laser printer (152)
light-emitting diode (LED) (148)
liquid crystal display (LCD) (148)
magnetic card reader (144)
magnetic-ink character recognition (MICR) (145)
MaxiCode (145)
monitor (147)
motion-sensing device (143)
mouse (142)
mouse pointer (142)
multifunctional device (MFD) (154)
multitouch screen (142)
optical-character recognition (OCR) (145)
optical-mark recognition (OMR) (145)
optical mouse (142)
optical scanner (144)
output (147)
output device (147)
personal laser printer (152)

picture element (147)
pixel (147)
pixel pitch (148)
platform scanner (144)
plotter (153)
pointing device (142)
portable scanner (144)
printer (151)
QR codes (145)
repetitive strain injury (RSI) (158)
resolution (147)
RFID reader (145)
RFID (radio-frequency identification) tag (145)
scanner (144)
scanning devices (144)
shared laser printer (152)
Skype (154)
soft copy (147)
speakers (153)
stylus (143)
technical writer (159)
telephony (154)
thermal printer (153)
thumb keyboard (141)
toggle key (141)
touch pad (142)
touch screen (142)
traditional keyboard (141)
Universal Product Code (UPC) (145)
virtual keyboard (141)
virtual reality (VR) (157)
voice over IP (VoIP) (154)
voice recognition system (146)
wand reader (144)
webcam (146)
wheel button (142)
wireless mouse (142)

CHAPTER REVIEW

Following the Visual Summary, the chapter review includes material designed to review and reinforce chapter content. It includes a key terms list that reiterates the terms presented in the chapter, multiple-choice questions to help test your understanding of information presented in the chapter, matching exercises to test your recall of terminology presented in the chapter, and open-ended questions or statements to help review your understanding of the key concepts presented in the chapter.

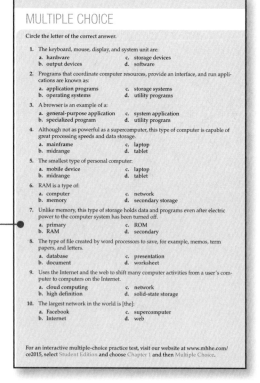

MULTIPLE CHOICE

Circle the letter of the correct answer.

1. The keyboard, mouse, display, and system unit are:
   a. hardware
   b. output devices
   c. storage devices
   d. software

2. Programs that coordinate computer resources, provide an interface, and run applications are known as:
   a. application programs
   b. operating systems
   c. storage systems
   d. utility programs

3. A browser is an example of a:
   a. general-purpose application
   b. specialized program
   c. system application
   d. utility program

4. Although not as powerful as a supercomputer, this type of computer is capable of great processing speeds and data storage.
   a. mainframe
   b. midrange
   c. laptop
   d. tablet

5. The smallest type of personal computer:
   a. mobile device
   b. midrange
   c. laptop
   d. tablet

6. RAM is a type of:
   a. computer
   b. memory
   c. network
   d. secondary storage

7. Unlike memory, this type of storage holds data and programs even after electric power to the computer system has been turned off.
   a. primary
   b. RAM
   c. ROM
   d. secondary

8. The type of file created by word processors to save, for example, memos, term papers, and letters.
   a. database
   b. document
   c. presentation
   d. worksheet

9. Uses the Internet and the web to shift many computer activities from a user's computer to computers on the Internet.
   a. cloud computing
   b. high definition
   c. network
   d. solid-state storage

10. The largest network in the world is [the]:
    a. Facebook
    b. Internet
    c. supercomputer
    d. web

For an interactive multiple-choice practice test, visit our website at www.mhhe.com/ce2015, select Student Edition and choose Chapter 1 and then Multiple Choice.

CAREERS IN IT

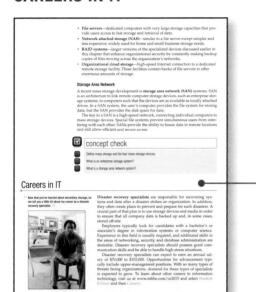

Some of the fastest-growing career opportunities are in information technology. Each chapter highlights one of the most promising careers in IT by presenting job titles, responsibilities, educational requirements, and salary ranges. Among the careers covered are webmaster, software engineer, and database administrator. You will learn how the material you are studying relates directly to a potential career path.

A LOOK TO THE FUTURE

Each chapter concludes with a brief discussion of a recent technological advancement related to the chapter material, reinforcing the importance of staying informed.

Unique End-of-Chapter Discussion Materials

MAKING IT WORK FOR YOU

Making IT Work for You discussion questions are carefully integrated with the chapter's Making IT Work for You topics. The questions facilitate in-class discussion or written assignments focusing on applying specific technologies into a student's day-to-day life. They are designed to expand a student's awareness of technology applications.

PRIVACY

Privacy discussion questions are carefully integrated with the chapter's marginal Privacy box. The questions facilitate in-class discussion or written assignments focusing on critical privacy issues. They are designed to develop a student's ability to think critically and communicate effectively.

DISCUSSION

Respond to each of the following questions.

1 Making IT Work for You: ONLINE ENTERTAINMENT

Are you one of the millions of people who regularly use streaming technology to watch favorite television programs, movies, and other video content? Review the Making IT Work for You: Online Entertainment on pages xx and xx and then respond to the following: (a) Do you currently have a subscription to Netflix, Hulu Plus, or another service that allows you to stream movies and TV shows? If so, which ones? If not, do you plan on using one in the future? Why or why not? (b) Name at least three TV shows that you currently watch or are interested in watching. Next, list a few services that include these shows as part of a subscription. If none does, list a few online stores where you can purchase and stream these episodes. (c) What device do you use most often to watch video content from the web? Would you consider purchasing a dedicated streaming device such as the Roku? Why or why not? (d) Could ever see yourself canceling or "cutting the cord" from your current cable or satellite service? Why or why not?

2 Privacy: Social Networking

When a Facebook friend posts a picture, video, or text that includes you, who can view that post? Review the Privacy box on page XX and respond to the following: (a) When it comes to protecting privacy on social networking sites, who should be responsible? Should the social networking site be responsible for making sure that people don't accidentally share private information? What about the responsibility of the user who posts the information—or the user who's privacy is damaged? (b) Do you think that most people are aware of their privacy settings on Facebook? Why or why not? Have you ever checked your settings? Why or why not? (c) Investigate the default security settings for a social networking website such as Facebook or Google+. In what ways do the default settings protect a new user from accidentally sharing private information and in what ways is a new user at risk? List a few example.

3 Ethics: FILTERING AND MONITORING

Parents can use content filters and monitoring software to restrict or monitor their child's Internet behavior. Review the Ethics box on page xx and respond to the following: (a) Is it ethical for parents to filter Internet content that they deem to be unsafe or inappropriate for their children? Does your answer depend on the age of the child? Defend your position. (b) Is it ethical for parents to monitor the Internet activity of their children? What if the monitoring software captures more than just web pages? What if it records instant messages, incoming e-mail, and even passwords? Explain your position. (c) Should parents inform their children that Internet activity is being filtered or monitored? Why or why not? (d) Do you feel that filtering or monitoring software is the best way to protect children? Do you feel that it hurts the trust between a parent and child? In your responses, be sure to include your opinion as to whether or not you would ever use such software.

DISCUSSION

Respond to each of the following questions.

1 Making IT Work for You: WINDOWS TASK MANAGER

Have you ever been working with a program when it simply stopped working and would not respond to you? Review the Making IT Work for You: Windows Task Manager on pages xxx and xxx and open Task Manager using a Windows-based computer. Then respond to the following: (a) List the top three processes in terms of memory usage. (b) List three processes that are using your CPU, even if it is only for a second or two as you look at that dialog box. (c) Find one process that you do not recognize. Using your favorite search engine, determine what the process does. Write down the name of the process, its description or purpose, and the URL of the website you used to research it.

2 Privacy: OPERATING SYSTEM SECURITY

Did you know that your computer or mobile device can provide others access to your personal information? Review the Privacy box on page xxx and respond to the following: (a) Have you ever lost a personal computer or mobile device? If so, what personal information was stored on it? If not, what personal information is stored on your current computer and/or mobile device? (b) Are you doing anything now that would make it difficult for someone to access personal information from your computing devices? If you are, discuss what that you are doing. If not, what could/should you be doing? Be specific. (c) Investigate the privacy setting on your devices and describe them. (d) Do you think computer manufacturers have a responsibility to provide better security and privacy features? Why or why not.

3 Ethics: VIRUS PROTECTION SCAMS

Everyone should be concerned about viruses infecting computer systems. Some report that this fear is being used to manipulate users into purchasing new or upgraded antivirus programs. Some even report specific antivirus scams. Review the Ethics box on page xxx and then respond to the following: (a) Have you ever been offered a free virus alert program? If so, describe the offer and whether you accepted the offer. (b) Almost all legitimate antivirus software manufacturers issue new virus alerts. Do you think these alerts are motivated by greed or by good consumer service? Why or why not? (c) Is this an ethical issue for antivirus software manufacturers? If so, create some ethical guidelines for antivirus software manufacturers to follow when issuing virus alerts. (d) What can users do to protect themselves against antivirus scams and against unethical manufacturers of antivirus programs? Be specific and defend your suggestions.

4 Environment: OS POWER MANAGEMENT

Did you know that some operating systems help protect the environment? Review the Environment box on page xx and then respond to the following: (a) In what ways do operating systems help the environment? (b) Do you leave your desktop or laptop computer on all day? Do you use sleep or hibernate modes? Explain the reasons behind your decision. (c) Find the power management options for your operating system. List a few options that you would consider adjusting in order to reduce your computer's energy consumption.

ETHICS

Ethics discussion questions are carefully integrated with the chapter's marginal Ethics boxes. The questions facilitate in-class discussion or written assignments focusing on ethical issues relating to technology. They are designed to develop a student's ability to think critically and communicate effectively.

ENVIRONMENT

Environment discussion questions are carefully integrated with the chapter's marginal Environment boxes. The questions facilitate in-class discussion or written assignments focusing on environmental issues relating to technology. They are designed to develop a student's ability to think critically and communicate effectively.

The Instructor's Manual offers lecture outlines with teaching notes and figure references. It provides definitions of key terms and solutions to the end-of-chapter material, including multiple-choice, matching, and open-ended questions.

The PowerPoint slides are designed to provide instructors with a comprehensive resource for lecture use. The slides include a review of key terms and topics, as well as artwork taken from the text to further explain concepts covered in each chapter.

The testbank contains over 2,200 questions categorized by level of learning (definition, concept, and application). This is the same learning scheme that is introduced in the text to provide a valuable testing and reinforcement tool. Text page references have been provided for all questions, including a level-of-difficulty rating. The testbank is offered in Word files, as well as in EZ Test format.

The instructor support materials can be downloaded at www.mhhe.com/ce2015

Students can access materials by going to www.mhhe.com/ce2015 and selecting **Student Edition.** Students can find a host of additional resources on the website, including animations of key concepts and in-depth coverage of select topics.

O'LEARY SERIES

The O'Leary Application Series for Microsoft® Office is available separately or packaged with *Computing Essentials*. The O'Leary Application Series offers a step-by-step case approach to learning computer applications.

SIMNET ONLINE TRAINING AND ASSESSMENT FOR OFFICE APPLICATIONS

SIMnet™ Online provides a way for you to test students' software skills in a simulated environment. SIMnet provides flexibility for you in your applications course by offering:

- Pretesting options
- Posttesting options
- Course placement testing
- Diagnostic capabilities to reinforce skills
- Web delivery of tests
- Learning verification reports

For more information on skills assessment software, please contact your local sales representative, or visit us at www.simnetkeepitsimple.com.

A special thank-you goes to the professors who took time out of their busy schedules to provide us with the feedback necessary to develop the 2015 edition of this text. The following professors offered valuable suggestions on revising the text:

Kurt Kominek
Northeast State Community College

Bernice Eng
Brookdale Community College

Mary Ann Zlotow
College of DuPage

Ronald Conway
Bowling Green State University

Hyo Joo Han
Georgia Southern University

Natalie Cooper
Madisonville Community College

Mark Jackson
Columbus State Community College

Candice Spangler
Columbus State Community College

Terri Holly
Indian River State College

Michael DeMaio
Brookdale Community College

Colin Gabriel Onita
University of Akron

Paulette Comet
Community College of Baltimore County

Diane Stark
Phoenix College

Terry Rigsby
Hill College

Lindsey Moore
Wiregrass Georgia Technical College

Paul Yaroslaski
Dodge City Community College

Laurence Hitterdale
Glendale Community College

Jean Insinga
Antonelli College

Cynthia Rumney
Middle Georgia Technical College

Lana LaBruyere
Mineral Area College

Diane Smith
Henry Ford Community College

Sandra Tavegia
The Community College of Baltimore County

Tahir Aziz
Long Beach City College

David Trimble
Park University at Fort Bliss

Brenda Nickel
Moraine Park Technical College

Gene Cabonaro
Long Beach City College

Russell Dulaney
Rasmussen College

Our sincere thanks also go to Laurie Zouharis at Suffolk College for revising probes for LearnSmart; to Brenda Nielsen at Mesa Community College for revising the Instructor's Manual, and online quizzes; to Rose Marie Kuebbing for revising the testbank; and to Rachelle Hall at Glendale Community College for revising the PowerPoint presentations to accompany this text.

About the Authors

Tim and Linda O'Leary live in the American Southwest and spend much of their time engaging instructors and students in conversation about learning. In fact, they have been talking about learning for over 25 years. Something in those early conversations convinced them to write a book, to bring their interest in the learning process to the printed page. Now, they are joined by their son Dan O'Leary as a coauthor. Dan is completing his PhD in Electrical Engineering with significant experience in teaching and consulting in information technology.

The O'Leary's form a unique team blending experience and youth. Tim has taught courses at Stark Technical College in Canton, Ohio, and at Rochester Institute of Technology in upstate New York, and is currently a professor emeritus at Arizona State University. Linda offered her expertise at ASU for several years as an academic advisor. She also presented and developed materials for major corporations such as Motorola, Intel, Honeywell, and AT&T, as well as various community colleges in the Phoenix area. Dan has taught at the University of California at Santa Cruz, developed energy-related labs at NASA, and worked as a database administrator and as a consultant in information systems.

Tim, Linda, and Dan have talked to and taught numerous students, all of them with a desire to learn something about computers and applications that make their lives easier, more interesting, and more productive.

Each new edition of an O'Leary text, supplement, or learning aid has benefited from these students and their instructors who daily stand in front of them (or over their shoulders).

Computing Essentials

Making IT work for you

INTRODUCTORY 2015

chapter 1

Information Technology, the Internet, and You

Learning Objectives

After you have read this chapter, you should be able to:

1   Explain the parts of an information system: people, procedures, software, hardware, data, and the Internet.

2   Distinguish between system software and application software.

3   Differentiate between the three kinds of system software programs.

4   Define and compare general-purpose, specialized, and mobile applications.

5   Identify the four types of computers and the four types of personal computers.

6   Describe the different types of computer hardware, including the system unit, input, output, storage, and communication devices.

7   Define data and describe document, worksheet, database, and presentation files.

8   Explain computer connectivity, the wireless revolution, the Internet, and cloud computing.

Why should I read this chapter?

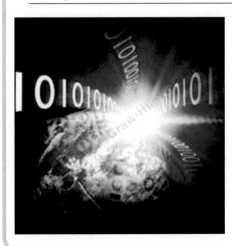

The future of computers and digital technology promises exciting challenges and opportunities. Powerful software and hardware systems are changing the way people and organizations interact in their daily life and on the Internet.

This chapter introduces you to the skills and concepts you need to be prepared for this ever changing digital world, including:

- Information systems—how the critical parts of technology interact.
- Efficiency and effectiveness—how to maximize the use of technology.
- Privacy, ethics, and environment—how to integrate technology with people.
- Connectivity and cloud computing—how the Internet, web, and the wireless revolution are changing how we communicate and interact.

Introduction

Welcome to Computing Essentials. I'm Alan and I work in information technology. On the following pages, we'll be discussing some of the most exciting new developments in computer technology including smartphones, tablet computers, and cloud computing. Let me begin in this chapter by giving you an overview of the book and showing you some of its special features.

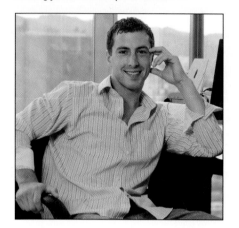

The purpose of this book is to help you become a highly efficient and effective computer user. This includes how to use (1) apps and application software; (2) all types of computer hardware including mobile devices like smartphones, tablets, and laptops; and (3) the Internet. Becoming a highly efficient and effective computer user also requires a full understanding of the potential impact of technology on privacy and the environment as well as the role of personal and organizational ethics.

In this chapter, we present an overview of an information system: people, procedures, software, hardware, data, and the Internet. It is essential to understand these basic parts and how connectivity through the Internet and the web expands the role of information technology in our lives. Later, we describe these parts of an information system in detail.

Not all that long ago, most people had little to do with computers, at least directly. Of course, they filled out computerized forms, took computerized tests, and paid computerized bills. But the real work was handled by specialists. Then personal computers came along and changed everything. Today it is easy for nearly everybody to use a computer.

- Personal computers are common tools in all areas of life. Writers write, artists draw, engineers and scientists calculate—all on personal computers. Students and businesspeople do all this and more.

- New forms of learning have developed. People who are homebound, who work odd hours, or who travel frequently may take online courses. A college course need not fit within a quarter or a semester.

- Computers offer new ways to communicate, to find people with similar interests, and to buy goods. People use electronic mail, electronic commerce, and the Internet to meet and to share ideas and products.

To effectively and efficiently use computers, you need to know the parts of an information system: people, procedures, software, hardware, data, and the Internet. You also need to understand the wireless revolution, the mobile Internet, and the web and to recognize the role of information technology in your personal and professional life.

Information Systems

When you think of a personal computer, perhaps you think of just the equipment itself. That is, you think of the screen or the keyboard. Yet, there is more to it than that. The way to think about a personal computer is as part of an information system. An **information system** has several parts: *people, procedures, software, hardware, data,* and *the Internet.* (See Figure 1-1.)

- **People:** It is easy to overlook people as one of the parts of an information system. Yet this is what personal computers are all about—making **people, end users** like you, more productive.

- **Procedures:** The rules or guidelines for people to follow when using software, hardware, and data are **procedures.** These procedures are typically documented in manuals written by computer specialists. Software and hardware manufacturers provide manuals with their products. These manuals are provided in either printed or electronic form.

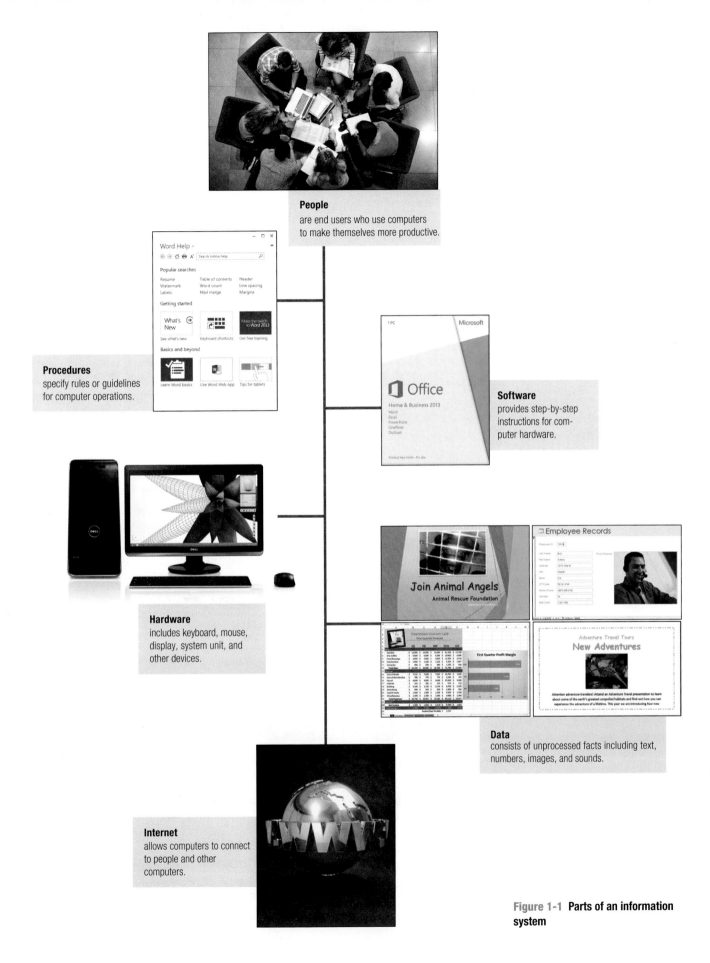

People
are end users who use computers to make themselves more productive.

Procedures
specify rules or guidelines for computer operations.

Software
provides step-by-step instructions for computer hardware.

Hardware
includes keyboard, mouse, display, system unit, and other devices.

Data
consists of unprocessed facts including text, numbers, images, and sounds.

Internet
allows computers to connect to people and other computers.

Figure 1-1 **Parts of an information system**

- **Software:** A **program** consists of the step-by-step instructions that tell the computer how to do its work. **Software** is another name for a program or programs. The purpose of software is to convert **data** (unprocessed facts) into **information** (processed facts). For example, a payroll program would instruct the computer to take the number of hours you worked in a week (data) and multiply it by your pay rate (data) to determine how much you are paid for the week (information).
- **Hardware:** The equipment that processes the data to create information is called **hardware.** It includes the keyboard, mouse, display, system unit, and other devices. Hardware is controlled by software.
- **Data:** The raw, unprocessed facts, including text, numbers, images, and sounds, are called data. Processed data yields information. Using the previous example of a payroll program, the data (number of hours worked and pay rate) is processed (multiplied) to yield information (weekly pay).
- **Internet:** Almost all information systems provide a way to connect to other people and computers typically using the Internet. This **connectivity** greatly expands the capability and usefulness of information systems.

concept check

What are the parts of an information system?

What is a program?

What is the difference between data and information?

People

People are surely the most important part of any information system. Our lives are touched every day by computers and information systems. Many times the contact is direct and obvious, such as when we create documents using a word processing program or when we connect to the Internet. (See Figure 1-2.) Other times, the contact is not as obvious.

Throughout this book you will find a variety of features designed to help you become an efficient and effective end user. These features include Making IT Work for You, Privacy, Environment, Ethics, Tips, Careers in IT, and the Computing Essentials website.

- **Making IT Work for You.** Throughout this

Figure 1-2 **People and computers**

Application	Description
Free Antivirus Program	Protect your computer by installing and using a free antivirus program. See page 10.
Online Entertainment	Use your computer to watch your favorite television programs, movies, and other video content. See page 30.
Google Docs	Create, collaborate, and access documents from almost anywhere with a free online office suite. See page 77.
SKYPE	Visit face to face with friends and family located almost anywhere at little or no cost. See page 155.
Cloud Storage	Send large files using a free tool and the cloud. See page 181.

To see additional applications, visit our website at www.mhhe.com/ce2015 and select Student Edition and then Making IT Work.

Figure 1-3 Making IT Work for You applications

book you will find Making IT Work for You features that present numerous interesting and practical IT applications. For just a few of the Making IT Work for You topics, see Figure 1-3. For a complete list, visit our website at www.mhhe.com/ce2015.

- **Tips.** We all can benefit from a few tips or suggestions. Throughout this book you will find numerous tips to make your computing safer, more efficient, and more effective. These tips range from the basics of keeping your computer system running smoothly to how to protect your privacy while surfing the web. For a partial list of the tips presented in the following chapters, see Figure 1-4. For a complete list, visit our website at www.mhhe.com/ce2015 and select Student Edition and then Tips.

Are you getting the most out of your computer? Here are just a few of the tips to make your computing safer, more efficient, and more effective.

1. **Low battery.** Do you find that your laptop's battery keeps its charge for less time than it used to? Here some ways to make your battery last longer. See page 126.

2. **Language translation.** Have you had trouble communicating with someone who does not speak English? If so, Google Translate may be just what you need. See page 147.

3. **Lost files.** Have you ever accidentally deleted or lost important files from your flash drive? Here are a few suggestions that might help. See page 179.

4. **Computer security.** With so many security threats out there, do you know how to protect your computer? Some steps to help protect your computer are on page xxx.

5. **Wireless networks.** Do you use your laptop to connect to wireless networks at school, coffee shops, airports, or hotels? If so, it is important to use caution to protect your computer and your privacy. A few suggestions are on page xxx.

To see additional tips, visit our website at www.mhhe.com/ce2015 and select Student Edition and then Tips.

Figure 1-4 Selected tips

- **Privacy.** One of the most critical issues today is how to protect the privacy of our personal information. Throughout this book you will find Privacy boxes in the margin that present information about protecting our privacy.

- **Environment.** Today it is more important than ever that we be aware of our impact on the environment. In this chapter and the following ones, you will find Environment boxes in the margin that present important relevant environmental information.

- **Ethics.** Most people agree that we should behave ethically. That is, we should follow a system of moral principles that direct our everyday lives. However, for any given circumstance, people often do not agree on the ethics of the situation. Throughout this book you will find numerous Ethics boxes posing a variety of different ethical/unethical situations for your consideration.

- **Careers in IT.** One of the most important decisions of your life is to decide upon your life's work or career. Perhaps you are planning to be a writer, an artist, or an engineer. Or you might become a professional in **information technology (IT)**. Each of the following chapters highlights a specific career in information technology. This feature provides job descriptions, projected employment demands, educational requirements, current salary ranges, and advancement opportunities.

- **Computing Essentials Website.** Throughout the text you will find numerous text references to the Computing Essentials website at www.mhhe.com/ce2015. This site is carefully integrated with the textbook. At the site, you'll find animations, career information, tips, test review materials, and much more.

concept check

 Which part of an information system is the most important?

 Describe the Making IT Work for You, Tips, Privacy, and Environment features.

 Describe the Ethics, the Careers in IT, and the Computing Essentials website features.

Software

Software, as we mentioned, is another name for programs. Programs are the instructions that tell the computer how to process data into the form you want. In most cases, the words *software* and *programs* are interchangeable. There are two major kinds of software: *system software* and *application software*. You can think of application software as the kind you use. Think of system software as the kind the computer uses.

System Software

The user interacts primarily with application software. **System software** enables the application software to interact with the computer hardware. System software is "background" software that helps the computer manage its own internal resources.

System software is not a single program. Rather it is a collection of programs, including the following:

- **Operating systems** are programs that coordinate computer resources, provide an interface between users and the computer, and run applications. Microsoft's Windows 8 and Apple's Mac OS X are two of the best-known operating systems for today's personal computer users. (See Figures 1-5 and 1-6.)
- **Utilities** perform specific tasks related to managing computer resources. One of the most essential utility programs that every computer system should have is an antivirus program. These programs protect your computer system from **viruses** or malicious programs that are all too often deposited onto your computer from the Internet. These programs can damage software and hardware, as well as compromise the security and privacy of your personal data. If your computer does not have an antivirus program installed on it, you need to get one. To see how you can install a free antivirus program on your computer, see Making IT Work for You: Free Antivirus Program on page 10.
- **Device drivers** are specialized programs designed to allow particular input or output devices to communicate with the rest of the computer system.

Figure 1-5 **Windows 8**   Figure 1-6 **Mac OS X**

Application Software

Application software might be described as end user software. Three types of application software are *general-purpose, specialized,* and *apps.*

General-purpose applications are widely used in nearly all career areas. They are the kinds of programs you have to know to be considered an efficient and effective end user. Some of the best-known are presented in Figure 1-7.

Specialized applications include thousands of other programs that are more narrowly focused on specific disciplines and occupations. Two of the best known are graphics and web authoring programs.

Mobile apps, also known as **mobile applications** or simply **apps,** are small programs primarily designed for mobile devices such as smartphones and for tablet computers. There are over half a million apps. The most popular mobile apps are for social networking, playing games, and dowloading music and videos.

concept check

Describe the two major kinds of software.

Describe three types of system software programs.

Define and compare general-purpose applications, specialized applications, and mobile apps.

Type	Description
Browsers	Connect to Web sites and display Web pages
Word processors	Prepare written documents
Spreadsheets	Analyze and summarize numerical data
Database management systems	Organize and manage data and information
Presentation graphics	Communicate a message or persuade other people

Figure 1-7 **General-purpose applications**

FREE ANTIVIRUS PROGRAM

Have you or someone you know had a slower computing experience due to a spyware infection? Even worse, perhaps a malicious piece of software stole crucial, personal information or caused a total system failure. Most of these problems can be averted by having an up-to-date antivirus program running in your computer's memory at all times. This exercise shows you how to download and install a free antivirus program if your computer does not yet have one.

Getting Started   First, make sure your computer does not have an antivirus or security suite running. If it does, be sure to completely uninstall that program, even if the subscription is expired. Now, follow these steps to install AVG, a popular, free antivirus program:

1 ● Visit http://free.avg.com and click the *Download* button. You will be asked to confirm that you want the free edition and then redirected to a download site.

2 ● Run the installation file and follow the prompts.

3 ● Select *basic protection* if you are asked which product you would like to install.

4 ● Choose *Express Install* and wait for files to be downloaded and installed.

Using AVG   Generally speaking, your antivirus program watches your system for malware and updates itself automatically. However, you can always download updates manually, set a schedule for full-system scans, and change basic settings for various components of the software.

1 ● After installation, verify that the software is downloading updates by clicking *Update* or *Updating . . . on the right* side. Wait for all updates to be downloaded.

2 ● Click *Scan now* to run a full scan on your computer.

3 ● Just to the right of that, click the button with the three white horizontal lines to see the scan options where you can set a schedule for automated scans.

4 ● Click the *back arrow* to reach the main screen, where you can click various elements of the program to configure them. For example, clicking *Web Browsing* will allow you turn on a feature that detects cookies that may be used to track your online activity.

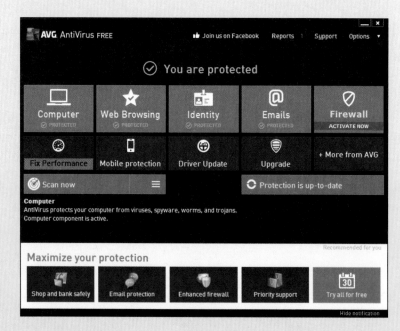

The web is continually changing, and some of the specifics presented in this Making IT Work for You may have changed. **To learn about other ways to make information technology work for you, visit our website at www.mhhe.com/ce2015 and select** Student Edition **and then** Making IT Work.

Figure 1-8 **Supercomputer**

Hardware

Computers are electronic devices that can follow instructions to accept input, process that input, and produce information. This book focuses principally on personal computers. However, it is almost certain that you will come in contact, at least indirectly, with other types of computers.

Types of Computers

There are four types of computers: supercomputers, mainframe computers, midrange computers, and personal computers.

- **Supercomputers** are the most powerful type of computer. These machines are special high-capacity computers used by very large organizations. IBM's Blue Gene supercomputer is one of the fastest computers in the world. (See Figure 1-8.)
- **Mainframe computers** occupy specially wired, air-conditioned rooms. Although not nearly as powerful as supercomputers, mainframe computers are capable of great processing speeds and data storage. For example, insurance companies use mainframes to process information about millions of policyholders.
- **Midrange computers,** also referred to as **servers,** are computers with processing capabilities less powerful than a mainframe computer yet more powerful than a personal computer. Originally used by medium-size companies or departments of large companies to support their processing needs, today midrange computers are most widely used to support or serve end users for such specific needs as retrieving data from a database or supplying access to application software.
- **Personal computers,** also known as **Pcs,** are the least powerful, yet the most widely used and fastest-growing type of computer. There are four types of personal computers: *desktop computers, laptop computers, tablet computers*, and *mobile devices.* **Desktop computers** are small enough to fit on top of or alongside a desk yet are too big to carry around. (See Figure 1-9.) **Laptop computers,**

Figure 1-9 **Desktop**

Figure 1-10 **Laptop**

Figure 1-11 **Tablet**

also known as **notebook computers,** are portable and lightweight and fit into most briefcases. (See Figure 1-10.) **Tablets,** also known as **tablet computers,** are smaller, lighter, and generally less powerful than laptops. Like a laptop, tablets have a flat screen but typically do not have a standard keyboard. (See Figure 1-11.) Instead tablets typically use a virtual keyboard that appears on the screen and is touch-sensitive. The best known tablet is Apple's iPad.

Mobile devices, also known as **handheld computers,** are the smallest and are designed to fit into the palm of one hand. These systems contain an entire computer system, including the electronic components, secondary storage, and input and output devices. **Smartphones** are the most widely used handheld computers. Smartphones are cell phones with wireless connections to the Internet and processing capabilities. (See Figure 1-12.) Their growth has been explosive in the past few years.

Personal Computer Hardware

Hardware for a personal computer system consists of a variety of different devices. This physical equipment falls into four basic categories: system unit, input/output, secondary storage, and communication. Because we discuss hardware in detail later in this book, here we will present just a quick overview of the four basic categories.

Figure 1-12 **Smartphone**

- **System unit:** The **system unit** is a container that houses most of the electronic components that make up a computer system. Two important components of the system unit are the *microprocessor* and *memory*. (See Figure 1-13.) The **microprocessor** controls and manipulates data to produce information. **Memory** is a holding area for data, instructions, and information. One type, **random-access memory (RAM),** holds the program and data that is currently being processed. This type of memory is sometimes referred to as *temporary storage* because its contents will typically be lost if the electric power to the computer is disrupted.

- **Input/output: Input devices** translate data and programs that humans can understand into a form that the computer can process. The most common input devices are the **keyboard** and the **mouse. Output devices** translate the processed information from the computer into a form that humans can understand. The most common output device is the computer **display,** also known as a **monitor.**

Microprocessor

Memory

Figure 1-13 **System unit**

- **Secondary storage:** Unlike memory, **secondary storage** holds data and programs even after electric power to the computer system has been turned off. The most important kinds of secondary media are *hard disks, solid-state storage,* and *optical discs.*

    Hard disks are typically used to store programs and very large data files. Using rigid metallic platters and read/write heads that move across the platters, data and information are stored using magnetic charges on the disk's surface. In contrast, **solid-state storage** does not have any moving parts, is more reliable, and requires less power. It saves data and information electronically similar to RAM except that it is not volatile. **Optical discs** use laser technology to store data and programs. (See Figure 1-14.) Three types of optical discs are **compact discs (CDs), digital versatile (or video) discs (DVDs),** and **Blu-ray discs.**
- **Communication:** At one time, it was uncommon for a personal computer system to communicate with other computer systems. Now, using **communication devices,** a personal computer can communicate with other computer systems located as near as the next office or as far away as halfway around the world, using the Internet. A **modem** is a widely used communication device that modifies audio, video, and other types of data into a form that can be transmitted across the Internet.

Figure 1-14 **Optical disc**

 concept check

 What are the four types of computers?

 Describe the four types of personal computers.

 Describe the four basic categories of personal computer hardware.

Figure 1-15 Four types of files: presentation, database, worksheet, and document

Data

Data is raw, unprocessed facts, including text, numbers, images, and sounds. As we mentioned earlier, processed data becomes information. When stored electronically in files, data can be used directly as input for the system unit.

Four common types of files (see Figure 1-15) are

- **Document files,** created by word processors to save documents such as memos, term papers, and letters.
- **Worksheet files,** created by electronic spreadsheets to analyze things like budgets and to predict sales.
- **Database files,** typically created by database management programs to contain highly structured and organized data. For example, an employee database file might contain all the workers' names, Social Security numbers, job titles, and other related pieces of information.
- **Presentation files,** created by presentation graphics programs to save presentation materials. For example, a file might contain audience handouts, speaker notes, and electronic slides.

Figure 1-16 Wireless communication devices

Connectivity and the Mobile Internet

Connectivity is the capability of your personal computer to share information with other computers. The two most dramatic changes in connectivity in the past five years have been the widespread use of mobile or wireless communication devices and cloud computing. For just a few of these mobile devices, see Figure 1-16. Many experts predict that these wireless applications are just the beginning of the **wireless revolution,** a revolution that will dramatically affect the way we communicate and use computer technology.

Central to the concept of connectivity is the **network.** A network is a communications system connecting two or more computers. The largest network in the world is the **Internet.** It is like a giant highway that connects you to millions of other people and organizations located throughout the world. The **web** provides a multimedia interface to the numerous resources available on the Internet. **Cloud computing** uses the Internet and the web to shift many computer activities from a user's computer to computers on the Internet. The wireless revolution and cloud computing promise the potential to dramatically affect the entire computer industry and how you and I will interact with computers. Each will be discussed in detail in the following chapters.

✓ concept check

Define data. List four common types of files.

Define connectivity and the wireless revolution.

What is a network? Describe the Internet, web, and cloud computing.

Careers in IT

❝ Now that you know the basic outline and important features of this book, I'd like to talk about some of the most exciting and well-paid careers in information technology. ❞

As mentioned previously, each of the following chapters highlights a specific career in information technology. Each provides specific job descriptions, salary ranges, advancement opportunities, and more. For a partial list of these careers, see Figure 1-17. For a complete list, visit our website at www.mhhe.com/ce2015 and select Student Edition and then Careers.

Career	Description
Webmaster	Develops and maintains websites and web resources. See page 48.
Software engineer	Analyzes users' needs and creates application software. See page 76.
Computer support specialist	Provides technical support to customers and other users. See page 103.
Computer technician	Repairs and installs computer components and systems. See page 128.
Technical writer	Prepares instruction manuals, technical reports, and other scientific or technical documents. See page 159.
Network administrator	Creates and maintains computer networks. See page 213.

Figure 1-17 **Careers in information technology**

A LOOK TO THE FUTURE

Using and Understanding Information Technology

The purpose of this book is to help you use and understand information technology. We want to help you become proficient and to provide you with a foundation of knowledge so that you can understand how technology is being used today and anticipate how technology will be used in the future. This will enable you to benefit from six important information technology developments.

The Internet and the Web

The Internet and the web are consid-ered by most to be the two most impor-tant technologies for the 21st century. Understanding how to efficiently and effectively use the Internet to browse, communicate, and locate information are essential skills. These issues are presented in Chapter 2, The Internet, the Web, and Electronic Commerce.

Powerful Software

The software that is now available can do an extraordinary number of tasks and help you in an endless number of ways. You can create professional-looking docu-ments, analyze massive amounts of data, create dynamic multimedia web pages, and much more. Today's employers are expecting the people they hire to be able to effectively and efficiently use a variety of different types of software. General-purpose, specialized, and mobile applica-tions are presented in Chapter 3. System software is presented in Chapter 4.

Powerful Hardware

Personal computers are now much more powerful than they used to be. Smartphones, tablets, and communication tech-nologies such as wireless networks are dramatically changing the ways to connect to other computers, networks, and the Internet. However, despite the rapid change of specific equip-ment, their essential features remain unchanged. To become an efficient and effective end user, you should focus on these features. Chapters 5 through 8 explain what you need to

know about hardware. For those considering the purchase of a computer, an appendix—The Computer Buyer's Guide— is provided at the end of this book. This guide provides a very concise comparison of desktops, laptops, tablets, and smartphones.

Privacy, Security, and Ethics

What about people? Experts agree that we as a society must be careful about the potential of technology to negatively affect our lives. Specifically, we need to be aware of how technology can impact our per-sonal privacy and our environment. Also, we need to understand the role and the importance of organizational and personal ethics. These critical issues are integrated in every chapter of this book as well as extensively covered in Chapter 9.

Organizations

Almost all organizations rely on the qual-ity and flexibility of their information sys-tems to stay competitive. As a member or employee of an organization, you will undoubtedly be involved in these infor-mation systems. In order to use, develop, modify, and maintain these systems, you need to understand the basic concepts of information systems and know how to safely, efficiently, and effectively use computers. These concepts are covered throughout this book.

Changing Times

Are the times changing any faster now than they ever have? Almost everyone thinks so. Whatever the answer, it is clear we live in a fast-paced age. The Evolution of the Computer Age section presented at the end of this book tracks the major developments since computers were first introduced.

After reading this book, you will be in a very favorable position compared with many other people in industry today. You will learn not only the basics of hardware, software, con-nectivity, the Internet, and the web but also the most cur-rent technology. You will be able to use these tools to your advantage.

INFORMATION SYSTEMS

The way to think about a personal computer is to realize that it is one part of an **information system**. There are several parts of an information system:

- **People** are an essential part of the system. The purpose of information systems is to make people, or **end users** like you, more productive.
- **Procedures** are rules or guidelines to follow when using software, hardware, and data. They are typically documented in manuals written by computer professionals.
- **Software (programs)** provides step-by-step instructions to control the computer to convert **data** into **information**.
- **Hardware** consists of the physical equipment. It is controlled by software and processes data to create information.
- **Data** consists of unprocessed facts including text, numbers, images, and sound. **Information** is data that has been processed by the computer.
- The **Internet** allows computers to connect and share information.

To efficiently and effectively use the computer, you need to understand **information technology (IT)**, including software, hardware, data, and connectivity.

PEOPLE

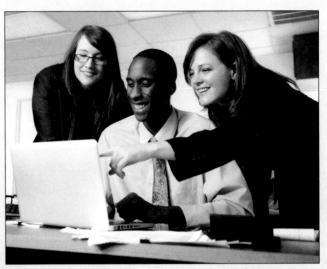

People are the most important part of an information system. This book contains several features to demonstrate how people just like you use computers. These features include the following:

- **Making IT Work for You** presents several interesting and practical applications. Topics include using digital video editing and locating job opportunities.
- **Tips** offer a variety of suggestions on such practical matters as how to improve slow computer performance and how to protect your privacy while on the web.
- **Privacy** marginal boxes discuss threats to your personal privacy and suggest ways to protect yourself.
- **Environment** boxes discuss important and relevant environmental issues. The impact of computers and other technologies is more critical today than ever before.
- **Ethics** boxes pose a variety of different ethical/unethical situations for your consideration.
- **Careers in IT** presents job descriptions, employment demands, educational requirements, salary ranges, and advancement opportunities.
- **Computing Essentials website** integrates the textbook with information on the web, including animations, career information, tips, test review materials, and much more.

To efficiently and effectively use computers, you need to understand the basic parts of an information system: people, procedures, software, hardware, data, and connectivity. Also you need to understand the Internet and the web and to recognize the role of technology in your professional and personal life.

SOFTWARE

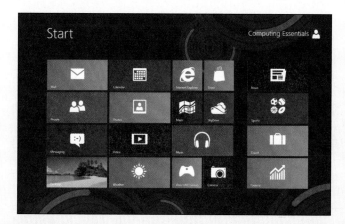

Software, or **programs**, consists of system and application software.

System Software

System software enables application software to interact with computer hardware.

- **Operating systems** coordinate resources, provide an interface, and run applications.
- **Utilities** perform specific tasks to manage computer resources.
- **Device drivers** are specialized programs to allow input and output devices to communicate with the rest of the computer system.

Application Software

Application software includes general-purpose, specialized, and mobile applications.

- **General purpose**—widely used in nearly all career areas; programs include browsers, word processors, spreadsheets, database management systems, and presentation graphics.
- **Specialized**—focus more on specific disciplines and occupations; programs include graphics and web authoring.
- **Apps (mobile apps, mobile applications)**—designed for mobile devices; most popular are for text messaging, Internet browsing, and connecting to social networks.

HARDWARE

Hardware consists of electronic devices that can follow instructions to accept input, process the input, and produce information.

Types of Computers

Supercomputer, mainframe, midrange (server), and personal computers (PCs) are four types of computers. Personal computers can be **desktop, laptop (notebook computer), tablet,** or **mobile devices (handheld computers). Smartphones** are the most widely used mobile device).

Personal Computer Hardware

There are four basic categories of hardware devices.

- **System unit** contains electronic circuitry, including the **microprocessor** and **memory. Random-access memory (RAM)** holds the program and data currently being processed.
- **Input/output devices** are translators between humans and computers. **Input devices** include the **keyboard** and **mouse.** The most common output device is the computer **display (monitor).**
- **Secondary storage** holds data and programs. Typical media include **hard disks, solid-state storage,** and **optical discs (CD, DVD,** and **Blu-ray).**
- **Communication devices** allow personal computers to communicate with other computer systems. **Modems** modify audio, video, and other types of data for transmission across the Internet.

DATA

Data is the raw unprocessed facts about something. Common file types include

- **Document files** created by word processors.

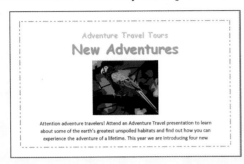

- **Worksheet files** created by spreadsheet programs.

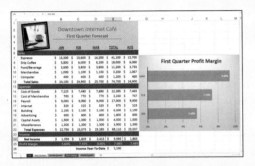

- **Database files** created by database management programs.

- **Presentation files** created by presentation graphics programs.

CONNECTIVITY

Connectivity

Connectivity describes the ability of end users to use resources well beyond their desktops.

The Wireless Revolution

The **wireless revolution** is the widespread and increasing use of mobile (wireless) communication devices.

Internet

The **Internet** is the world's largest computer **network**. The **web** provides a multimedia interface to resources available on the Internet.

Cloud Computing

Cloud computing uses the Internet and the web to shift many activities from users' computers to computers on the Internet.

CAREERS IN IT

Career	Description
Webmaster	Develops and maintains websites and web resources. See page 48.
Software engineer	Analyzes users' needs and creates application software. See page 76.
Computer support specialist	Provides technical support to customers and other users. See page 103.
Computer technician	Repairs and installs computer components and systems. See page 128.
Technical writer	Prepares instruction manuals, technical reports, and other scientific or technical documents. See page 159.
Network administrator	Creates and maintains computer networks. See page 213.

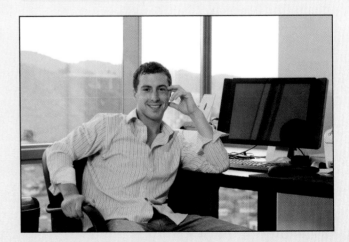

KEY TERMS

application software (9)
apps (9)
Blu-ray disc (13)
cloud computing (16)
communication device (13)
compact disc (CD) (13)
connectivity (6, 15)
data (6)
database file (14)
desktop computer (11)
device driver (8)
digital versatile disc (DVD) (13)
digital video disc (DVD) (13)
display (12)
document file (14)
end user (4)
general-purpose application (9)
handheld computer (12)
hard disk (13)
hardware (6)
information (6)
information system (4)
information technology (IT) (8)
input device (12)
Internet (15)
keyboard (12)
laptop computer (11)
mainframe computer (11)
memory (12)
microprocessor (12)
midrange computer (11)
mobile app (application) (9)

mobile device (12)
modem (13)
monitor (12)
mouse (12)
network (15)
notebook computer (12)
operating system (8)
optical disc (13)
output device (12)
PC (11)
people (4)
personal computer (11)
presentation file (14)
procedures (4)
program (6)
random-access memory (RAM) (12)
secondary storage (13)
server (11)
smartphone (12)
software (6)
solid-state storage (13)
specialized application (9)
supercomputer (11)
system software (8)
system unit (12)
tablet (12)
tablet computer (12)
utility (8)
virus (8)
web (16)
wireless revolution (15)
worksheet file (14)

To test your knowledge of these key terms with animated flash cards, visit our website at www.mhhe.com/ce2015, select Student Edition, and choose Chapter 1 and then Flashcards.

MULTIPLE CHOICE

Circle the letter of the correct answer.

1. The keyboard, mouse, display, and system unit are:
   - a. hardware
   - b. output devices
   - c. storage devices
   - d. software

2. Programs that coordinate computer resources, provide an interface, and run applications are known as:
   - a. application programs
   - b. operating systems
   - c. storage systems
   - d. utility programs

3. A browser is an example of a:
   - a. general-purpose application
   - b. specialized program
   - c. system application
   - d. utility program

4. Although not as powerful as a supercomputer, this type of computer is capable of great processing speeds and data storage.
   - a. mainframe
   - b. midrange
   - c. laptop
   - d. tablet

5. The smallest type of personal computer:
   - a. mobile device
   - b. midrange
   - c. laptop
   - d. tablet

6. RAM is a type of:
   - a. computer
   - b. memory
   - c. network
   - d. secondary storage

7. Unlike memory, this type of storage holds data and programs even after electric power to the computer system has been turned off.
   - a. primary
   - b. RAM
   - c. ROM
   - d. secondary

8. The type of file created by word processors to save, for example, memos, term papers, and letters.
   - a. database
   - b. document
   - c. presentation
   - d. worksheet

9. Uses the Internet and the web to shift many computer activities from a user's computer to computers on the Internet.
   - a. cloud computing
   - b. high definition
   - c. network
   - d. solid-state storage

10. The largest network in the world is [the]:
    - a. Facebook
    - b. Internet
    - c. supercomputer
    - d. web

For an interactive multiple-choice practice test, visit our website at www.mhhe.com/ce2015, select Student Edition and choose Chapter 1 and then Multiple Choice.

MATCHING

Match each numbered item with the most closely related lettered item. Write your answers in the spaces provided.

a. desktop
b. modem
c. network
d. output
e. presentation
f. program
g. software
h. solid-state
i. system software
j. system unit

____ 1. Consists of the step-by-step instructions that tell the computer how to do its work.

____ 2. Another name for a program.

____ 3. Enables the application software to interact with the computer hardware.

____ 4. Type of computer that is small enough to fit on top of or alongside a desk yet is too big to carry around.

____ 5. A container that houses most of the electronic components that make up a computer system.

____ 6. Devices that translate the processed information from the computer into a form that humans can understand.

____ 7. Unlike hard disks, this type of storage does not have any moving parts, is more reliable, and requires less power.

____ 8. The most widely used communication device.

____ 9. A type of a file that might contain, for example, audience handouts, speaker notes, and electronic slides.

____ 10. A communications system connecting two or more computers.

For an interactive matching practice test, visit our website at www.mhhe.com/ce2015, select Student Edition and choose Chapter 1 and then Matching.

OPEN-ENDED

On a separate sheet of paper, respond to each question or statement.

1. Explain the parts of an information system. What part do people play in this system?

2. What is system software? What kinds of programs are included in system software?

3. Define and compare general-purpose applications, specialized applications, and apps. Describe some different types of general-purpose applications. Describe some types of specialized applications.

4. Describe the different types of computers. What is the most common type? What are the types of personal computers?

5. What is connectivity? What are wireless devices and the wireless revolution? What is a computer network? What are the Internet and the web? What is cloud computing?

DISCUSSION

Respond to each of the following questions.

1 Making IT Work for You

Making it a habit of keeping current with technology applications can be a key to your success. Numerous full-page spreads identified as *Making IT Work for You* are presented in the following chapters. These sections address some of today's most interesting and useful applications. They include online entertainment in Chapter 2, Skype in Chapter 6, and cloud storage in Chapter 7. Select one that you find the most interesting, and then respond to the following: (a) Why did you select this application? (b) Have you used this application? If so when and how? If not, do you plan to in the near future? (c) Go to the chapter containing your selected application, and locate the application's Making IT Work for You coverage. Review and briefly describe its contents. (d) Did you find the coverage useful? Why or why not?

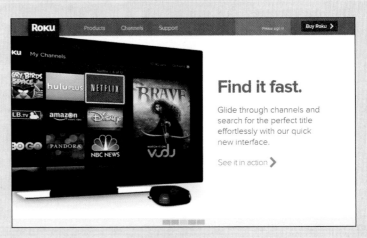

2 Privacy

Privacy is one of the most critical issues facing society today. Numerous Privacy boxes appear in the margins of the upcoming chapters presenting a variety of privacy issues. These issues include apps that track smartphone and tablet user locations without their knowledge or consent in Chapter 3, access by government and organization networks to obtain unauthorized detailed personal information in Chapter 8, and protection of personal privacy while using social networking sites such as Facebook in Chapter 9. Select one that you find the most interesting, and then respond to the following: (a) Why did you select this issue? (b) Do you have knowledge or experience with the issue? If so, describe your knowledge or experience. If not, do you consider the issue to be important for protecting your privacy? (c) Go to the chapter containing your selected issue, locate the Privacy box, read it, and describe its contents. (d) Did you find the coverage thought-provoking? Why or why not?

3 Environment

Almost everyone agrees that protecting our environment today is more important than ever before. Numerous Environment boxes appear in the margins of the upcoming chapters. These boxes present a variety of environmental topics including e-mail benefits in Chapter 2, operating systems reducing energy consumption in Chapter 4, and recycling old inkjet cartridges in Chapter 6. Select one that you find the most interesting, and then respond to the following: (a) Why did you select this topic? (b) Do you have knowledge or experience with the topic? If so, describe your knowledge or experience. If not, do you consider the topic to be important for protecting the environment? (c) Go to the chapter containing your selected topic, locate the Environment box, read it, and describe its contents. (d) Did you find the coverage thought-provoking? Why or why not?

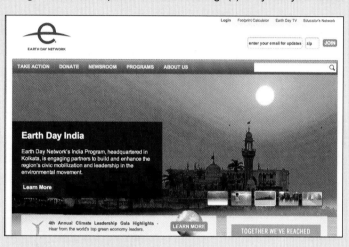

4 Ethics

Computer ethics are guidelines for the morally acceptable use of computers in our society. Numerous Ethics boxes appear in the margins of the upcoming chapters presenting a variety of ethical issues. These issues include image editing in Chapter 3, unauthorized use of webcams in Chapter 6, and unauthorized monitoring or eavesdropping of Internet activity in Chapter 8. Select one issue that you find the most interesting, and then respond to the following: (a) Why did you select this issue? (b) Do you have knowledge or experience with the issue? If so, describe your knowledge or experience. If not, do you consider the issue critical for individuals or organizations? (c) Go to the chapter containing your selected issue, locate the Ethics box, read it, and describe its contents. (d) Did you find the coverage thought-provoking? Why or why not?

chapter 2

The Internet, the Web, and Electronic Commerce

Learning Objectives

After you have read this chapter, you should be able to:

1 Explain the origins of the Internet and the web.

2 Explain how to access the web using providers and browsers.

3 Compare different web utilities, including plug-ins, filters, file transfer utilities, and Internet security suites.

4 Compare different Internet communications, including e-mail, text messaging, instant messaging, social networking, blogs, microblogs, webcasts, podcasts, and wikis.

5 Describe search tools, including search engines and specialized search engines.

6 Evaluate the accuracy of information presented on the web.

7 Identify electronic commerce, including B2C, C2C, B2B, and security issues.

8 Describe cloud computing, including the three-way interaction of clients, Internet, and service providers.

Why should I read this chapter?

The Internet is changing our world. For example, cars promise to soon be able to drive themselves, avoid traffic accidents and congestion, respond to voice commands, monitor and automatically adjust personal schedules and much more – all through the Internet.

This chapter covers the things you need to know to be prepared for this ever changing digital world, including:

- The impact of the Internet—how Internet technology is changing your world.
- Internet hardware—how to connect your life to the Internet, including Wi-Fi, smartphones, and tablets.
- Internet uses—how to get ahead using social media, streaming technology, and cloud computing.

ONLINE ENTERTAINMENT

Are you one of the millions of people who regularly use their computers to watch their favorite television programs, movies, and other video content? Many have "cut the cord" from their cable or satellite TV providers and have turned to online content. It's easy and convenient. Typically, the content is provided by a subscription or a pay-as-you-go service. Users watch the content on their TVs or their computers (including tablets and smartphones).

Subscription Services   These services provide access to their library of videos for a fee. You can select and view as many of these videos as you want. Three of the most popular subscription services are Netflix, Hulu Plus, and Amazon Prime.

1 ● **Netflix and Amazon Prime offer content similar to a DVD rental store that is delivered either online or through the mail. Netflix offers the largest library of movies and TV programs for a low monthly fee. Amazon Prime, a newer service, provides similar content for an annual fee.**

2 ● **Hulu Plus focuses on current TV programs. Although it does use limited advertising, Hulu Plus's low monthly subscription and current content make it attractive.**

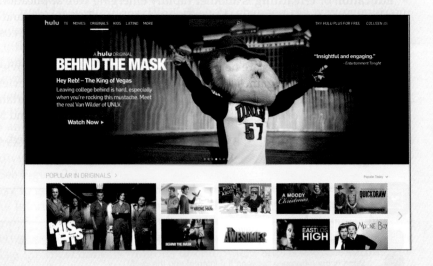

3 NBA League Pass provides access to live broadcasts of NBA basketball games for a fee. CNN and C-SPAN provide live content for free. Unlike Hulu, which often offers programming with a delay of a day or longer, these services are simulcast with TV programming.

Pay-As-You-Go Services These services provide online access to specific titles in their libraries for a charge. Amazon, iTunes, and Vudu are just a few of the companies that let you rent or purchase movies and TV programs. Movie rentals cost only a few dollars and can be viewed several times over a 24-hour period. The price can increase by one or two dollars for HD quality.

Viewing Video Content Many people own Internet-ready TVs that will directly accept content from the Internet. Most Blu-ray disc players and many gaming consoles also provide this access. You can also purchase specialized devices like Roku, which will connect TVs to many of the services listed above.

Many viewers use their computer and a browser to display the video content. Also, many services provide apps for tablet and smartphone viewing.

To learn about other ways to make information technology work for you, visit our website at www.mhhe.com/ce2015 and select Student Edition **and then** Making IT Work**.**

Figure 2-2 **Browser**

Internet Access

The Internet and the telephone system are similar—you can connect a computer to the Internet much like you connect a phone to the telephone system. Once you are on the Internet, your computer becomes an extension of what seems like a giant computer— a computer that branches all over the world. When provided with a connection to the Internet, you can use a browser program to search the web.

Providers

The most common way to access the Internet is through an **Internet service provider (ISP).** The providers are already connected to the Internet and provide a path or connection for individuals to access the Internet.

The most widely used commercial Internet service providers use telephone lines, cable, and/or wireless connections. Some of the best-known providers in the United States are AT&T, Comcast, Sprint, T-Mobile, and Verizon.

As we will discuss in Chapter 8, users connect to ISPs using one of a variety of connection technologies including **DSL, cable,** and **wireless modems.**

Browsers

Browsers are programs that provide access to web resources. This software connects you to remote computers; opens and transfers files; displays text, images, and multimedia; and provides in one tool an uncomplicated interface to the Internet and web documents. Four well-known browsers are Apple Safari, Google Chrome, Microsoft Internet Explorer, and Mozilla Firefox. (See Figure 2-2.)

For browsers to connect to resources, the **location** or **address** of the resources must be specified. These addresses are called **uniform resource locators (URLs).** All URLs have at least two basic parts. (See Figure 2-3.)

Figure 2-3 **Basic parts of a URL**

- The first part presents the protocol used to connect to the resource. As we will discuss in Chapter 8, **protocols** are rules for exchanging data between computers. The protocol *http* is used for web traffic and is the most widely used Internet protocol.
- The second part presents the **domain name.** It indicates the specific address where the resource is located. In Figure 2-3 the domain is identified as www. mtv.com. The last part of the domain name following the dot (.) is the **top-level domain (TLD).** Also known as the **web suffix,** it typically identifies the type of organization. For example, *.com* indicates a commercial site. (See Figure 2-4.)

Once the browser has connected to the website, a document file is sent back to your computer. This document typically contains **Hypertext Markup Language (HTML),** a markup language for displaying web pages. The browser interprets the HTML formatting instructions and displays the document as a **web page.** For example, when your browser first connects to the Internet, it opens up to a web page specified in the browser settings. Web pages present information about the site along with references and **hyperlinks** or **links** that connect to other documents containing related information—text files, graphic images, audio, and video clips.

Domain	Type
.com	Commercial
.edu	Educational
.gov	Government
.mil	U.S. military
.net	Network
.org	Organization

Figure 2-4 **Traditional top-level domains**

There are various technologies used to provide highly interactive and animated websites. These technologies include

- **Cascading style sheets (CSS)** are separate files referenced by or lines inserted into an HTML document that control the appearance of a web page. CSS help ensure that related web pages have a consistent presentation or look. Netflix uses CSS to visually connect all its web pages.
- **JavaScript** is a language often used within HTML documents to trigger interactive features, such as opening new browser windows and checking information entered in online forms. The Microsoft search engine Bing.com uses JavaScript to make its website more interactive and to assist its users by auto-filling search requests as they type content into the search box.
- **AJAX,** an advanced use of JavaScript, is used to create interactive websites that respond quickly. Google Maps uses AJAX to make the maps fast loading, dynamic, and interactive.
- **Applets** are programs that can be downloaded quickly and run by most browsers. They are used to display graphics, provide interactive games, and much more. For example, many of the online games at Yahoo! Games are JAVA applets.

Today it is common to access the Internet from a variety of mobile devices like smartphones and tablets. Special browsers called **mobile browsers** are designed to run on these portable devices. Unlike a traditional web browser that is typically displayed on a large screen, a mobile browser is displayed on a very small screen, and special navigational tools are required to conveniently view web content. The Apple iPhone, for example, enables you to "pinch" or "stretch" the screen with two fingers to zoom web content in and out. (See Figure 2-5.)

To learn more about browsers, visit our website at www.mhhe.com/ce2015, select Student Edition, then Explore, and then Browsers.

Figure 2-5 **Zoom web content**

 concept check

 What is the function of an ISP, a browser, and a mobile browser?

 What are URLs, HTML, web pages, hyperlinks, CSS, JavaScript, AJAX, and applets?

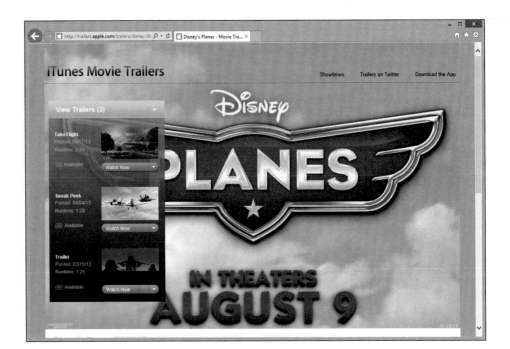

Figure 2-6 **QuickTime movie at Apple.com**

Web Utilities

Utilities are programs that make computing easier. **Web utilities** are specialized utility programs that make using the Internet and the web easier and safer. Some of these utilities are browser-related programs that either become part of your browser or are executed from your browser. Others are designed to protect children from dangerous and inappropriate website material. File transfer utilities allow you to efficiently copy files to and from your computer across the Internet. Internet security suites enhance security and privacy.

Plug-ins

Plug-ins are programs that are automatically started and operate as a part of your browser. Many websites require you to have one or more plug-ins to fully experience their content. Some widely used plug-ins include

- Acrobat Reader from Adobe—for viewing and printing a variety of standard forms and other documents saved in a special format called PDF.
  - Flash Player from Adobe—for viewing videos, animations, and other media.
  - QuickTime from Apple—for playing audio and video files. (See Figure 2-6.)
  - Windows Media Player from Microsoft—for playing audio files, video files, and much more.

Some of these utilities are included in many of today's browsers and operating systems. Others must be installed before they can be used by your browser. To learn more about plug-ins and how to download them, visit some of the sites listed in Figure 2-7.

Plug-in	Source
Reader	get.adobe.com/reader
Flash Player	get.adobe.com/flashplayer
QuickTime	www.apple.com/quicktime
Silverlight	www.microsoft.com/silverlight

Figure 2-7 **Plug-in sites**

Filters

Filters block access to selected sites. The Internet is an interesting and multifaceted arena. But not all aspects of the Internet are appropriate

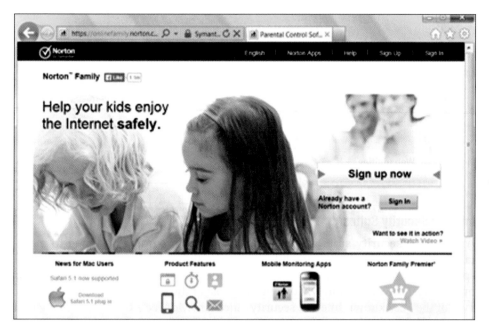

Figure 2-8 **Norton Online Family is a web filter**

for all audiences. Parents, in particular, are concerned about children roaming unrestricted across the Internet. Filter programs allow parents as well as organizations to block out selected sites and set time limits. (See Figure 2-8.) Additionally, these programs can monitor use and generate reports detailing the total time spent on the Internet and the time spent at individual websites. For a list of some of the best-known filters, see Figure 2-9.

File Transfer Utilities

Using file transfer utility software, you can copy files to your computer from specially configured servers. This is called **downloading.** You also can use file transfer utility software to copy files from your computer to another computer on the Internet. This is called **uploading.** Three popular types of file transfer are FTP, web-based, and BitTorrent.

- **File transfer protocol (FTP)** and **secure file transfer protocol (SFTP)** allow you to efficiently copy files to and from your computer across the Internet, and are frequently used for uploading changes to a website hosted by an Internet service provider. FTP has been used for decades and still remains one of the most popular methods of file transfer.
- **Web-based file transfer services** make use of a web browser to upload and download files. This eliminates the need for any custom software to be installed. A popular web-based file transfer service is Dropbox.com.
- **BitTorrent** distributes file transfers across many different computers for more efficient downloads, unlike other transfer technologies where a file is copied from one computer on the Internet to another. A single file might be located on dozens of individual computers. When you download the file, each computer sends you a tiny piece of the larger file, making BitTorrent well-suited for transferring very large files. Unfortunately, BitTorrent technology often has been used for distributing unauthorized copies of copyrighted music and video. For a summary of web utilities, see Figure 2-10.

Filter	Site
CyberPatrol	www.cyberpatrol.com
Pearl Echo	www.pearlsw.com
Norton Online Family	onlinefamily.norton.com
Net Nanny	www.netnanny.com
Symantec Web Gateway	symantec.com/web-gateway

Figure 2-9 **Filters**

INTERNET AND WEB

Internet

Launched in 1969 with **ARPANET**, the **Internet** consists of the actual physical network.

Web

Introduced in 1991 at **CERN**, the **web** provides a multimedia interface to Internet resources. Three generations: **Web 1.0** (existing information), **Web 2.0** (content creation and social interaction), **Web 3.0** (computer-generated information).

Common Uses

The most common uses of the Internet and the web include

- Communication—the most popular Internet activity.
- Shopping—one of the fastest-growing Internet activities.
- Searching—access libraries and local, national, and international news.
- Education—**e-learning** or taking online courses.
- Entertainment—music, movies, magazines, and computer games.

INTERNET ACCESS

Once connected to the Internet, your computer seemingly becomes an extension of a giant computer that branches all over the world.

Providers

Internet service providers are connected to the Internet, providing a path for individuals to access the Internet. Connection technologies include **DSL**, **cable**, and **wireless modems**.

Browsers

Browsers provide access to web resources. Some related terms are

- **URLs**—**locations** or **addresses** to web resources; two parts are **protocol** and **domain name**; **top-level domain (TLD)** or **web suffix** identifies type of organization.
- **HTML**—commands to display **web pages**; **hyperlinks (links)** are connections.

Technologies providing interactive, animated websites include **cascading style sheets**, or **CSS** (to control the appearance of web pages); **JavaScript** (to trigger interactive features); **AJAX** (to create quick response interactive websites; and **applets** (to display graphics, provide interactive games, and more).

Mobile browsers run on portable devices.

To efficiently and effectively use computers, you need to be aware of resources available on the Internet and web, to be able to access these resources, to effectively communicate electronically, to efficiently locate information, to understand electronic commerce, and to use web utilities.

WEB UTILITIES

Web utilities are specialized utility programs that make using the Internet and the web easier and safer.

Plug-ins

Plug-ins are automatically loaded and operate as part of a browser. Many websites require specific plug-ins to fully experience their content. Some plug-ins are included in many of today's browsers; others must be installed.

Filters

Filters are used by parents and organizations to block certain sites and to monitor use of the Internet and the web.

File Transfer Utilities

File transfer utilities copy files to (**downloading**) and from (**uploading**) your computer. Three types are

- **File transfer protocol (FTP)** and **secure file transfer protocol (SFTP)** allow you to efficiently copy files across the Internet.
- **BitTorrent** distributes file transfers across many different computers.
- **Web-based file transfer services** make use of a web browser to upload and download files.

Internet Security Suite

An **Internet security suite** is a collection of utility programs designed to protect your privacy and security on the Internet.

COMMUNICATION

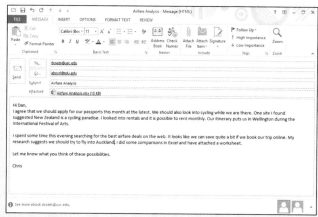

E-mail

E-mail (electronic mail) is the transmission of electronic messages. There are two basic types of e-mail systems:

- **Client-based e-mail systems** use **e-mail clients** installed on your computer.
- **Web-based e-mail systems** use **webmail clients** located on the e-mail provider's computer. This is known as **webmail**.

A typical e-mail has three basic elements: **header** (including **address, subject**, and perhaps **attachment**), **message**, and **signature**.

Spam is unwanted and unsolicited e-mail that may include a *computer* **virus** or destructive programs often attached to unsolicited e-mail. **Spam blockers**, also known as **spam filters**, are programs that identify and eliminate spam.

Messaging

While e-mail is the most widely used, two other messaging systems are

- **Text messaging**, also known as **texting** and **SMS (short message service)**, is a process of sending short electronic messages typically less than 160 characters. Texting while driving is very dangerous and illegal in several states.
- **Instant messaging (IM)**—supports live communication between **friends**. Most instant messaging programs also include video conferencing features, file sharing, and remote assistance.

Social Networking

Social networks connect individuals to one another. Many sites support a variety of different activites. Three of the best known are Facebook, Google+, and LinkedIn.

- **Facebook** provides access to **Facebook Profiles**, **Facebook Pages**, and **Facebook groups**.
- **Google+** provides access to **Circles**, **Hangouts**, and **Sparks**.
- **LinkedIn** is a premier business-oriented social networking site.

Blogs, Webcasts, and Wikis

Other sites that help individuals communicate across the web are blogs, microblogs, webcasts, podcasts, and wikis.

- **Blogs (web logs)** are typically personal websites to keep in touch with friends and family. Some are like online diaries. Businesses, newspapers, and others also use blogs as a quick publishing method.
- **Microblogs** unlike traditional blogs only use short sentences that only take a few seconds to write. **Twitter** is the most popular microblogging site. A **Twitter** message is known as a **Tweet**.
- **Webcasts** deliver media content over the Internet. Using **streaming** technology (audio and video files continuously downloaded while you are listening to and/or viewing the file content) no files remain on your computer at the conclusion of the webcast.
- **Podcasts**, like webcasts, deliver media content but do not use streaming technology. Before content can be accessed, the entire media files has to be downloaded and saved to your computer.
- A **wiki** is a website designed to allow visitors to use their browsers to add, edit, or delete the site's content. Wikis are often used to support collaborative writing. **Wikipedia** is one of the most popular wikis.

Search Service	Site
Ask	www.ask.com
Bing	www.bing.com
Google	www.google.com
Yahoo!	www.yahoo.com

Search services maintain huge databases relating to website content. **Spiders** are programs that update these databases.

Search Engines

Search engines are specialized programs to help locate information. To use, enter a keyword or phrase and a list of **hits** or links to references is displayed.

Specialized Search Engines

Specialized search engines focus on subject-specific websites.

Topic	Site
Environment	www.ecoearth.info
Fashion	www.shopstyle.com
History	www.historynet.com
Law	www.findlaw.com
Medicine	www.webmd.com

Content Evaluation

To evaluate the accuracy of information found on the web, consider the following:

- Authority. Is the author an expert? Is the site official or does it present one individual's or organization's opinion.
- Accuracy. Has the information been critically reviewed? Does the site provide a method to report inaccurate information?
- Objectivity. Is the information factual or does the author have a bias? Does the author appear to have a personal agenda to convince or form a reader's opinion?
- Currency. Is the information up to date? Does the site specify when information is updated? Are the site's links operational?

ELECTRONIC COMMERCE

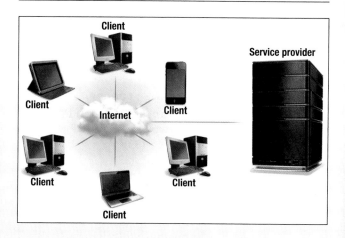

Electronic commerce, or e-commerce, is the buying and selling of goods over the Internet. Three basic types of e-commerce are **business-to-consumer**, **consumer-to-consumer**, and **business-to-business**.

- **Business-to-consumer (B2C)** commerce involves sales from business to the general public. It is the fastest-growing type. Three of the most widely used applications are online banking, financial trading, and shopping.
- **Consumer-to-consumer (C2C)** commerce involves sales between individuals, often as the electronic version of classified ads or an auction. **Web auctions** are similar to traditional auctions except buyers and sellers rarely, if ever, meet face to face.
- **Business-to-business (B2B)** commerce involves sales from one business to another, typically a manufacturer-supplier relationship.

Organization	Site
QuiBids	www.quibids.com
eBay	www.ebay.com
uBid	www.ubid.com

Security

The two greatest challenges for e-commerce are the development of

- Safe, secure payment methods. Two types are credit cards and **digital cash** (third party sells digital cash to buyers and redeems for sellers).
- Convenient ways to provide required information such as mailing addresses and credit card information.

CLOUD COMPUTING

Cloud computing uses the Internet and the web to shift many computer activities from the user's computer to other computers on the Internet.

Components

There are three basic components to cloud computing:

- Clients are corporations and end users who want access to data, programs, and storage.
- The Internet provides the connection between the clients and providers. Two critical factors are the speed and reliability of the user's access and the Internet's capability to provide safe and reliable access.
- Service providers are organizations with computers connected to the Internet that are willing to provide access to software, data, and storage.

CAREERS IN IT

Webmasters develop and maintain websites and web resources. Bachelor's or associate's degree in computer science or information systems and knowledge of common programming languages and web development software are required. Salary range is $56,000 to $80,000.

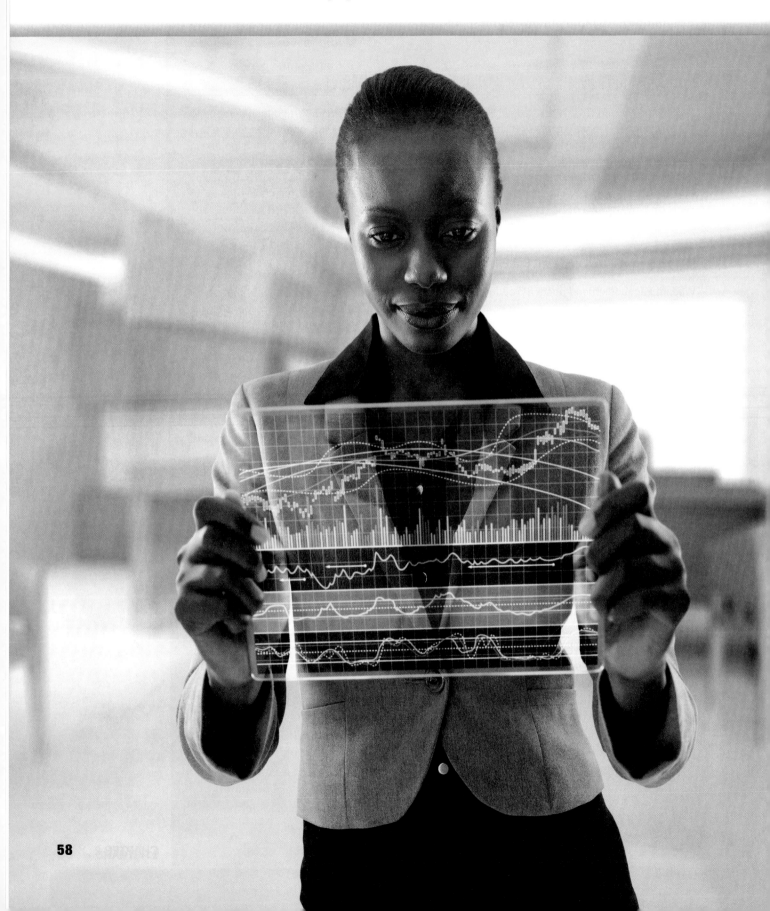

chapter 3

Application Software

Learning Objectives

After you have read this chapter, you should be able to:

1 Identify general-purpose applications.

2 Describe word processors, spreadsheets, presentation programs, and database management systems.

3 Identify specialized applications.

4 Describe graphics programs, web authoring programs, and other specialized professional applications.

5 Describe mobile apps and app stores.

6 Identify software suites.

7 Describe office suites, cloud suites, specialized suites, and utility suites.

Why should I read this chapter?

The power and capability of application software is exploding. The way users interact is rapidly advancing as well. For example, we can expect applications beyond our imagination and to control these applications entirely with our voice, gestures, and in some cases even our entire body.

This chapter covers the things you need to know to be prepared for this ever changing digital world, including:

- General purpose applications—learn how to create documents, analyze data, make presentations, and organize information.
- Special purpose applications—learn how to use graphics programs for image editing and creating web pages and how to locate and use mobile apps.
- Software suites—how to use suites and cloud based applications.

Mobile Apps

Mobile apps or **mobile applications** are add-on programs for a variety of mobile devices including smartphones and tablets. Sometimes referred to simply as **apps,** mobile apps have been widely used for years. The traditional applications include address books, to-do lists, alarms, and message lists. With the introduction of smartphones, tablets, and wireless connections to the Internet, mobile capabilities have exploded. Now, any number of applications are available.

Apps

The breadth and scope of available mobile applications for smartphones and other mobile devices are ever expanding. There are over 500,000 apps just for Apple's iPhone alone. Some of the most widely used are for listening to music, viewing video, social networking, shopping, and scanning QR codes.

- Music. For many, their smartphone and/or tablet is their primary source for music. The mobile app Pandora offers free streaming music with ads and playlists that you can customize in a limited way. Spotify is another streaming music service that requires a monthly fee but offers direct control of what music you listen to and no ads.
- Video. With faster data speeds and higher resolution screens, smartphones and tablets are becoming a favorite way to watch TV shows, movies, or video clips. The YouTube app offers access to free online videos such as movie trailers and video blogs. The Netflix app provides access to more professional videos for a fee.
- Social networking. Mobile apps are ideal for sharing a picture while on vacation, checking in at your favorite coffee shop, or sending out invites to a last-minute party. The Facebook mobile app offers many of the features of the Facebook website, with additional features that take advantage of a mobile device's camera and GPS capability. The Instagram app provides a more specialized and artistic flair by focusing on sharing photos.
- Shopping. A recent poll concluded that well over half of all smartphone users in the United States regularly use their phones for shopping. By scanning a product's barcode, shopping apps search for the product and provide price comparisons as well as product reviews. Using Amazon's Price Check app, all you need to do is take a picture of the product.
- QR codes. **QR codes,** also known as **quick response codes,** are graphics that link mobile devices to a variety content including games, text, videos, and websites. You have likely see QR codes in magazines, newspapers, and even books. (See Figure 3-16.) Popular QR reader apps include QR Reader for iPhone and QR Droid. The ShopSavvy app focuses on shopping by scanning products with QR codes and providing online and local stores that sell that product.

Many apps are written for a particular type of mobile device and will not run on other types. For example, an app designed for Apple's iPhone may not work with Google's Android.

App Stores

An **app store** is typically a website that provides access to specific mobile apps that can be downloaded either for a nominal fee or free of charge. Three of the best-known stores are Apple's App Store, Google Play, and Windows Phone Marketplace. (See Figure 3-17.) Although most of the best-known app stores specialize in applications for a particular line of mobile device, other less well-known stores provide apps for a wide variety of mobile devices. For a list of some more widely used app stores, see Figure 3-18.

Figure 3-16 **QR Code**

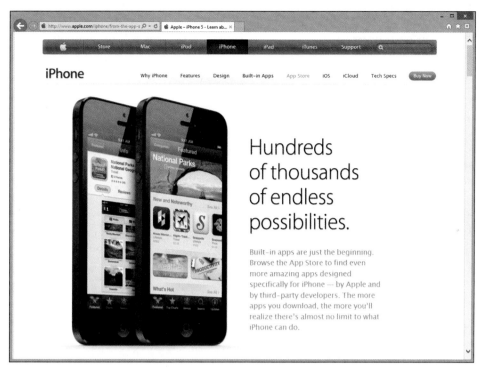

Figure 3-17 Apple's App Store

concept check

What are mobile apps? What are some of the most widely used? What are QR codes?

What are app stores?

Software Suites

A **software suite** is a collection of separate application programs bundled together and made available as a group. Four types of suites are office suites, cloud suites, specialized suites, and utility suites.

Office Suites

Office suites, also known as **office software suites** and **productivity suites,** contain general-purpose application programs that are typically used in a business situation. Productivity suites commonly include a word processor, spreadsheet, database manager, and a presentation application. The best known is Microsoft Office. Other well-known productivity suites are Apple iWork and OpenOffice.

App	Focus	Site
Apple App Store	iOS devices	www.appstore.com
Google Play	Android devices	play.google.com
Windows Phone Marketplace	Windows phones	windowsphone.com/marketplace

Figure 3-18 App stores

Cloud Computing

Cloud suites or **online office suites** are stored at a server on the Internet and are available anywhere you can access the Internet. Documents created using online applications can also be stored online, making it easy to share and collaborate on documents with others. One downside to cloud applications is that you are dependent on the server providing the application to be available whenever you need it. For this reason, when using online applications, it is important to have backup copies of your documents on your computer and to have a desktop office application available to use. Popular online office suites include Google Docs, Zoho, and Microsoft Office Web Apps. To learn more about one of the most widely used online office suites, see Making IT Work for You: Google Docs on page 77.

Specialized and Utility Suites

Two other types of suites that are more narrowly focused are specialized suites and utility suites.

- **Specialized suites** focus on specific applications. These include graphics suites like CorelDRAW Graphics Suite X6, financial planning suites like Moneytree Software's TOTAL Planning Suite, and many others.
- **Utility suites** include a variety of programs designed to make computing easier and safer. Two of the best known are Norton SystemWorks and Norton Internet Security Suite. (Utility suites will be discussed in detail in Chapter 4.)

 concept check

 What is a software suite? What are the advantages of purchasing a suite?

 What is the difference between a traditional office suite and a cloud or online suite?

 What is a specialized suite? What is a utility suite?

Careers in IT

Now, that you have learned about application software, I'd like to tell you about my career as a software engineer.

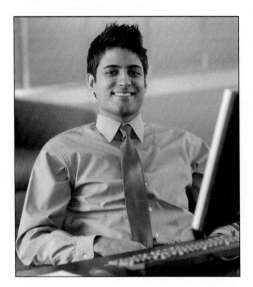

Software engineers analyze users' needs and create application software. Software engineers typically have experience in programming but focus on the design and development of programs using the principles of mathematics and engineering.

A bachelor's or an advanced specialized associate's degree in computer science or information systems and an extensive knowledge of computers and technology are required by most employers. Internships may provide students with the kinds of experience employers look for in a software engineer. Those with specific experience with web applications may have an advantage over other applicants. Employers typically look for software engineers with good communication and analytical skills.

Software engineers can expect to earn an annual salary in the range of $53,000 to $97,000. Starting salary is dependent on both experience and the type of software being developed. Experienced software engineers are candidates for many other advanced careers in IT. To learn about other careers in information technology, visit us at www.mhhe.com/ce2015 and select Student Edition and then Careers.

GOOGLE DOCS

Do you need to create and collaborate with others on a document, presentation, or spreadsheet? Do you need access from different computers in different locations? If so, an online office suite, such as Google Docs, might be just what you need.

Creating a Document   You must have a free Google account in order to start creating and sharing documents. To get started:

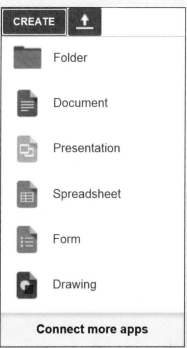

1 ● Go to www.google.com. If you are not currently signed in or you do not have a Google account, click the *Sign in* button and follow the appropriate instructions.

2 ● Once you are signed in, click *Drive* at the top of the page. If the Google Drive screen appears, click the *Get start*ed button to continue.

3 ● Click the *Create* button; then select *Document.*

4 ● Start typing in the blank document. You will notice many familiar buttons in the toolbar above the document area.

5 ● Click the *Untitled document* area at the top left, and you will be prompted to enter a name for the document.

6 ● Close the browser tab (or window) in order to close the document.

You may have noticed that there is no save option. This is because your document is automatically being saved as you work on it.

Sharing a Document   Any document that you create can be shared with one or more individuals. Those individuals can be granted read-only access, or they could be allowed to edit the document, even at the same time that you are working on it. To share a document:

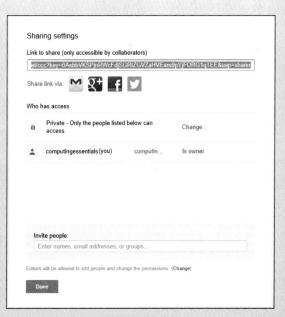

1 ● With the document open, click the *Share* button at the top right.

2 ● Type in the e-mail addresses of those with whom you wish to share the document.

3 ● To the right of this text box, select the permission these individuals will have for the document.

4 ● Click the *Done* button to finish.

The web is continually changing, and some of the specifics presented in this Making IT Work for You may have changed.

To learn about other ways to make information technology work for you, visit our website at www.mhhe.com/ce2015 and select Student Edition and then Making IT Work.

A LOOK TO THE FUTURE

Next-Generation User Interfaces

How will you be interacting with computers in the future? Will you continue using a mouse and keyboard for your desktop, or will touch screen and voice recognition replace them? Will a new type of interface emerge? One thing is for sure: We humans interact with the world around us in many ways, ranging from using our fingers to manipulate objects to making verbal requests. The goal of any future user interface is to bring that same level of interaction to a computer.

There are several challenges with designing interfaces. First is the simple fact that individuals have varying preferences. Some might prefer to interact with a friend through text messages, while others prefer voice communication. Therefore, it is doubtful that a single interface will become dominant. The second challenge is ergonomic in nature; that is, it must be comfortable to use.

Since tablets and smartphones have touch-screen interfaces, many people believe that all home and business computers will eventually have them too. In futuristic movies individuals use both hands to interact with a large screen. Such a setup allows a person to interact with multiple objects at the same time. The only problem with a multitouch, multigesture screen is that it is not comfortable to extend our arms for prolonged periods. Knowing this, many companies are looking toward large, interactive surfaces that perform the same function while lying flat on a desk. Microsoft has already developed a product called "PixelSense" that acts like a large, interactive table. It responds to both human interactions and objects that are placed on top of it. Although costs prevent it from replacing the desktop of today, the strain on a person's neck from looking down could prevent it from being used for long periods of time. The ideal use of PixelSense appears to be activities involving collaboration and teamwork.

Voice recognition is another form of input that is already available, but much improvement is needed. Computers are becoming better at following specific voice commands, but they cannot engage in everyday conversation or follow complex requests. Researchers in the field of artificial intelligence are working to improve natural language processing to help computers understand our writing and speech. When that is fully developed, you will be able to speak to your computer in the same way you would speak to another person.

The field of interactivity generating the most buzz involves using the entire body. Both cameras and software are becoming sophisticated enough to observe and interpret our movements and gestures. The "Kinect" system for the Xbox One has the ability to use body movements to interact with various games and fitness programs. Researchers at MIT are also working with cameras that can observe our gestures and the physical objects we interact with in order to communicate with a computer. In the future, computers could become so attuned to our emotions and expressions that they will be able to see our frustration with the current operation and take various corrective actions to relieve that frustration.

Which type of interface do you currently enjoy using the most? Do you think that touch-screen interfaces will replace keyboards? Do you believe that a computer can ever understand your speech as well as another human does?

APPLICATION SOFTWARE

The three categories of application software are **general purpose**, **specialized**, and **mobile**.

User Interface

You control and interact with a program using a **user interface**. A **graphical user interface (GUI)** uses **icons** selected by a mouse-controlled **pointer**. A **window** contains a document, program, or message. Software programs with a traditional GUI have

- **Menus**—present commands listed on the **menu bar**.
- **Toolbars**—contain **buttons** for quick access to commonly used commands.
- **Dialog box**—provides additional information or requests user input.

Software programs with a **Ribbon GUI** have

- **Ribbons**—replace menus and toolbars.
- **Tabs**—divide ribbons into **groups. Contextual tabs** automatically appear when needed.
- **Galleries**—graphically display alternatives before they are selected.

Common Features

Common features include spell checkers, alignment, fonts and font sizes, character effects, and edit options.

GENERAL-PURPOSE APPLICATIONS

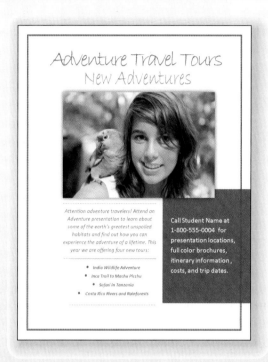

General-purpose applications include word processors, spreadsheets, presentation graphics, and database management systems.

Word Processors

Word processors create text-based documents. Individuals and organizations use word processors to create memos, letters, and faxes. Organizations also create newsletters, manuals, and brochures to provide information to their customers. Microsoft Word is the most widely used word processor. Others include Corel WordPerfect, Apple Pages, OpenOffice Writer, and Google Docs.

Spreadsheets

Spreadsheets organize, analyze, and graph numeric data such as budgets and financial reports. They are widely used by nearly every profession. Microsoft Excel is the most widely used spreadsheet program. Others include Apple Numbers and OpenOffice Calc.

To efficiently and effectively use computers, you need to understand the capabilities of general-purpose and specialized application software. Additionally, you need to know about mobile applications and software suites.

GENERAL-PURPOSE APPLICATIONS

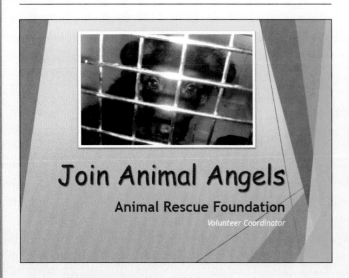

Presentation Graphics

Presentation graphics are programs that combine a variety of visual objects to create attractive, visually interesting presentations. They are excellent tools to communicate a message and to persuade people. People in a variety of settings and situations use presentation graphics programs to make their presentations more interesting and professional. Three of the most widely used presentation graphics programs are Microsoft PowerPoint, OpenOffice Impress, and Apple Keynote.

Database Management Systems

A **database** is a collection of related data. A **database management system (DBMS)** or **database manager** is a program that structures a database. It provides tools to enter, edit, and retrieve data from the database. Organizations use databases for many purposes including maintaining employee records. Two widely used database management systems designed for personal computers are Microsoft Access and OpenOffice Base.

SPECIALIZED APPLICATIONS

Specialized applications are widely used within specific professions. They include graphics programs and web authoring programs.

Graphics Programs

Graphics programs are used by graphic arts professionals.

* **Desktop publishing programs (page layout programs)** mix text and graphics to create professional-quality publications.
* **Image editors (photo editors)** edit digital photographs consisting of thousands of dots or **pixels** that form **bitmap** or **raster** images.
* **Illustration programs (drawing programs)** create and edit vector images. **Vector images (vector illustrations)** use geometric shapes.
* **Image galleries** are libraries of electronic images. Two basic types are **stock photographs** and **clip art**.

Web Authoring Programs

Web authoring is the process of creating a website. Individuals create online diaries called **blogs**. Many sites have **animations** (moving graphics) and **Flash** movies (interactive animation). Website design is represented by a **graphical site map.**

Web authoring programs (web page editors, HTML editors) create sophisticated commercial websites. Some are WYSIWYG (what you see is what you get) editors.

MOBILE APPS

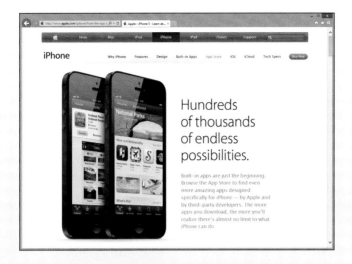

Mobile apps (mobile applications, apps) are add-on programs for a variety of mobile devices. Traditional applications include address books, to-do lists, alarms, and message lists. Recently mobile capabilities have exploded.

Apps

Popular apps include those for music, videos, social networking, shopping, and scanning QR codes.

QR codes (quick response codes) are graphics that automatically link mobile devices to content, including games, text, videos, and websites.

App Stores

An app store is typically a website that provides access to specific mobile apps that can be downloaded either for a nominal fee or free of charge. Two of the best-known stores are Apple's App Store and Google Play.

App	Focus	Site
Apple App Store	iOS devices	www.appstore.com
Google Play	Android devices	play.google.com
Windows Phone Marketplace	Windows phones	windowsphone.com/marketplace

SOFTWARE SUITES

A software suite is a collection of individual application packages sold together.

- Office suites (office software suites or productivity suites) contain professional-grade application programs.
- Cloud suites (online office suites) are stored on servers and available through the Internet.
- Specialized suites focus on specific applications such as graphics.
- Utility suites include a variety of programs designed to make computing easier and safer.

CAREERS IN IT

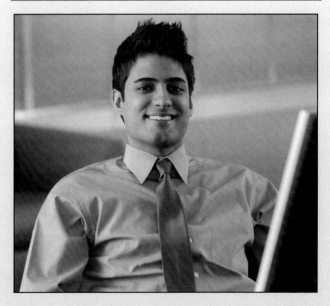

Software engineers analyze users' needs and create application software. Bachelor's or advanced specialized associate's degree in computer science or information systems and extensive knowledge of computers and technology are required. Salary range is $53,000 to $97,000.

KEY TERMS

animation   (72)
app   (74)
application software   (60)
app store   (75)
bitmap   (70)
blog   (71)
button   (60)
clip art   (71)
cloud suite   (76)
contextual tab   (61)
database   (68)
database management system
(DBMS)   (68)
database manager   (68)
desktop publishing program   (68)
dialog box   (60)
document   (62)
drawing program   (70)
Flash   (72)
gallery   (62)
general-purpose application   (60)
graphical site map   (72)
graphical user interface (GUI)   (60)
group   (61)
HTML editor   (72)
icon   (60)
illustration program   (70)
image editor   (70)
image gallery   (70)
menu   (60)
menu bar   (60)
mobile app   (60, 74)
mobile application   (74)
office software suite   (75)

office suite   (75)
online office suite   (76)
page layout program   (68)
photo editor   (70)
pixel   (70)
pointer   (60)
presentation graphics   (67)
productivity suite   (75)
QR code   (74)
quick response code   (74)
raster   (70)
ribbon   (61)
Ribbon GUI   (61)
software engineer   (76)
software suite   (75)
specialized application   (60)
specialized suite   (76)
spreadsheet   (65)
stock photograph   (71)
system software   (60)
tab   (61)
toolbar   (60)
user interface   (60)
utility suite   (76)
vector illustration   (70)
vector image   (70)
web authoring   (72)
web authoring program   (72)
web page editor   (72)
window   (60)
word processor   (62)
WYSIWYG (what you see is
what you get) editor   (72)

To test your knowledge of these key terms with animated flash cards, visit our website at www.mhhe.com/ce2015, select Student Edition, and choose Chapter 3 and then Flashcards.

MULTIPLE CHOICE

Circle the correct answer.

1. This type of software works with end users, application software, and computer hardware to handle the majority of technical details.
   a. application
   b. specialized
   c. system
   d. utility

2. A rectangular area that can contain a document, program, or message.
   a. dialog box
   b. form
   c. frame
   d. window

3. Programs that create text-based documents.
   a. DBMS
   b. suites
   c. spreadsheets
   d. word processors

4. Programs that organize, analyze, and graph numerical data such as budgets and financial reports.
   a. DBMS
   b. suites
   c. spreadsheets
   d. word processors

5. Program that allows you to mix text and graphics to create publications of professional quality.
   a. database
   b. desktop publishing
   c. presentation
   d. productivity

6. The type of image that consists of geometric shapes.
   a. bitmap
   b. raster
   c. ribbon
   d. vector

7. An online diary or commentary.
   a. bitmap
   b. blog
   c. HTML
   d. vector

8. Programs that combine a variety of visual objects to create attractive, visually interesting presentations.
   a. DBMS
   b. presentation graphics
   c. spreadsheet
   d. word processor

9. Graphics that typically appear as black and white boxes that automatically link mobile devices to various content.
   a. Flash
   b. animation
   c. vector
   d. QR codes

10. Also known as an online suite.
    a. cloud
    b. integrated
    c. office
    d. utility

For an interactive multiple-choice practice test, visit our website at www.mhhe.com/ce2015, select Student Edition, and choose Chapter 3 and then Multiple Choice.

MATCHING

Match each numbered item with the most closely related lettered item. Write your answers in the spaces provided.

a. buttons
b. cloud
c. database
d. galleries
e. image editor
f. map
g. spreadsheet
h. store
i. utility
j. word processor

___ 1. Toolbars typically appear below the menu bar and include small graphic elements called _____.

___ 2. Simplifies the process of making a selection from a list of alternatives by graphically displaying the effect of alternatives before being selected.

___ 3. A general-purpose program that creates text-based documents.

___ 4. Program that organizes, analyzes, and graphs numerical data.

___ 5. A collection of related data.

___ 6. Also known as a photo editor, this specialized graphics program edits or modifies digital photographs.

___ 7. The overall site design for a website is commonly represented in a graphical site _____.

___ 8. A website that provides access to specific mobile apps is known as an app _____.

___ 9. A type of suite that is stored at a server on the Internet and is available anywhere you can access the Internet.

___ 10. A type of specialized suite that includes a variety of programs designed to make computing easier and safer.

For an interactive matching practice test, visit our website at www.mhhe.com/ce2015, select Student Edition, and choose Chapter 3 and then Matching.

OPEN-ENDED

On a separate sheet of paper, respond to each question or statement.

1. Explain the difference between general-purpose and specialized applications. Also discuss the common features of application programs, including those with traditional and ribbon graphical user interfaces.

2. Discuss general-purpose applications, including word processors, spreadsheets, database management systems, and presentation graphics.

3. Discuss specialized applications, including graphics programs, web authoring programs, and other professional specialized applications.

4. Describe mobile apps, including popular apps and app stores.

5. Describe software suites, including office suites, cloud suites, specialized suites, and utility suites.

DISCUSSION

Respond to each of the following questions.

① Making IT Work for You: GOOGLE DOCS

Would you like to try free alternatives to traditional office software suites? Review the Making IT Work for You: Google Docs on page 77, and then respond to the following: (a) Do you currently use Google Docs? If so, what types of documents do you typically create? If not, then list some possible benefits Google Docs could provide. (b) Do you share documents and/or collaborate with others? How do you do it? If you have used Google Docs, describe how you would share documents. (c) Using a search engine or your own research, list a few differences between Google Docs and Microsoft Office Web Apps. Which one do you prefer? Why?

② Privacy: SMARTPHONE TRACKING

If you have a smartphone, then it is likely that your movements are recorded and stored. Review the Privacy box on page 75, and respond to the following: (a) Do you think that smartphone tracking is a violation of your privacy? If yes, what can be done? If no, explain your position. (b) Does a company that tracks your movements have the right to sell this information to other companies? Would your opinion change if the company sells your location information but does not reveal your identity? State and defend your position. (c) Does the government have the right to subpoena GPS information from an app maker? Why or why not? (d) Are there any circumstances in which it would be acceptable/justifiable for a company to reveal location data to the government or another company? Give some examples.

③ Ethics: IMAGE EDITING

Various image and video editing applications have made it easy for both professionals and amateurs to alter photographs and videos. Some of these edits raise ethical concerns when they are used inappropriately. Review the Ethics box on page 71. Research examples of digital photo or video editing that have resulted in controversy, and then respond to the following: (a) Do you see any ethical issues related to altering photographs or videos? (b) What do you consider the boundary to be between acceptable editing and deceptive or misleading practices? (c) How does such editing affect courtrooms where visual evidence is often presented? (d) Do you feel the old saying "seeing is believing" needs to be reconsidered for the digital age? Defend your answers.

④ Environment: APPS

Did you know that using mobile devices and apps can benefit the environment? Review the Environment box on page 74, and then respond to the following: (a) In what ways are mobile devices helping the environment? (b) Do you currently read any books on mobile devices? If so, list a few of your most recent ones. If you do not, name three of your traditional textbooks that are available as e-books. (c) List and briefly describe three apps that allow you to take notes on your mobile device. If you do not own a mobile device, research these apps for any mobile operating system. (d) Is it possible that mobile devices could actually be worse for the environment? Discuss your response.

Learning Objectives

After you have read this chapter, you should be able to:

1 Describe the differences between system software and application software.

2 Identify the four types of system software programs.

3 Explain the basic functions, features, and categories of operating systems.

4 Compare mobile operating systems, including iOS, Android, and Windows Phone.

5 Compare desktop operating systems, including Windows, Mac OS, UNIX, Linux, and virtualization.

6 Explain the purpose of utilities and utility suites.

7 Identify the four most essential utilities.

8 Describe Windows utility programs.

9 Describe device drivers, including Windows' Add a Device Wizard and Update.

Why should I read this chapter?

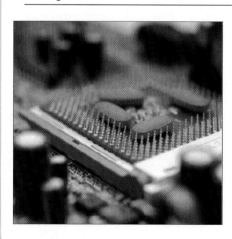

Someday soon, your computer will be able to automatically diagnose and repair problems, much like you body's immune system. For now, however, your electronics are at risk from dangerous viruses and software failures.

This chapter covers the things you need to know to protect your computer and data today and to prepare you for tomorrow, including:

- Desktop operating systems—discover how operating systems control and protect desktop and laptop computers.
- Mobile operating systems—learn the key features of the operating systems that control tablets and cell phones.
- Utilities—protect your computer from viruses and perform important maintenance tasks.

Introduction

"Hi, I'm Ann, and I'm a computer support specialist. I'd like to talk with you about system software, programs that do a lot of the work behind the scenes so that you can run applications and surf the web. I'd also like to talk about the mobile operating systems that control smartphones and other small portable computers."

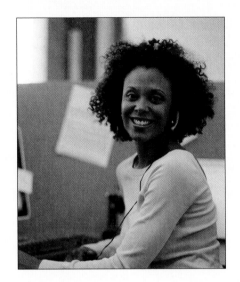

When most people think about computers, they think about surfing the web, creating reports, analyzing data, storing information, making presentations, and any number of other valuable applications. We typically think about applications and application software. Computers and computer applications have become a part of the fabric of our everyday lives. Most of us agree that they are great . . . as long as they are working.

We usually do not think about the more mundane and behind-the-scenes computer activities: loading and running programs, coordinating networks that share resources, organizing files, protecting our computers from viruses, performing periodic maintenance to avoid problems, and controlling hardware devices so that they can communicate with one another. Typically, these activities go on behind the scenes without our help.

That is the way it should be, and the way it is, as long as everything is working perfectly. But what if new application programs are not compatible and will not run on our current computer system? What if we get a computer virus? What if our hard disk fails? What if we buy a new digital video camera and can't store and edit the images on our computer system? What if our computer starts to run slower and slower?

These issues may seem mundane, but they are critical. This chapter covers the vital activities that go on behind the scenes. A little knowledge about these activities can go a long way to making your computing life easier. To efficiently and effectively use computers, you need to understand the functionality of system software, including operating systems, utility programs, and device drivers.

System Software

End users use application software to accomplish specific tasks. For example, we use word processing programs to create letters, documents, and reports. However, end users also use system software. **System software** works with end users, application software, and computer hardware to handle the majority of technical details. For example, system software controls where a word processing program is stored in memory, how commands are converted so that the system unit can process them, and where a completed document or file is saved. (See Figure 4-1.)

System software is not a single program. Rather it is a collection or a system of programs that handle hundreds of technical details with little or no user intervention. System software consists of four types of programs:

- **Operating systems** coordinate computer resources, provide an interface between users and the computer, and run applications.
- **Utilities** perform specific tasks related to managing computer resources.
- **Device drivers** are specialized programs that allow particular input or output devices to communicate with the rest of the computer system.
- **Language translators** convert the programming instructions written by programmers into a language that computers understand and process.

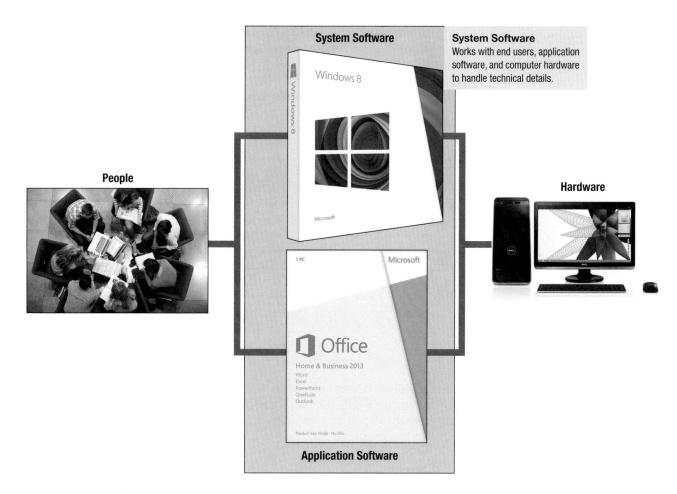

System Software
Works with end users, application software, and computer hardware to handle technical details.

People

Hardware

Application Software

Figure 4-1 System software handles technical details

Operating Systems

An **operating system** is a collection of programs that handle many of the technical details related to using a computer. In many ways, an operating system is the most important type of computer program. Without a functioning operating system, your computer would be useless.

Functions

Every computer has an operating system, and every operating system performs a variety of functions. These functions can be classified into three groups:

- **Managing resources:** Operating systems coordinate all the computer's resources including memory, processing, storage, and devices such as printers and monitors. They also monitor system performance, schedule tasks, provide security, and start up the computer.
- **Providing user interface:** Operating systems allow users to interact with application programs and computer hardware through a **user interface.** Many older operating systems used a character-based interface in which users communicated with the operating system through written commands such as "Copy A: report.txt C:". Almost all newer operating systems use a **graphical user interface (GUI).** As we discussed in Chapter 3, a graphical user interface uses graphical elements such as icons and windows.

- **Running applications:** Operating systems load and run applications such as word processors and spreadsheets. Most operating systems support **multi-tasking,** or the ability to switch between different applications stored in memory. With multitasking, you could have Word and Excel running at the same time and switch easily between the two applications. The program that you are currently working on is described as running in the **foreground.** The other program or programs are running in the **background.**

Features

Starting or restarting a computer is called **booting** the system. There are two ways to boot a computer: a warm boot and a cold boot. A **warm boot** occurs when the computer is already on and you restart it without turning off the power. A warm boot can be accomplished in several ways. For many computer systems, they can be restarted by simply pressing a sequence of keys. Starting a computer that has been turned off is called a **cold boot.** To learn more about booting your computer system and POST (power on self-test), visit our website at www.mhhe.com/ce2015 and select Student Edition, then Explore, and then Boot.

You typically interact with the operating system through the graphical user interface. Most provide a place, called the **desktop,** that provides access to computer resources. (See Figure 4-2.) Operating systems have several features in common with application programs, including

- **Icons**—graphic representations for a program, type of file, or function.
- **Pointer**—controlled by a mouse, trackpad, or touch screen, the pointer changes shape depending on its current function. For example, when shaped like an arrow, the pointer can be used to select items such as an icon.

Figure 4-2 Desktop

- **Windows**—rectangular areas for displaying information and running programs.
- **Menus**—provide a list of options or commands that can be selected.
- **Tabs**—divide menus into major activity areas such as format and page layout.
- **Dialog boxes**—typically provide information or request input.
- **Help**—provides online assistance for operating system functions and procedures.
- **Gesture control**—ability to control operations with finger movements, such as swiping, sliding, and pinching.

Most operating systems store data and programs in a system of files and folders. **Files** are used to store data and programs. Related files are stored within a **folder,** and, for organizational purposes, a folder can contain other folders, or subfolders. For example, you might organize your electronic files in the *Documents* folder on your hard disk. This folder could contain other folders, each named to indicate its contents. One might be "Computer Class" and could contain all the files you have created (or will create) for this course.

Categories

While there are hundreds of different operating systems, there are only three basic categories: embedded, network, or stand-alone.

- **Embedded operating systems** are operating systems that are entirely stored within (i.e., embedded in) a device. Examples of embedded devices are smartphones, cable and satellite television tuner boxes, video game systems, and other small electronics. (See Figure 4-3.)

Figure 4-3 Handheld devices use embedded operating systems

- **Network operating systems (NOS)** are used to control and coordinate computers that are networked or linked together. Many networks are small and connect only a limited number of personal computers. Other networks, like those at colleges and universities, are very large and complex. These networks may include other smaller networks and typically connect a variety of different types of computers.

  Network operating systems are typically located on one of the connected computers' hard disks. Called the **network server,** this computer coordinates all communication between the other computers. Popular network operating systems include Linux, Windows Server, and UNIX.

- **Stand-alone operating systems**, also called **desktop operating systems,** control a single desktop or laptop computer. (See Figure 4-4.) These operating systems are located on the computer's hard disk. Often desktop computers and laptops are part of a network. In these cases, the desktop operating system works with the network's NOS to share and coordinate resources. In these situations, the desktop operating system is referred to as the *client operating system.*

Figure 4-4 Laptops use stand-alone operating systems

The operating system is often referred to as the **software environment** or **software platform.** Almost all application programs are designed to run with a specific platform. For example, Apple's iMovie software is designed to run with the Mac OS environment. Many applications, however, have different versions, each designed to operate with a particular platform. For example, one version of Microsoft Office is designed to operate with Windows. Another version is designed to operate with Mac OS.

concept check

What is system software? What are the four kinds of system software programs?

What is an operating system? Discuss operating system functions and features.

Describe each of the three categories of operating systems.

Figure 4-5 **Apple's iPad and iPhone use iOS mobile operating system**

Mobile Operating Systems

Mobile operating systems, also known as **mobile OS,** are a type of embedded operating system. Just like other computer systems, mobile computers including smartphones and tablets require an operating system. These mobile operating systems are less complicated and more specialized for wireless communication.

While there are numerous mobile operating systems, some of the best known are Android, iOS, and Windows Phone.

- **Android** was introduced in 2007. It was originally developed by Android Inc. and later purchased by Google. Android is widely used in many of today's smartphones.
- **iOS,** formerly known as **iPhone OS,** was originally developed in 2007 by Apple. It is based on Mac OS and is used as the platform for Apple's iPad and iPhone. (See Figure 4-5.)
- **Windows Phone 8** was introduced in 2012 by Microsoft to support a variety of mobile devices, including smartphones. It has the ability to run many powerful programs designed for desktop and laptop computers.

In the last chapter, we discussed that not all mobile applications will run on all smartphones. That is because an app is designed to run on a particular software platform or operating system. Before downloading an app, be sure that it is designed to run with the mobile operating system on your mobile device.

concept check

What is a mobile operating system?

List the three most widely used mobile operating systems.

Which mobile operating system works with the iPhone? Which mobile operating system was developed by Microsoft?

Figure 4-6 **Windows 7**

Figure 4-7 **Windows 8**

Desktop Operating Systems

Every personal computer has an operating system controlling its operations. The most widely used desktop operating systems are Windows, Mac OS, Unix, and Linux.

Windows

Microsoft's **Windows** is the most widely used personal computer operating system. Because its market share is so large, more application programs have been developed to run under Windows than any other operating system. Windows comes in a variety of different versions and is designed to run with a variety of different microprocessors.

The two recent versions are Windows 7 and Windows 8.

- **Windows 7** was released in 2009 and has a traditional user interface similar to previous versions of Windows. (See Figure 4-6.) It provided enhanced features, including improved handwriting recognition and advanced searching capabilities for finding files and other content on a computer.
- **Windows 8** was released in 2012 and was created to better integrate Microsoft's desktop operating systems with its mobile operating systems. (See Figure 4-7.) It provided support for gestures, cloud integration, and apps. Windows 8 also introduced a new interface. This interface is very similar to the interface for Microsoft's mobile operating system, Windows Phone, and is a dramatic shift from the traditional Windows interface. Windows 8 offers a **start screen** consisting of tiles. Each **tile** displays active content linked to an application. A desktop similar to the traditional Windows desktop can be accessed various ways. **Windows RT** is a version of Windows 8 designed to run with tablets using a particular microprocessor from ARM.

Mac OS

Apple has been the leader in the development of powerful and easy-to-use personal computer operating systems since its introduction of the Macintosh personal computer in 1984. Designed to run only with Apple computers, **Mac OS** is not as widely used as the Windows operating system. As a result, fewer application programs have been written for it. However, with dramatically increasing sales of Apple computers, the use of Mac OS has been rapidly increasing and is widely recognized as one of the most innovative operating systems.

Figure 4-8 Mac OS X Mavericks

Figure 4-9 Linux

Mac OS X is the most widely used Mac desktop operating system. Its two most recent versions are

- **OS X Mountain Lion** was released in 2012 and designed for desktops and laptops. Its user interface is very similar to the interface used with its tablets and smartphones. The functionality of Mountain Lion is similar to Windows 8, although it is generally regarded as easier to use.
- **OS X Mavericks** was announced in 2013 and introduce several improvements, including better power management for longer laptop battery life, enhanced workflow options for multiple monitor setups, and better integration with cloud computing. (See Figure 4-8.)

UNIX and Linux

The **UNIX** operating system was originally designed in the late 1960s to run on minicomputers in network environments. Over the years, UNIX has evolved with numerous different version. Now, it is widely used by servers on the web, mainframe computers, and very powerful personal computers. There are a large number of different versions of UNIX.

Linux is an operating system that extended one of the UNIX versions. It was originally developed by a graduate student at the University of Helsinki, Linus Torvalds, in 1991. He allowed free distribution of the operating system code and encouraged others to modify and further develop the code. Programs released in this way are called **open source.** Linux is a popular and powerful alternative to the Windows operating system. (See Figure 4-9.)

Linux has been the basis of several other operating systems. For example, Google's **Chrome OS** is based on Linux. This operating system is designed for netbook computers and other mobile devices. Chrome OS focuses on Internet connectivity and cloud computing.

Virtualization

As we have discussed, application programs are designed to run with particular operating systems. What if you wanted to run two or more applications each requiring a different operating system? One solution would be to install each of the operating systems on a different computer. There is, however, a way in which a single physical computer can support multiple operating systems that operate independently. This approach is called **virtualization.**

When a single physical computer runs a special program known as **virtualization software,** it operates as though it were two or more separate and independent computers, known as **virtual machines.** Each virtual machine appears to the user as a separate independent computer with its own operating system. The operating system of the physical machine is known as the **host operating system.** The operating system for each virtual machine is known as the **guest operating system.** Users can readily switch between virtual computers and programs running on them. There are several programs that create and run virtual machines. One such program, Microsoft's **Hyper-V,** is included with the Windows 8 Professional version. (See Figure 4-10.)

Figure 4-10 **Ubuntu Linux running in a Windows 8 Hyper-V virtual machine**

concept check

What is Windows? What are the two most recent versions?

What is Mac OS? What are Mountain Lion and Mavericks?

What is UNIX? What is Linux? What is Chrome OS?

Utilities

Ideally, personal computers would continuously run without problems. However, that simply is not the case. All kinds of things can happen—internal hard disks can crash, computers can freeze up, operations can slow down, and so on. These events can make computing very frustrating. That's where utilities come in. **Utilities** are specialized programs designed to make computing easier. There are hundreds of different utility programs. The most essential are

- **Troubleshooting** or **diagnostic programs** that recognize and correct problems, ideally before they become serious. To learn more about using a troubleshooting program, see Making IT Work for You: Windows Task Manager on pages 96 and 97.
- **Antivirus programs** that guard your computer system against viruses or other damaging programs that can invade your computer system. Popular antivirus programs include Norton Antivirus and Webroot Secure Anywhere AntiVirus.
- **Backup programs** that make copies of files to be used in case the originals are lost or damaged. Windows 8 comes with a free backup program, the File History tool, and Mac OS X has a backup feature named Time Machine.
- **File compression programs** that reduce the size of files so they require less storage space and can be sent more efficiently over the Internet. Most operating systems handle unzipping files automatically when you open a .zip file.

Most operating systems provide some utility programs. Even more powerful utility programs can be purchased separately or in utility suites.

WINDOWS TASK MANAGER

Have you ever been working with a program when it simply stopped working and would not respond to you? Does your computer seem to be getting slower and slower? Windows Task Manager, which gives you a live view of every program that is currently in RAM, is designed to help with these and many other operational problems.

Starting Task Manager   You can open Task Manager from anywhere by following these steps:

1 ● **Press and momentarily hold the Ctrl + Alt + Del keys.**

2 ● **Select the *Start Task Manager* option.**

As you can see, the Task Manager window provides a list of active programs; more information can be seen by clicking on the *More details* button; and you can return to the compact view by clicking the *Fewer details* button. Please note that it may look slightly different in your version of Windows.

Closing an Application   Use Task Manager when a program you are using becomes stuck and stops responding.

1 ● **If you are not currently in the compact view of Task Manager, click the *Fewer details* button.**

2 ● **Find the program that is stuck. Next to the program name there should read, "Not Responding."**

3 ● **Select it and click the *End task* button.**

The program that was not responding has been closed, and you can now continue using Windows normally.

Viewing Processes   This is the most powerful area of Task Manager. Here, you will see a list of every process (running program) that is currently residing in your computer's RAM.

1 ● **If you are not currently in the expanded view of Task Manager, click the *More details* button. Go to the *Processes* tab of Task Manager.**

2 ● **Click the *Memory* heading. All the processes will be sorted from highest (occupying the most RAM) to the lowest.**

3 ● **Click the *CPU* heading. This will show any processes that the CPU is currently working on.**

It is normal for the numbers to fluctuate for running programs, especially those for the CPU. Also note that a very high number on "System Idle Process" is normal.

Ending a Process   Some problematic processes could be spyware, while others represent background services you don't need. Other processes are crucial for your system and should never be ended. *Warning:* Before ending a process, you must truly understand the risks (or benefits) of doing so. Using a search engine, type the name of the process, and the results will list several websites that explain what it does. If you want to end a process:

1 While in the *Processes* tab, click the *Name* heading (to avoid the fluctuating positions of each process).

2 Click the process you want to end.

3 Select the *End task* button.

That particular program file will be removed from the list and from your computer's memory. Keep in mind that if this program is configured to load automatically, you will see it again when you restart your computer.

Managing Startup Programs If you are wondering why you have so many processes running in your computer's memory, it is likely because many of your software titles have small programs or services that begin running each time you start Windows. Some services are crucial, while others are not always needed and do little except slow down your computer. To manage these services:

1 Go to the *Startup* tab of Task Manager.

2 Review the list of startup processes, perform research online, and select any programs that you do not want to load automatically each time you start Windows.

3 Click the *Disable* button to stop that program from running at startup in the future.

Before making any changes to startup programs or active processes, be sure that you have carefully researched the program and/or consulted with a professional.

To learn about other ways to make information technology work for you, visit our website at www. mhhe.com/ce2015 and select Student Edition **and then** Making IT Work.

Windows Utilities

The Windows operating systems are accompanied by several utility programs, including File History, Disk Cleanup, and Disk Defragmenter.

File History is a utility program included with Windows 8 that makes a copy of all files that are in the libraries, contacts, and favorites and on the desktop. It helps protect you from the effects of a disk failure. For example, you can select *File History* from the Windows 8 System and Security window to create a backup for your hard disk as shown in Figure 4-11.

1 Go to the Windows 8 start screen, type "control panel," and select *Control Panel*.

In the Control Panel window, select *Systems and Security* and click on *File History*.

Choose the destination for the backup.

Click the *Turn on* button.

Figure 4-11 File History utility

When you surf the web, a variety of programs and files are saved on your hard disk. Many of these and other files are not essential. **Disk Cleanup** is a trouble-shooting utility that identifies and eliminates nonessential files. This frees up valuable disk space and improves system performance.

For example, by opening Disk Cleanup from the Windows 8 search results, you can eliminate unneeded files on your hard disk as shown in Figure 4-12.

1

Go to the Windows 8 start screen, type "disk cleanup," and select *Settings*.

Click on *Free up disk space by deleting unnecessary files* in the search results.

Review the files suggested for cleanup, and then click *OK*.

If you have multiple drives, select the drive you want to clean up, and then click *OK*.

2

The utility cleans the selected files.

Figure 4-12 Disk Cleanup utility

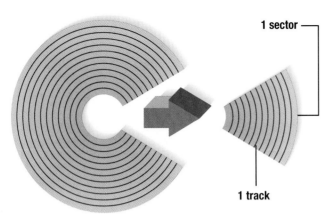

1 sector

1 track

Figure 4-13 **Tracks and sectors**

As we will discuss in detail in Chapter 7, files are stored and organized on a disk according to tracks and sectors. A **track** is a concentric ring. Each track is divided into wedge-shaped sections called **sectors.** (See Figure 4-13.) The operating system tries to save a file on a single track across contiguous sectors. Often, however, this is not possible, and the file has to be broken up, or **fragmented,** into small parts that are stored wherever space is available. Whenever a file is retrieved, it is reconstructed from the fragments. After a period of time, a hard disk becomes highly fragmented, slowing operations.

Optimize Drives is a utility program that locates and eliminates unnecessary fragments and rearranges files and unused disk space to optimize operations. For example, by selecting Optimize Drives from the Windows 8 search results, you can defrag your hard disk as shown in Figure 4-14.

1 From the start screen, type "disk cleanup" and click *Settings.*

From the search results, select *Defragment and optimize your drives.*

2 In the Optimize Drives window, in the section labeled Status, select the drive you would like to defrag.

Click the *Optimize* button to defrag the highlighted drive.

When defragmentation is complete for the selected drive, view the report or close the window.

Figure 4-14 **Optimize Drives utility**

Utility Suites

Like application software suites, **utility suites** combine several programs into one package. Buying the package is less expensive than buying the programs separately. Some of the best-known utility suites are BitDefender, Norton Utilities, and

Figure 4-15 **Norton Utilities**

ZoneAlarm. (See Figure 4-15.) These suites provide a variety of utilities, including programs that will protect your system from dangerous computer **viruses.** You can "catch" a computer virus many ways, including by opening attachments to e-mail messages and downloading software from the Internet. (We will discuss computer viruses in detail in Chapter 9.)

concept check

Discuss four essential utilities.

Describe Windows File History, Disk Cleanup, and Optimize Drives.

What is the difference between a utility and a utility suite?

Device Drivers

Every device, such as a mouse or printer, that is connected to a computer system has a special program associated with it. This program, called a **device driver** or simply a **driver,** works with the operating system to allow communication between the device and the rest of the computer system. Each time the computer system is started, the operating system loads all of the device drivers into memory.

Whenever a new device is added to a computer system, a new device driver must be installed before the device can be used. Windows supplies hundreds of different device drivers with its system software. For many devices, the appropriate drivers are automatically selected and installed when the device is first connected to the computer system. For others, the device driver must be manually installed. Fortunately, Windows provides wizards to assist in this process. For example, Windows' **Add a Device Wizard** provides step-by-step guidance for selecting the appropriate hardware driver and installing that driver. If a particular device driver is not included with the Windows system software, the product's manufacturer will supply one. Many times these drivers are available directly from the manufacturer's website.

You probably never think about the device drivers in your computer. However, when your computer behaves unpredictably, you may find reinstalling or updating your device drivers solves your problems. Windows 8 makes it easy to update the drivers on your computer using **Windows Update,** as shown in Figure 4-16.

1 • From the start screen, type "windows update" and click on *Settings.*

 • Click *Check for updates.*

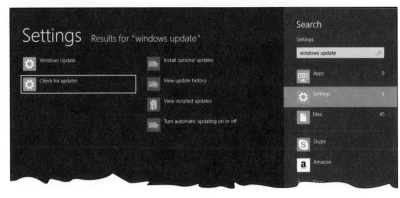

2 • Click *See details* to review the list of recommended updates.

3 • Click *Install updates* to download updates to your computer.

Figure 4-16 **Windows Update**

☑ concept check

What are device drivers, and what do they do?

What is Windows' Add a Device Wizard, and what does it do?

What is Windows Update? What does it do?

Careers in IT

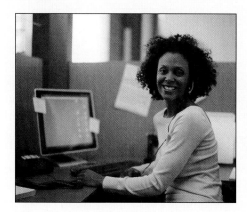

Computer support specialists provide technical support to customers and other users. They also may be called technical support specialists or help-desk technicians. Computer support specialists manage the everyday technical problems faced by computer users. They resolve common networking problems and may use troubleshooting programs to diagnose problems. Most computer support specialists are hired to work within a company and provide technical support for other employees and divisions. However, it is increasingly common for companies to provide technical support as an outsourced service.

Employers generally look for individuals with either an advanced associate's degree or a bachelor's degree to fill computer support specialist positions. Degrees in computer science or information systems may be preferred. However, because demand for qualified applicants is so high, those with practical experience and certification from a training program increasingly fill these positions. Employers seek individuals with customer service experience that demonstrate good analytical, communication, and people skills.

Computer support specialists can expect to earn an annual salary of $31,000 to $58,000. Opportunities for advancement are very good and may involve design and implementation of new systems. To learn about other careers in information systems, visit us at www.mhhe.com/ce2015 and select Student Edition and then Careers.

A LOOK TO THE FUTURE

Self-Healing Computers Could Mean an End to Computer Crashes and Performance Problems

Wouldn't it be nice if computers could fix themselves? What if your computer could continually fine-tune its operations to maintain peak performance? And wouldn't it be a relief if you never had to help your computer recover after a virus or other intrusion? For many people, this sounds too good to be true. Maintenance and troubleshooting tasks like these can be time-consuming and frustrating.

Now imagine you run a business, and unless these tasks are performed, you will lose time and money. It is not a pleasant daydream, and it quickly becomes a nightmare without properly trained systems administrators to keep servers running smoothly. Yet many experts predict that supercomputers and business systems are not far from becoming too complex for humans to manage and secure. Recent news from IBM makes the dream of a self-repairing, self-updating, and self-protecting server seem closer.

IBM has announced plans to concentrate research efforts on developing just such a server. The project, called the Autonomic Computing Initiative (ACI), hopes to free businesses from time-consuming computer maintenance. IBM hopes the new system will be self-regulating and virtually invisible. It believes autonomic computing has the potential to revolutionize the way businesses run.

Autonomic computing is a system that allows machines to run with little human intervention. Such computers would not have self-awareness but would be self-correcting. Autonomic processes in machines are modeled after autonomic processes in the human body. For example, you are not consciously breathing. Instead, your body monitors and maintains your respiration without your input. Scientists hope autonomic computing will behave in a similar manner and maintain systems without intervention.

Autonomic machines would be able to identify security flaws and repair them. They would be able to sense slow computer operations and take corrective action. They would be able to detect new equipment, format it, and test it. Computer usage will become less complex so that you can focus on getting work done instead of worrying about the machine's operation. These goals are impressive, and the autonomic computer is still in development.

It is important to note that autonomic computing is not artificial intelligence because autonomic machines do not have human cognitive abilities or intelligence. Instead, these machines have knowledge of their own systems and the capability to learn from experience to correct errors.

Given the potential for a self-maintaining server, the possibility of a similar system designed for a personal computer seems less like a dream and more like a reality. What do you think? Will personal computers ever care for themselves? Do you think it is possible to have a computer managing its own security? Will hackers find a way to outsmart these "intelligent" systems?

SYSTEM SOFTWARE

System software works with end users, application programs, and computer hardware to handle many details relating to computer operations.

Not a single program but a collection or system of programs, these programs handle hundreds of technical details with little or no user intervention.

Four kinds of systems programs are operating systems, utilities, device drivers, and language translators.

- **Operating systems** coordinate resources, provide an interface between users and the computer, and run programs.
- **Utilities** perform specific tasks related to managing computer resources.
- **Device drivers** allow particular input or output devices to communicate with the rest of the computer system.
- **Language translators** convert programming instructions written by programmers into a language that computers can understand and process.

OPERATING SYSTEMS

Operating systems (software environments, software platforms) handle technical details.

Functions

Functions include managing resources, providing a **user interface** (most operating systems use a **graphical user interface**, or GUI), and running applications. **Multitasking** allows switching between different applications stored in memory; current programs run in **foreground**; other programs run in **background**.

Features

Booting starts (**cold**) or restarts (**warm**) a computer system. The **desktop** provides access to computer resources. Common features include **icons, pointers, windows, menus, tabs, dialog boxes, Help,** and **gesture control**. Data and programs are stored in a system of **files** and **folders**.

Categories

Three categories of operating systems are

- **Embedded**—used with handheld computers; operating system stored within device.
- **Network (NOS)**—controls and coordinates networked computers; located on the **network server**.
- **Stand-alone (desktop)**—controls a single computer; located on the hard disk.

Operating systems are often called **software environments** or **software platforms**.

To efficiently and effectively use computers, you need to understand the functionality of system software, including operating systems, utility programs, and device drivers.

MOBILE OPERATING SYSTEMS

Mobile operating systems (mobile OS) are embedded in every smartphone and tablet. These systems are less complicated and more specialized for wireless communication than desktop operating systems.

Some of the best known are Android, iOS (iPhone OS), and Windows Phone.

- **Android** was originally developed by Android Inc. and later purchased by Google. It is a widely used mobile OS.
- **iOS (iPhone OS)** was developed by Apple to support iPhone and iPad.
- **Windows Phone 8** was introduced in 2012 by Microsoft to support a variety of mobile devices, including smartphones. It can run many powerful programs designed for laptop and desktop computers.

Not all mobile applications will run on all smartphones. That is because an app is designed to run on a particular software platform or operating system. Before downloading an app, be sure that it is designed to run with the mobile operating system on your mobile device.

DESKTOP OPERATING SYSTEMS

Windows

Windows is designed to run with many different microprocessors. The two recent versions are **Windows 7** and **Windows 8**. Windows 8 offers an interface very similar to the Windows Phone interface; supports desktops, laptops, and tablets; uses a **start screen** and **tiles**; and provides support for gestures, cloud integration, and apps. **Windows RT**, a version of Windows 8, is designed to run with ARM tablets.

Mac OS

Mac OS, an innovative, powerful, easy-to-use operating system, runs on Macintosh computers. The two most recent versions are **Mountain Lion** and **Mavericks**. Mountain Lion's interface is very similar to the interfaces on Apple's smartphone and tablets. It is designed for Apple's desktops and laptops. Its functionality is similar to Windows 8, but it generally is considered easier to use. Mavericks supports longer laptop battery life and multiple monitor setups.

UNIX and Linux

UNIX was originally designed to run on minicomputers in network environments. Now, it is widely used by servers on the web, mainframe computers, and very powerful personal computers. There are many different versions of UNIX. One version, **Linux**, a popular and powerful alternative to the Windows operating system, is **open source** software. Google's **Chrome OS** is based on Linux and designed for netbooks and other mobile devices. Chrome OS focuses on Internet connectivity and cloud computing.

Virtualization

Virtualization allows a single physical computer to support multiple operating systems. Using a special program (**virtualization software**) allows the single physical computer to operate as two or more separate and independent computers known as **virtual machines**. **Host operating systems** run on the physical machine. **Guest operating systems** operate on virtual machines. Microsoft's **Hyper-V** creates and runs virtual machines.

Utilities make computing easier. The most essential are **troubleshooting (diagnostic)**, **antivirus**, **backup**, and **file compression**.

Windows Utilities

Windows operating systems are accompanied by several utility programs, including **File History**, **Disk Cleanup**, and **Optimize Drives** (eliminates unnecessary **fragments**; **tracks** are concentric rings; **sectors** are wedge-shaped).

Utility Suites

Utility suites combine several programs into one package. Computer **viruses** are dangerous programs.

DEVICE DRIVERS

Device drivers (drivers) allow communication between hardware devices. **Add a Device Wizard** gives step-by-step guidance to install printer drivers. **Windows Update** automates the process of updating device drivers.

CAREERS IN IT

Computer support specialists provide technical support to customers and other users. Degrees in computer science or information systems are preferred plus good analytical and communication skills. Salary range is $31,000 to $58,000.

Learning Objectives

After you have read this chapter, you should be able to:

1 Differentiate between the four basic types of system units.

2 Describe system boards, including sockets, slots, and bus lines.

3 Recognize different microprocessors, including microprocessor chips and specialty processors.

4 Compare different types of computer memory, including RAM, ROM, and flash memory.

5 Explain expansion slots and cards.

6 Describe bus lines, bus widths, and expansion buses.

7 Describe ports, including standard and specialized ports.

8 Identify power supplies for desktop, laptop, tablet, and mobile devices.

9 Explain how a computer can represent numbers and encode characters electronically.

Why should I read this chapter?

System units are getting smaller, faster, cheaper, and more powerful. These staggering improvements are resulting in microchips integrating with all aspects of our lives. For example, in the future we will see everything from microchips embedded in the brain that improve mental capacity to sensors that can literally read your mind.

This chapter covers the things you need to know to be prepared for this ever changing digital world, including:

- Types of microcomputers—learn the strengths and weaknesses of desktops, laptops, tablets, and mobile devices.
- Computer components—understand the impact microprocessors and memory have on the power of a computer.
- Peripherals and upgrades—expand your computer's abilities and speed.

Introduction

Why are some computers more powerful than others? The answer lies in three words: speed, capacity, and flexibility. After reading this chapter, you will be able to judge how fast, powerful, and versatile a particular personal computer is. As you might expect, this knowledge is valuable if you are planning to buy a new personal computer system or to upgrade an existing system. (The Computer Buyer's Guide at the end of this book provides additional information.) This knowledge will help you evaluate whether or not an existing system is powerful enough for today's new and exciting applications.

Sometime you may get the chance to watch when a technician opens up a personal computer. You will see that it is basically a collection of electronic circuitry. While there is no need to understand how all these components work, it is important to understand the principles. Armed with this knowledge, you will be able to confidently make sound purchasing and upgrading decisions.

To efficiently and effectively use computers, you need to understand the functionality of the basic components in the system unit, including the system board, microprocessor, memory, expansion slots and cards, bus lines, ports, cables, and power supply units.

System Unit

The **system unit,** also known as the **system chassis,** is a container that houses most of the electronic components that make up a computer system.

At one time all system units were in a separate case. Advances in the miniaturization of electronic components, however, have led to smaller and smaller computers with system units that share containers with other parts of the computer system.

As we have previously discussed, a **personal computer** is the most widely used type of computer. It is the most affordable and designed to be operated directly by an end user. The four most common types are desktop, laptop, tablet, and mobile devices. Each has a unique type of system unit.

Desktops

This is the most powerful type of personal computer. Most **desktops** have their system unit in a separate case. This case contains the system's electronic components and selected secondary storage devices. Input and output devices, such as a mouse, keyboard, and monitor, are located outside the system unit. This type of system unit is designed to be placed either horizontally or vertically. Desktop system units that are placed vertically are sometimes referred to as a **tower unit** or **tower computer.** (See Figure 5-1.)

Some desktop computers, like Apple's iMac, have their monitor and system unit housed together in the same case. These computers are known as an **all-in-one.** (See Figure 5-2.)

Laptops

Although typically not as powerful as desktops, **laptops** are portable and much smaller. Their system units are housed with selected secondary storage devices and input devices (keyboard and pointing device). Located outside the system unit, the monitor is attached by hinges. Laptops are often called **notebooks.**

Figure 5-1 **Tower unit**

Figure 5-2 **All-in-one**

Ultrabooks, also known as **ultraportables** or **mini notebooks,** are a type of very portable laptop. They are lighter and thinner and have a longer battery life than other laptops. They accomplish these advantages by leaving out components such as optical drives and using energy-efficient microprocessors. (See Figure 5-3.)

Tablets

Tablets, also known as **tablet computers,** are the newest and one of the most popular types of computer. They are effectively a thin slab that is almost all monitor with the system unit located behind the monitor.

Tablets are smaller, lighter, and generally less powerful than laptop computers. Like a laptop, tablets have a flat screen but typically do not have a standard keyboard. Instead, most tablets use a virtual keyboard that appears on the screen and is touch-sensitive.

Mini tablets are a type of tablet with a smaller screen. While mini tablets operate like a traditional tablet, they typically do not have all the functionality of the bigger tablets. Their most significant advantage is that they are easier to transport in pockets and purses. (See Figure 5-4.)

Figure 5-3 **Ultrabook**

Figure 5-4 **Mini tablet**

Mobile Devices

Mobile devices, also known as **handheld computers,** are the smallest and are designed to comfortably fit into the palm of one hand. These systems contain an entire computer system, including the electronic components, secondary storage, and input and output devices. These devices are smaller and generally less powerful than tablets.

By far the most popular mobile device is the **smartphone.** It greatly extends the capabilities of a cell phone by providing computing power. In addition to capturing and sending audio and video, smartphones run apps, connect to the Internet, and more. Their system unit is located behind the display screen.

Components

Personal computers come in a variety of different sizes, shapes, and capabilities. While they look different and each has its own unique features, they share surprisingly similar components, including system boards, microprocessors, and memory. (See Figure 5-5.)

Desktop

Laptop

Tablet

Smartphone

Figure 5-5 **System unit components**

Bus lines

Socket

Slot

Figure 5-6 **System board**

   concept check

What is the system unit?

Describe and compare the four most common types of personal computers.

What are tower units? What is an all-in-one? What is an ultrabook? What is a mini tablet?

System Board

The **system board** is also known as the **mainboard** or **motherboard.** The system board controls communications for the entire computer system. All devices and components connect to the system board, including external devices like keyboards and monitors and internal components like hard disk drives and microprocessors. The system board acts as a data path and traffic monitor, allowing the various components to communicate efficiently with one another.

On a desktop computer, the system board is typically located at the bottom of the system unit or along one side. It is a large flat circuit board covered with a variety of different electronic components including sockets, slots, and bus lines. (See Figure 5-6.)

- **Sockets** provide a connection point for small specialized electronic parts called chips. **Chips** consist of tiny circuit boards etched onto squares of sandlike material called silicon. These circuit boards can be smaller than the tip of your finger. (See Figure 5-7.) A chip is also called a **silicon chip, semiconductor,** or **integrated circuit.** Chips typically are mounted onto **chip carriers.** (See Figure 5-8.) These carriers plug either directly into sockets on the system board or onto cards that are then plugged into slots on the system board. Sockets are used to connect the system board to a variety of different types of chips, including microprocessor and memory chips.

Figure 5-7 **Chip**

Figure 5-8 Chip mounted onto a chip carrier

- **Slots** provide a connection point for specialized cards or circuit boards. These cards provide expansion capability for a computer system. For example, a wireless networking card plugs into a slot on the system board to provide a connection to a local area network.
- Connecting lines called **bus lines** provide pathways that support communication among the various electronic components that are either located on the system board or attached to the system board.

Generally, the system board found on a desktop is larger than that found on a laptop, and much larger than one found on a tablet or a mobile device. Although these system boards vary in size, they nevertheless all perform the same function of communicating between the components of the personal computer.

concept check

 What is the system board, and what does it do?

 Define and describe sockets, slots, and bus lines.

 What are chips? How are chips attached to the system board?

Microprocessor

In most personal computer systems, the **central processing unit (CPU)** or **processor** is contained on a single chip called the **microprocessor**. The microprocessor is the "brains" of the computer system. It has two basic components: the control unit and the arithmetic-logic unit.

- **Control unit:** The **control unit** tells the rest of the computer system how to carry out a program's instructions. It directs the movement of electronic signals between memory, which temporarily holds data, instructions, and processed information, and the arithmetic-logic unit. It also directs these control signals between the CPU and input and output devices.
- **Arithmetic-logic unit:** The **arithmetic-logic unit,** usually called the **ALU,** performs two types of operations: arithmetic and logical. **Arithmetic operations** are the fundamental math operations: addition, subtraction, multiplication, and division. **Logical operations** consist of comparisons such as whether one item is equal to ($=$), less than ($<$), or greater than ($>$) the other.

Microprocessor Chips

Chip processing capacities are often expressed in word sizes. A **word** is the number of bits (such as 16, 32, or 64) that can be accessed at one time by the CPU. The more bits in a word, the more data a computer can process at one time. Eight bits group together to form a byte. A 32-bit-word computer can access 4 bytes at a time. A 64-bit-word computer can access 8 bytes at a time. Therefore, the computer designed to process 64-bit words has greater processing capacity. Other factors affect a computer's processing capability including how fast it can process data and instructions.

The processing speed of a microprocessor is typically represented by its **clock speed,** which is related to the number of times the CPU can fetch and process data or instructions in a second. Older microcomputers typically process data and instructions in millionths of a second, or microseconds. Newer microcomputers are much faster and process data and instructions in billionths of a second, or nanoseconds. Supercomputers, by contrast, operate at speeds measured in picoseconds—1,000 times as fast as microcomputers. (See Figure 5-9.) Logically, the higher a microprocessor's clock speed, the faster the microprocessor. However, some processors can handle multiple instructions per cycle or tick of the clock; this means that clock speed comparisons can only be made between processors that work the same way.

At one time, personal computers were limited by microprocessors that could support a single CPU that controlled operations. These computers were limited to processing one program at a time. Now, many personal computers have **multicore processors** that can provide two or more separate and independent CPUs. For example, a quad-core processor could have one core computing a complex Excel spreadsheet, a second core creating a report using Word, a third core locating a record using Access, and a fourth core running a multimedia presentation all at the same time. More significantly, however, is the potential for personal computers to run very large, complex programs that previously required expensive and specialized hardware.

For multicore processors to be used effectively, computers must understand how to divide tasks into parts that can be distributed across each core—an operation called **parallel processing.** Operating systems such as Windows 8 and Mac OS X support parallel processing. Software developers use this technology for a wide range of applications from scientific programs to sophisticated computer games.

See Figure 5-10 for a table of popular microprocessors.

Unit	Speed
Microsecond	Millionth of a second
Nanosecond	Billionth of a second
Picosecond	Trillionth of a second

Figure 5-9 **Processing speeds**

Processor	Manufacturer
A-Series	AMD
E-Series	AMD
Atom	Intel
i7	Intel

Figure 5-10 **Popular microprocessors**

Specialty Processors

In addition to microprocessor chips, a variety of more specialized processing chips have been developed.

- **Coprocessors** are specialty chips designed to improve specific computing operations. One of the most widely used is the **graphics coprocessor,** also called a **GPU (graphics processing unit).** These processors are designed to handle a variety of specialized tasks such as displaying 3-D images and encrypting data.
- Many cars have more than 70 separate specialty processors to control nearly everything from fuel efficiency to satellite entertainment and tracking systems.

☑ concept check

Name and describe the two components of a microprocessor.

Define word, clock speed, multicore chip, and parallel processing.

What are specialty processors? Describe coprocessors.

privacy

Did you know that one type of specialty processor is devoted exclusively to protecting your privacy? Called cryptoprocessors, these microchips perform encoding and decoding of data faster and more securely than a CPU. These specialized chips exist in ATMs, TV set-top boxes, and smartcards.

To see more privacy facts, visit our website at www.mhhe. com/ce2015 and select Student Edition **and then** Privacy.

Chip

Circuit board

Figure 5-11 RAM chips mounted on circuit board

Memory

Memory is a holding area for data, instructions, and information. Like microprocessors, **memory** is contained on chips connected to the system board. There are three well-known types of memory chips: random-access memory (RAM), read-only memory (ROM), and flash memory.

RAM

Random-access memory (RAM) chips hold the program (sequence of instructions) and data that the CPU is presently processing. (See Figure 5-11.) RAM is called temporary or volatile storage because everything in most types of RAM is lost as soon as the computer is turned off. It is also lost if there is a power failure or other disruption of the electric current going to the computer. Secondary storage, which we shall describe in Chapter 7, does not lose its contents. It is permanent or nonvolatile storage, such as the data stored on a hard disk. For this reason, as we mentioned earlier, it is a good idea to frequently save your work in progress to a secondary storage device. That is, if you are working on a document or a spreadsheet, every few minutes you should save, or store, the material.

Cache (pronounced "cash") **memory** improves processing by acting as a temporary high-speed holding area between the memory and the CPU. The computer detects which information in RAM is most frequently used and then copies that information into the cache. When needed, the CPU can quickly access the information from the cache.

Having enough RAM is important! For example, to use the standard version of Microsoft Office 2013, you need 2 GB, or 2 billion bytes, of RAM. Some applications, such as photo editing software, may require even more. Fortunately, additional RAM can be added to a computer system by inserting an expansion module called a **DIMM (dual in-line memory module)** into the system board. The capacity or amount of RAM is expressed in bytes. There are three commonly used units of measurement to describe memory capacity. (See Figure 5-12.)

Other types of RAM include DRAM, SDRAM, DDR, and direct RDRAM. To learn more about these other types of RAM, visit our website at www.mhhe.com/ce2015 and select Student Edition, then Explore, and then RAM.

Even if your computer does not have enough RAM to hold a program, it might be able to run the program using **virtual memory.** Most of today's operating systems support virtual memory. With virtual memory, large programs are divided into parts and the parts are stored on a secondary device, usually a hard disk. Each part is then read into RAM only when needed. In this way, computer systems are able to run very large programs. To learn more about how virtual memory works, visit our website at www.mhhe.com/ce2015 and select Student Edition, then Explore, and then Memory.

Unit	Capacity
Megabyte (MB)	1 million bytes
Gigabyte (GB)	1 billion bytes
Terabyte (TB)	1 trillion bytes

Figure 5-12 Memory capacity

ROM

Read-only memory (ROM) chips have information stored in them by the manufacturer. Unlike RAM chips, ROM chips are not volatile and cannot be changed by the user. "Read only" means that the CPU can read, or retrieve, data and programs written on the ROM chip. However, the computer cannot write—encode or change—the information or instructions in ROM.

Not long ago, ROM chips were typically used to contain almost all the instructions for basic computer operations. For example, ROM instructions are needed to start a computer, to access memory, and to handle keyboard input. Recently, however, flash memory chips have replaced ROM chips for many applications.

Flash Memory

Flash memory offers a combination of the features of RAM and ROM. Like RAM, it can be updated to store new information. Like ROM, it does not lose that information when power to the computer system is turned off.

Flash memory is used for a wide range of applications. For example, it is used to store the start-up instructions for a computer. This information is called the system's **BIOS (basic input/output system).** This information would include the specifics concerning the amount of RAM and the type of keyboard, mouse, and secondary storage devices connected to the system unit. If changes are made to the computer system, these changes are reflected in flash memory. To learn more about how a computer starts up and BIOS, visit our website at www.mhhe.com/ce2015 and select Student Edition, then Explore, and then Boot.

See Figure 5-13 for a summary of the three types of memory.

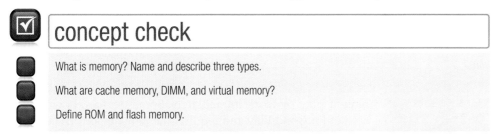

Type	Use
RAM	Programs and data
ROM	Fixed start-up instructions
Flash	Flexible start-up instructions

Figure 5-13 **Memory**

concept check

What is memory? Name and describe three types.

What are cache memory, DIMM, and virtual memory?

Define ROM and flash memory.

Expansion Slots and Cards

As previously mentioned, many personal computers allow users to expand their systems by providing **expansion slots** on the system board. Users can insert optional devices known as **expansion cards** into these slots. (See Figure 5-14.) Ports on the cards allow cables to be connected from the expansion cards to devices outside the system unit. (See Figure 5-15.) There are a wide range of different types of expansion cards. Some of the most commonly used expansion cards are:

- **Graphics cards** provide high-quality 3-D graphics and animation for games and simulations.
- **Sound cards** accept audio input from a microphone and convert it into a form that can be processed by the computer. Also, these cards convert internal electronic signals to audio signals so they can be heard from external speakers or home theater systems.
- **Network interface cards (NIC),** also known as **network adapter cards,** are used to connect a computer to a network. (See Figure 5-16.) The network allows connected computers to share data, programs, and hardware. The network adapter card typically connects the system unit to a cable that connects to the network.
- **Wireless network cards** allow computers to be connected without cables. As we will discuss in Chapter 9, wireless networks in the home are widely used to share a common Internet connection. Each device on the network is equipped with a wireless network card that communicates with the other devices.

Plug and Play was originally a set of specific hardware and software standards developed by Intel, Microsoft, and others. As hardware and software have evolved, however, Plug and Play has become a generic term that is associated with the ability to plug any device such as a printer or monitor into a computer and

Slot

Figure 5-14 **Expansion cards fit into slots on the system board**

Figure 5-15 **Expansion card with three ports**

Figure 5-16 **Network interface card**

Figure 5-17 **PC card**

have it play or work immediately. Some devices, however, are not Plug and Play and require that new device drivers be installed, as discussed in Chapter 4.

To meet the size constraints of laptop computers, tablets, and mobile devices, small credit card–sized expansion cards known as **PC cards** have been developed. These cards plug into **PCMCIA slots** (called **PC card slots**) or, most recently, **ExpressCard** slots. (See Figure 5-17.)

concept check

 What are expansion slots and cards? Name four expansion cards.

 Discuss Plug and Play.

 What are PC cards, PCMCIA slots, and ExpressCard slots?

Bus Lines

As mentioned earlier, a **bus line**—also known simply as a **bus**—connects the parts of the CPU to each other. Buses also link the CPU to various other components on the system board. (See Figure 5-18.) A bus is a pathway for bits representing data and instructions. The number of bits that can travel simultaneously down a bus is known as the **bus width.**

A bus is similar to a multilane highway that moves bits rather than cars from one location to another. The number of traffic lanes determines the bus width. A highway (bus line) with more traffic lanes (bus width) can move traffic (data and instructions) more efficiently. For example, a 64-bit bus can move twice as much information at a time as a 32-bit bus. Why should you even care about what a bus line is? Because as microprocessor chips have changed, so have bus lines. Bus design or bus architecture is an important factor relating to the speed and power for a particular computer. Additionally, many devices, such as expansion cards, will work with only one type of bus.

Every computer system has two basic categories of buses. One category, called **system buses,** connects the CPU to memory on the system board. The other category, called **expansion buses,** connects the CPU to other components on the system board, including expansion slots.

Expansion Buses

Computer systems typically have a combination of different types of expansion buses. The principal types are USB, FireWire, and PCIe.

- **Universal serial bus (USB)** is widely used today. External USB devices are connected from one to another or to a common point or hub and then onto the USB bus. The USB bus then connects to the PCI bus on the system board. The current USB standard is USB 3.0.
- **FireWire buses** are similar to USB buses but more specialized. They are used primarily to connect audio and video equipment to the system board.
- **PCI Express (PCIe)** is widely used in many of today's most powerful computers. Unlike most other buses that share a single bus line or path with several devices, the PCIe bus provides a single dedicated path for each connected device.

Figure 5-18 **Bus is a pathway for bits**

concept check

 What is a bus, and what is bus width?

 What is the difference between a system and an expansion bus?

 Discuss three types of expansion buses.

Ports

A **port** is a socket for external devices to connect to the system unit. (See Figure 5-19.) Some ports connect directly to the system board, while others connect to cards that are inserted into slots on the system board. Some ports are standard features of most computer systems, and others are more specialized.

Standard Ports

Most desktop and laptop computers come with a standard set of ports for connecting a monitor, keyboard, and other peripheral devices. The most common ports include

- **VGA (Video Graphics Adapter)** and **DVI (Digital Video Interface) ports** provide connections to analog and digital monitors, respectively. DVI has become the most commonly used standard, but VGA ports are still provided on almost all systems for compatibility with older/lower-cost monitors.
- **Universal serial bus (USB) ports** can be used to connect several devices to the system unit and are widely used to connect keyboards, mice, printers, storage devices, and a variety of specialty devices. One such device, a USB TV tuner card, allows users to view and record television programs. To learn how you can use a TV tuner card, see Making IT Work for You: TV Tuners on page 1250. A single USB port can be used to connect many USB devices to the system unit.
- **FireWire ports** provide high-speed connections to specialized FireWire devices such as camcorders and storage devices.

Ethernet

FireWire

USB

Figure 5-19 **Ports**

DVI   HDMI   VGA

- **Ethernet ports** are a high-speed networking port that has become a standard for many of today's computers. Ethernet allows you to connect multiple computers for sharing files, or to a DSL or cable modem for high-speed Internet access.

Specialized Ports

In addition to standard ports, there are numerous specialty ports including eSATA, HDMI, MIDI, MiniDP, and Thunderbolt.

- **External Serial Advanced Technology Attachment (eSATA)** ports provide high-speed connections for external hard disk drives, optical discs, and other large secondary storage devices.
- **High Definition Multimedia Interface (HDMI)** ports provide high-definition video and audio, making it possible to use a computer as a video jukebox or an HD video recorder.
- **Musical instrument digital interface (MIDI)** ports are a special type of port for connecting musical instruments like an electronic keyboard to a sound card. The sound card converts the music into a series of digital instructions. These instructions can be processed immediately to reproduce the music or saved to a file for later processing.
- **Mini DisplayPort (MiniDP or mDP)** ports are an audiovisual port typically used to connect large monitors. These ports are used with many Apple Macintosh computers.
- **Thunderbolt** ports, first introduced in Apple's MacBook Pro computer, provide high-speed connections. A single port can connect up to seven separate devices connected one to another. Thunderbolt ports promise to replace a number of different types of ports including Mini DisplayPorts.

Cables

Cables are used to connect exterior devices to the system unit via the ports. One end of the cable is attached to the device, and the other end has a connector that is attached to a matching connector on the port. (See Figure 5-20.)

USB   DVI   FireWire   Ethernet

Figure 5-20 **Cables**

TV TUNERS

Do you already use a DVR (digital video recorder) in order to record your favorite TV shows? Although many cable and satellite companies offer this device, did you know that Windows Media Center can perform the same function? All you need is a device called a TV tuner that connects your antenna or cable to your computer. Below are the steps to turn your Windows-based computer into a DVR.

Installing a TV Tuner   A TV tuner is essentially a piece of hardware that allows your computer to process and display a cable or TV signal. Although some (usually pricey) PCs may include this technology, it is usually necessary to purchase it separately. The easiest ones to install are those that connect externally to a USB port, such as the AverTV Hybrid Volar Max.

1 ● Plug the TV tuner into an available USB port on your computer.

2 ● Connect a coaxial cable directly from your cable outlet or over-the-air antenna to the back of the TV tuner. If Windows does not automatically install the tuner, consult the user manual for instructions.

3 ● Start *Windows Media Center.*

4 ● With your TV tuner installed, it will guide you through a setup process, including a long scan for all available channels from your cable or antenna.

Using Windows Media Center   This utility is included with Windows 7 and can be purchased as an upgrade for Windows 8. Although it contains many tools to manage your music, photos, and movies, we focus on its DVR capabilities for TV and cable.

1 ● Once setup is complete, click the *TV* option from the main menu.

2 ● Click *Guide,* and scroll up/down and left/right until you find a show you wish to record.

3 ● Right-click the show, and choose *Record* from the menu.

4 ● To play back a recorded show, choose *Recorded TV* from the TV menu, and click the show you wish to play back.

5 ● Once you have watched a recording, choose the *Delete* option to free up space on your hard drive. The number of hours you can record is limited by your available hard drive space.

If you have a high-speed wireless network and several PCs in your home, you will have the capability to watch your recorded shows via Media Center's streaming ability. The web is continually changing, and some of the specifics presented in this Making IT Work for You may have changed.

To learn about other ways to make information technology work for you, visit our website at www.mhhe.com/ce2015 and select Student Edition **and then** Making IT Work**.**

Power Supply

Computers require direct current (DC) to power their electronic components and to represent data and instructions. DC power can be provided indirectly by converting alternating current (AC) from standard wall outlets or directly from batteries.

- Desktop computers have a **power supply unit** located within the system unit. (See Figure 5-21.) This unit plugs into a standard wall outlet, converts AC to DC, and provides the power to drive all of the system unit components.
- Laptops and tablets use **AC adapters** that are typically located outside the system unit. (See Figure 5-22.) AC adapters plug into a standard wall outlet, convert AC to DC, provide power to drive the system unit components, and can recharge the batteries. These computers can be operated either using an AC adapter plugged into a wall outlet or using battery power. Their batteries typically provide sufficient power for up to eight hours before they need to be recharged.
- Like laptops and tablets, mobile devices use AC adapters located outside the system unit. Unlike laptops and tablets, however, ultrabooks and mobile devices typically operate only using battery power. The AC adapter is used to recharge the batteries.

☑ concept check

What are ports? What do they do?

Describe four standard ports and five specialized ports.

What is a power supply unit? What is an AC adapter?

Figure 5-21 Power supply unit

Figure 5-22 AC adapter

Electronic Data and Instructions

Have you ever wondered why it is said that we live in a digital world? It's because computers cannot recognize information the same way you and I can. People follow instructions and process data using letters, numbers, and special characters. For example, if we wanted someone to add the numbers 3 and 5 together and record the answer, we might say "please add 3 and 5." The system unit, however, is electronic circuitry and cannot directly process such a request.

Our voices create **analog,** or continuous, signals that vary to represent different tones, pitches, and volume. Computers, however, can recognize only **digital** electronic signals. Before any processing can occur within the system unit, a conversion must occur from what we understand to what the system unit can electronically process.

Numeric Representation

What is the most fundamental statement you can make about electricity? It is simply this: It can be either on or off. Indeed, there are many forms of technology that can make use of this two-state on/off, yes/no, present/absent arrangement. For instance, a light switch may be on or off, or an electric circuit open or closed. A specific location on a tape or disk may have a positive charge or a negative charge. This is the reason, then, that a two-state or binary system is used to represent data and instructions.

The decimal system that we are all familiar with has 10 digits (0, 1, 2, 3, 4, 5, 6, 7, 8, 9). The **binary system,** however, consists of only two digits—0 and 1. Each 0 or 1 is called a **bit**—short for binary digit. In the system unit, the 1 can be represented by a negative charge and the 0 by no electric charge. In order to represent numbers, letters, and special characters, bits are combined into groups of eight called **bytes.** Whenever you enter a number into a computer system, that number must be converted into a binary number before it can be processed. To learn more about binary systems and binary arithmetic, visit our website at www.mhhe.com/ce2015 and select Student Edition, then Explore, and then Binary.

Any number can be expressed as a binary number. Binary numbers, however, are difficult for humans to work with because they require so many digits. Instead, binary numbers are often represented in a format more readable by humans. The **hexadecimal system, or hex,** uses 16 digits (0, 1, 2, 3, 4, 5, 6, 7, 8, 9, A, B, C, D, E, F) to represent binary numbers. Each hex digit represents four binary digits, and two hex digits are commonly used together to represent 1 byte (8 binary digits). (See Figure 5-23.) You may have already seen hex when selecting a color in a website design or drawing application, or when entering the password for access to a wireless network.

Character Encoding

As we've seen, computers must represent all numbers with the binary system internally. What about text? How can a computer provide representations of the nonnumeric characters we use to communicate, such as the sentence you are reading now? The answer is character encoding schemes or standards.

Character encoding standards assign a unique sequence of bits to each character. Historically, personal computers used the **ASCII (American Standard Code for Information Interchange)** to represent characters, while mainframe computers used **EBCDIC (Extended Binary Coded Decimal Interchange Code)**. These schemes were quite effective; however, they are limited. ASCII, for example, only uses 7 bits to represent each character, which means that only 128 total characters could be represented. This was fine for most characters in

Decimal	Binary	Hex
00	00000000	00
01	00000001	01
02	00000010	02
03	00000011	03
04	00000100	04
05	00000101	05
06	00000110	06
07	00000111	07
08	00001000	08
09	00001001	09
10	00001010	0A
11	00001011	0B
12	00001100	0C
13	00001101	0D
14	00001110	0E
15	00001111	0F

Figure 5-23 **Numeric representations**

the English language but was not large enough to support other languages such as Chinese and Japanese. These languages have too many characters to be represented by the 7-bit ASCII code.

The explosion of the Internet and subsequent globalization of computing have led to a new character encoding called **Unicode,** which uses 16 bits. The Unicode standard is the most widely used character encoding standard and is recognized by virtually every computer system. The first 128 characters are assigned the same sequence of bits as ASCII to maintain compatibility with older ASCII-formatted information. However, Unicode uses a variable number of bits to represent each character, which allows non-English characters and special characters to be represented.

concept check

 What is the difference between an analog and a digital signal?

 What are decimal and binary systems? How are they different?

 Compare EBCDIC, ASCII, and Unicode.

Careers in IT

❝ Now that you know about system units, I'd like to tell you about my career as a computer technician. ❞

Computer technicians repair and install computer components and systems. They may work on everything from personal computers and mainframe servers to printers. Some computer technicians are responsible for setting up and maintaining computer networks. Experienced computer technicians may work with computer engineers to diagnose problems and run routine maintenance on complex systems. Job growth is expected in this field as computer equipment becomes more complicated and technology expands.

Employers look for those with certification in computer repair or associate degrees from professional schools. Computer technicians also can expect to continue their education to keep up with technological changes. Good communication skills are important in this field.

Computer technicians can expect to earn an annual salary in the range of $31,000 to $46,000. Opportunities for advancement typically come in the form of work on more advanced computer systems. Some computer technicians move into customer service positions or go into sales. To learn more about other careers in information technology, visit us at www.mhhe.com/ce2015 and select Student Edition and then Careers.

A LOOK TO THE FUTURE

Chips inside Your Brain

Have you ever thought it would be possible to be able to communicate with a computer . . . by merely thinking? Researchers are working with various devices (usually worn on the head) that can use your basic thoughts to move objects, such as wheelchairs. However, the future will lie in implanted microchips that can communicate directly with our nerve cells. Although their initial purpose will be to treat a variety of medical conditions, they could eventually (and controversially) be used to improve various brain functions of otherwise healthy individuals.

For over a decade, doctors have been able to use deep brain stimulation (DBS) to treat several disorders such as Parkinson's disease. As successful as it has been for many patients, those implants simply send preset electrical impulses to the brain. They do not involve an active communication between nerve cells and machines. Researchers working on a chip known as ReNaChip hope to change this by using a programmable computer chip that is responsive to what is going on in the patient's brain. This silicon chip can measure the brain's electrical activity and then deliver the appropriate stimulation when and where it is needed.

Another brain implant that is currently being developed aims to help the blind regain some sight. A microchip is implanted in the brain's visual cortex, which is responsible for processing images. This chip would communicate wirelessly with a camera located inside special eyeglasses worn by the individual. The images captured by that camera would be processed by the chip and then fed directly to the nerves in this area of the brain.

Getting close to the world of the unbelievable, researchers are improving on the ability of computers to actually read human thoughts. Currently, one research team has been able to use a chip implant and computer to read the thoughts of a stroke victim in order to allow her to move a robotic hand. Although the success rate is not 100 percent and the processing is limited to basic movements, the patient has already been able to get the robotic arm to hold a cup of coffee by thinking about it. This research will hopefully lead to improved, thought-controlled prosthetic devices for millions of disabled individuals.

Many ethicists are concerned by the potential use of such chips to improve human abilities instead of treating medical conditions. For example, with tiny chips being able to store so much, people could use brain implants to improve their memory. This can lead to a variety of scenarios where the individual with the implants could have an unfair advantage over those who don't have them. However, others disagree, arguing that the integration of technology and biology is to be expected, and it is nothing more than the next step in human evolution.

If such a technology became widespread and affordable, would you opt to receive a chip implant? Would you make a distinction between using one for a medical condition and simply for improving your mental abilities? Do you think the future of humanity lies in the merging of technology with human biology?

129

SYSTEM UNIT

System unit (system chassis) contains electronic components. The most common **personal computers are desktop, laptop, tablet,** and **mobile device.**

Desktop

Desktop system units located in separate case; **tower unit (tower computer)** has vertical system unit; **all-in-one** computer combines system unit and monitor.

Laptop

Laptop (notebook) system units contain secondary storage devices and input devices. **Ultrabooks (ultraportables, mini notebooks)** are lighter, thinner, and have longer battery life than other laptops.

Tablet

Tablet system units are located behind the monitor. They are smaller, lighter, and generally less powerful than laptops and use a virtual keyboard. **Mini tablets** are smaller version of a traditional tablet.

Mobile Devices

Mobile devices (handheld computers) fit comfortably in one hand. **Smartphones** are most popular **type.** System unit is located behind the display screen.

Components

Each type of system unit has the same basic components including system board, microprocessor, and memory.

SYSTEM BOARD

The **system board (mainboard** or **motherboard)** controls all communication for the computer system. All external and internal devices and components connect to it.

*   **Sockets** provide connection points for **chips (silicon chips, semiconductors, integrated circuits).** Chips are mounted on **chip carriers.**
*   **Slots** provide connection points for specialized cards or circuit boards.
*   **Bus lines** provide pathways to support communication.

To efficiently and effectively use computers, you need to understand the functionality of the basic components in the system unit: system board, microprocessor, memory, expansion slots and cards, bus lines, ports, and cables. Additionally, you need to understand how data and programs are represented electronically.

MICROPROCESSOR

In most personal computers, the **central processing unit (CPU)** or **processor** is contained on a single chip called the **microprocessor**. It has two basic components: a **control unit** and **ALU**.

Microprocessor Chips

A **word** is the number of bits that can be accessed by the microprocessor at one time. **Clock speed** represents the number of times the CPU can fetch and process data or instructions in a second.

Multicore processors can provide multiple independent CPUs. **Parallel processing** requires programs that allow multiple processors to work together to run large complex programs.

Specialty Processors

Specialty processors include **graphics coprocessors**, also known as **GPU** or **graphics processing unit** (processes graphic images), and processors in automobiles (monitor fuel efficiency, satellite entertainment, and tracking systems).

MEMORY

Memory holds data, instructions, and information. There are three types of memory chips.

RAM

RAM (random-access memory) chips are called temporary or volatile storage because their contents are lost if power is disrupted.

- **Cache memory** is a high-speed holding area for frequently used data and information.
- **DIMM (dual in-line memory module)** is used to expand memory.
- **Virtual memory** divides large programs into parts that are read into RAM as needed.

ROM

ROM (read-only memory) chips are nonvolatile storage and control essential system operations.

Flash Memory

Flash memory does not lose its contents when power is removed.

EXPANSION SLOTS AND CARDS

Most computers allow users to expand their systems by providing **expansion slots** on their system boards to accept **expansion cards**.

Examples of expansion cards include **graphics cards, sound cards, network interface cards (NIC; network adapter cards)**, and **wireless network cards**.

Plug and Play is the ability for a computer to recognize and configure a device without human interaction.

PC cards plug into **PCMCIA slots**, and **ExpressCard** slots accept credit card–sized expansion cards.

BUS LINES

Bus lines, also known as **buses**, provide data pathways that connect various system components. **Bus width** is the number of bits that can travel simultaneously.

System buses connect CPU and memory. **Expansion buses** connect CPU and slots.

Expansion Buses

Three principal expansion bus types are

- **USB (universal serial bus)** can connect from one USB device to another or to a common point (hub) and then onto the system board.
- **FireWire bus** is similar to USB bus but more specialized.
- **PCI Express (PCIe) bus** is widely used; provides a single dedicated path for each connected device.

PORTS

Ports are connecting sockets on the outside of the system unit.

Standard Ports

Four standard ports are

- **VGA (Video Graphics Adapter)** and **DVI (Digital Video Interface)**—provide connections to monitors.
- **USB (universal serial bus)**—widely used to connect keyboards, mice, printers, and storage devices; one port can connect several devices to system unit.
- **FireWire**—provides high-speed connections to FireWire devices such as camcorders and storage devices.
- **Ethernet**—high-speed networking port that has become a standard for many of today's computers.

Specialized Ports

Five specialty ports are **eSATA (external Serial Advanced Technology Attachment)** for high-speed connections to large secondary storage devices, **HDMI (High Definition Multimedia Interface)** for high-definition digital audio and video, **MIDI** for digital music, **Mini DisplayPort (MiniDP, mDP)** for large monitors, and **Thunderbolt** for high-speed connections to up to seven separate devices connected one to another.

Cables

Cables are used to connect external devices to the system unit via ports.

POWER SUPPLY

Power supply units convert AC to DC and power desktops. **AC adapters** power laptops and tablets and recharge batteries.

ELECTRONIC REPRESENTATION

Human voices create **analog** (continuous) signals; computers only recognize **digital** electronic signals.

Numeric Representation

Data and instructions can be represented electronically with a two-state or **binary system** of numbers (0 and 1). Each 0 or 1 is called a **bit**. A **byte** consists of 8 bits. **Hexadecimal system (hex)** uses 16 digits to represent binary numbers.

Character Encoding

Character encoding standards assign unique sequences of bits to each character. Three standards are

- **ASCII**—American Standard Code for Information Interchange. Historically used for personal computers.
- **EBCDIC**—Extended Binary Coded Decimal Interchange Code. Historically used for mainframe computers.
- **Unicode**—16-bit code, most widely used standard.

CAREERS IN IT

Computer technicians repair and install computer components and systems. Certification in computer repair or associate degree from professional schools is required. Salary range is $31,000 to $46,000.

KEY TERMS

AC adapter (126)
all-in-one (114)
analog (127)
arithmetic-logic unit (ALU) (118)
arithmetic operation (118)
ASCII (127)
binary system (127)
BIOS (basic input/output system) (121)
bit (127)
bus (122)
bus line (118, 122)
bus width (122)
byte (127)
cable (124)
cache memory (120)
central processing unit (CPU) (118)
character encoding standards (127)
chip (117)
chip carriers (117)
clock speed (119)
computer technician (128)
control unit (118)
coprocessor (119)
desktop (114)
digital (127)
DIMM (120)
DVI (Digital Video Interface) port (123)
EBCDIC (127)
Ethernet port (123)
expansion bus (123)
expansion card (121)
expansion slot (121)
ExpressCard (122)

external Serial Advanced Technology Attachment (eSATA) (124)
FireWire bus (123)
FireWire port (123)
flash memory (121)
GPU (119)
graphics card (121)
graphics coprocessor (119)
handheld computer (116)
hexadecimal system (hex) (127)
High Definition Multimedia Interface (HDMI) (124)
integrated circuit (117)
laptop (114)
logical operation (118)
mainboard (117)
memory (120)
microprocessor (118)
Mini DisplayPort (MiniDP, mDP) (124)
mini notebook (115)
mini tablets (115)
mobile device (116)
motherboard (117)
multicore processor (119)
musical instrument digital interface (MIDI) (124)
network adapter card (121)
network interface card (NIC) (121)
notebook (115)
parallel processing (119)
PC card (122)

PC card slot (122)
PCI Express (PCIe) (123)
PCMCIA slot (122)
personal computer (114)
Plug and Play (121)
port (123)
power supply unit (126)
processor (118)
random-access memory (RAM) (120)
read-only memory (ROM) (120)
semiconductor (117)
silicon chip (117)
slot (118)
smartphone (116)
socket (117)
sound card (121)
system board (117)
system bus (123)
system chassis (114)
system unit (114)
tablet (115)
tablet computer (115)
Thunderbolt (124)
tower computer (114)
tower unit (114)
ultrabooks (115)
ultraportables (115)
Unicode (128)
universal serial bus (USB) (123)
universal serial bus (USB) port (123)
VGA (Video Graphics Adapter) port (123)
virtual memory (120)
wireless network card (121)
word (119)

To test your knowledge of these key terms with animated flash cards, visit our website at www.mhhe.com/ce2015, select Student Edition, and choose Chapter 5 and then Flashcards.

MULTIPLE CHOICE

Circle the correct answer.

1. This container houses most of the electrical components for a computer system.
   a. chip carrier
   b. system board
   c. system unit
   d. Unicode

2. The most popular mobile device.
   a. all-in-one
   b. handheld
   c. smartphone
   d. ultrabook

3. The mainboard or motherboard is also known as the:
   a. computer
   b. board processor
   c. mobile system
   d. system board

4. How many bytes can a 32-bit-word computer access at one time?
   a. 1
   b. 4
   c. 8
   d. 16

5. In a personal computer system, the central processing unit is typically contained on a single:
   a. bus
   b. chip
   c. module
   d. RAM

6. This type of memory divides large programs into parts and stores the parts on a secondary storage device.
   a. direct
   b. expanded
   c. random access
   d. virtual

7. Also known as NIC, this adapter card is used to connect a computer to a(n):
   a. AIA
   b. expansion
   c. graphics
   d. network

8. This provides a pathway to connect parts of the CPU to each other.
   a. bus
   b. Plug and Play
   c. wired
   d. wireless

9. The specialized port that connects musical instruments like an electronic keyboard to a sound card.
   a. eSATA
   b. HDMI
   c. MIDI
   d. Thunderbolt

10. Computers can only recognize this type of electronic signal.
    a. analog
    b. bus
    c. digital
    d. maximum

For an interactive multiple-choice practice test, visit our website at www.mhhe.com/ce2015, select Student Edition, and choose Chapter 5 and then Multiple Choice.

MATCHING

Match each numbered item with the most closely related lettered item. Write your answers in the spaces provided.

a. cache
b. flash
c. multicore
d. Plug and Play
e. port
f. random access
g. slots
h. sockets
i. system
j. USB

___ 1. A type of multiprocessor chip that provides two or more separate and independent CPUs.

___ 2. A type of memory that is volatile or loses its contents when power is turned off.

___ 3. System board component that provides a connection point for specialized cards or circuit boards.

___ 4. Provide connection points for chips.

___ 5. A type of memory that improves processing by acting as a temporary high-speed holding area between the memory and the CPU.

___ 6. A type of memory that provides a combination of features of RAM and ROM.

___ 7. A generic term that is associated with the ability to attach any device onto a computer and have it play or work immediately.

___ 8. This bus connects the CPU to memory on the system board.

___ 9. This port can be used to connect many USB devices to the system.

___10. A socket for external devices to connect to the system unit.

For an interactive matching practice test, visit our website at www.mhhe.com/ce2015, select Student Edition, and choose Chapter 5 and then Matching.

OPEN-ENDED

On a separate sheet of paper, respond to each question or statement.

1. Describe the four most common types of personal computers.
2. Describe system boards including sockets, chips, chip carriers, slots, and bus lines.
3. Discuss microprocessor components, chips, and specialty processors.
4. Define computer memory including RAM, ROM, and flash memory.
5. Define expansion slots, cards, Plug and Play, PC cards, PCMCIA slots, and ExpressCard slots.
6. Describe bus lines, bus width, system bus, and expansion bus.
7. Define ports including standard and specialized ports. Give examples of each.
8. Describe power supply including power supply units and AC adapters.
9. Discuss electronic data and instructions.

chapter 6 Input and Output

Learning Objectives

After you have read this chapter, you should be able to:

1 Define input.

2 Describe keyboard entry including types and features of keyboards.

3 Identify different pointing devices including game controllers and styluses.

4 Describe scanning devices including optical scanners, RFID readers, and recognition devices.

5 Recognize image capturing and audio-input devices.

6 Define output.

7 Identify different monitor features and types including flat panels and e-books.

8 Define printing features and types including inkjet and cloud printers.

9 Recognize different audio and video devices including portable media devices.

10 Define combination input and output devices including multifunctional devices, Internet telephones, and VR headgear and gloves.

11 Explain ergonomics and ways to minimize physical damage.

Why should I read this chapter?

Input and output devices have seen staggering advances in recent years. A typical cell phone now has dozens of input sensors and display options. In the future, input devices will include tiny attachments to clothes or eyewear. Augmented reality displays or wearable glasses will integrate what you see with extensive databases of relevant information.

This chapter covers the things you need to know to be prepared for this ever changing digital world, including:

- Keyboards design—discover how wireless and virtual keyboards improve the speed and ease of typing.
- Intuitive input devices—learn about advances in touch screens and voice recognition systems.
- Display technology—discover how webcams and digital whiteboards can create videos and share presentations.
- Evolving output devices—learn about advances in HDTVs, 3D printers, and ebooks.

Introduction

"Hi, I'm Marie, and I'm a technical writer. I'd like to talk with you about input and output devices . . . all those devices that help us to communicate with a computer. I'd also like to talk about emerging technologies such as virtual reality."

How do you send instructions and information to the CPU? How do you get information out? Here we describe one of the most important places where computers interface with people. We input text, music, and even speech, but we probably never think about the relationship between what we enter and what the computer processes. People understand language, which is constructed of letters, numbers, and special characters. However, at a basic level, computers can understand only the binary machine language of 0s and 1s. Input devices are essentially translators. Input devices translate numbers, letters, special characters, and gestures that people understand into a form that computers can process.

Have you ever wondered how information processed by the system unit is converted into a form that you can use? That is the role of output devices. While input devices convert what we understand into what the system unit can process, output devices convert what the system unit has processed into a form that we can understand. Output devices translate machine language into letters, numbers, sounds, and images that people can understand.

To efficiently and effectively use computers, you need to know about the most commonly used input devices, including touch screens, game controllers, scanners, digital cameras, voice recognition, and audio-input devices. Additionally, you need to know about the most commonly used output devices, including monitors, printers, and audio and video output devices. You also need to be aware of combination input and output devices such as multifunctional devices and Internet telephones.

What Is Input?

Input is any data or instructions that are used by a computer. They can come directly from you or from other sources. You provide input whenever you use system or application programs. For example, when using a word processing program, you enter data in the form of numbers and letters and issue commands such as to save and to print documents. You also can enter data and issue commands by pointing to items or using your voice. Other sources of input include scanned or photographed images.

Input devices are hardware used to translate words, numbers, sounds, images, and gestures that people understand into a form that the system unit can process. For example, when using a word processor, you typically use a keyboard to enter text and a mouse to issue commands. In addition to keyboards and mice, there are a wide variety of other input devices. These include pointing, scanning, image capturing, and audio-input devices.

Keyboard Entry

One of the most common ways to input data is by a **keyboard.** As mentioned in Chapter 5, keyboards convert numbers, letters, and special characters that people understand into electrical signals. These signals are sent to, and processed

Figure 6-1 **Traditional keyboard**

Laptop keyboard

Virtual keyboard

Thumb keyboard

Figure 6-2 **Keyboards**

by, the system unit. Most keyboards use an arrangement of keys given the name QWERTY. This name reflects the keyboard layout by taking the letters of the first six alphabetic characters found on the top row of keys displaying letters.

Keyboards

There are a wide variety of different keyboard designs. They range from the full-sized to miniature and can even be virtual. There are four basic categories of keyboards: traditional, laptop, virtual, and thumb.

- **Traditional keyboards**—these full-size keyboards are widely used on desktops and larger computers. The standard U.S. traditional keyboard has 101 keys. Some traditional keyboards include a few additional special keys. For example, the Windows keyboard includes a Windows key to directly access the Start menu. Traditional keyboards provide function keys, navigation keys, and a numeric keypad. Some keys, such as the Caps Lock key, are **toggle keys.** These keys turn a feature on or off. Others, such as the Ctrl key, are **combination keys,** which perform an action when held down in combination with another key. (See Figure 6-1.)

- **Laptop keyboards**—these keyboards are smaller than traditional keyboards and are widely used on laptop computers. While the precise location and number of keys may differ among manufactures, laptop keyboards typically have fewer keys, do not include a numeric keypad, and do not have a standard location for the function and navigation keys. (See Figure 6-2, top.)

- **Virtual keyboards**—these keyboards are used primarily with mobile devices and tablets. Unlike other keyboards, virtual keyboards do not have a physical keyboard. Rather, the keys are typically displayed on a screen and selected by touching their image on the screen. (See Figure 6-2, middle.)

- **Thumb keyboards**—these keyboards are used on smartphones and other small mobile devices. Designed primarily for communicating via texting and connecting to the web, these keyboards are very small. (See Figure 6-2, bottom.)

☑ concept check

What is input? What are input devices?

List and compare the four categories of keyboards.

What are toggle keys? What are combination keys?

Pointing Devices

Pointing is one of the most natural of all human gestures. **Pointing devices** provide an intuitive interface with the system unit by accepting physical movements or gestures such as a finger pointing or moving across a screen and converting these movements into machine-readable input. There are a wide variety of different pointing devices, including the mouse, touch screen, game controller, and stylus.

Mouse

A **mouse** controls a pointer that is displayed on the monitor. The **mouse pointer** usually appears in the shape of an arrow. It frequently changes shape, however, depending on the application. A mouse can have one, two, or more buttons, which are used to select command options and to control the mouse pointer on the monitor. Some mice have a **wheel button** that can be rotated to scroll through information that is displayed on the monitor.

Although there are several different designs, the **optical mouse** is the most widely used. It emits and senses light to detect mouse movement. Traditionally, the detected movements are communicated to the system unit through a cord. Alternatively, the **cordless** or **wireless mouse** uses radio waves or infrared light waves to communicate with the system unit. (See Figure 6-3.) These devices eliminate the mouse cord and free up desk space.

Like a mouse, a **touch pad** is used to control the mouse pointer and to make selections. Unlike a mouse, however, a touch pad operates by moving or tapping your finger on the surface of a pad. These devices are widely used instead of a mouse with laptops and some types of mobile devices. (See Figure 6-4.)

Figure 6-3 **Optical mouse**

Figure 6-4 **Touch pad**

Touch Screen

A **touch screen** allows users to select actions or commands by touching the screen with a finger or penlike device. **Multitouch screens** can be touched with more than one finger, which allows for interactions such as rotating graphical objects on the screen with your hand or zooming in and out by pinching and stretching your fingers. Multitouch screens are commonly used with tablets and smartphones, as well as some laptop computers and desktop monitors. (See Figure 6-5.)

Game Controllers

Game controllers are devices that provide input to computer games. While keyboards and mice can be used as game controllers, the four most popular and specialized game

Figure 6-5 **Multitouch screen**

Joystick

Dance pad

Gamepad

Motion-sensing device

Figure 6-6 **Game controllers**

controllers are joysticks, dance pads, gamepads, and motion-sensing devices. (See Figure 6-6.)

- **Joysticks** control game actions by users varying the pressure, speed, and direction of a control stick.
- **Dance pads** provide input for dance games. Users move (dance) on a pressure-sensitive mat that provides input to the game.
- **Gamepads** are designed to be held by two hands and provide a wide array of inputs including motion, turning, stopping, and firing.
- **Motion-sensing devices** control games by user movements. For example, Microsoft's Kinect motion-sensing device accepts user movements and spoken commands to control games on the Xbox 360.

Stylus

A **stylus** is a penlike device typically used with tablets and mobile devices. (See Figure 6-7.) A stylus uses pressure to draw images on a screen. Often, a stylus interacts with the computer through handwriting recognition software. **Handwriting recognition software** translates handwritten notes into a form that the system unit can process.

Figure 6-7 **Stylus**

concept check

What is a pointing device? Describe four pointing devices.

What is an optical mouse? What is a multitouch screen?

Describe four game controllers. What is a stylus?

Scanning Devices

Scanning devices convert scanned text and images into a form that the system unit can process. There are five types of scanning devices: optical scanners, card readers, RFID readers, bar code readers, and character and mark recognition devices.

Optical Scanners

An **optical scanner,** also known simply as a **scanner,** accepts documents consisting of text and/or images and converts them to machine-readable form. These devices do not recognize individual letters or images. Rather, they recognize light, dark, and colored areas that make up individual letters or images. Typically, scanned documents are saved in files that can be further processed, displayed, printed, or stored for later use. There are three basic types of optical scanners: flatbed, document, and portable.

- **Flatbed scanner** is much like a copy machine. The image to be scanned is placed on a glass surface, and the scanner records the image.

- **Document scanner** is similar to a flatbed scanner except that it can quickly scan multipage documents. It automatically feeds one page of a document at a time through a scanning surface. (See Figure 6-8.)

Figure 6-8 Document scanner

- **Portable scanner** is typically a handheld device that slides across the image, making direct contact.

Optical scanners are powerful tools for a wide variety of end users, including graphics and advertising professionals who scan images and combine them with text.

Card Readers

Nearly everyone uses a credit card, debit card, access (parking or building) card, and/or some type of identification card. These cards typically have the user's name, some type of identification number, and signature on the card. Additionally, encoded information is often stored on the card. **Card readers** interpret this encoded information.

Although there are several different types, by far the most common is the **magnetic card reader.** The encoded information is stored on a thin magnetic strip located on the back of the card. When the card is swiped through the magnetic card reader, the information is read.

Bar Code Readers

You are probably familiar with **bar code readers** or **scanners** from grocery stores. These devices are either handheld **wand readers** or **platform scanners.** They contain photoelectric cells that scan or read **bar codes,** or the vertical zebra-striped marks printed on product containers.

There are a variety of different codes including the UPC, MaxiCode, and QR codes.

- **UPCs (Universal Product Codes)** are widely used by retail stores to automate the processes to check out customers, to change product prices, and to maintain inventory records.
- **MaxiCode** is widely used by the United Parcel Service (UPS) and others to automate the process of routing packages, tracking in-transit packages, and locating lost packages.
- **QR codes,** as mentioned in Chapter 3, are widely used to provide consumer information.

Smartphones with the appropriate app can also scan codes. (See Figure 6-9.) For example, after scanning the bar code from a product you are thinking of buying, the app Price Check by Amazon will provide in-store and online price comparisons as well as provide other customer product reviews.

RFID Readers

RFID (radio-frequency identification) tags are tiny chips that can be embedded in most everything. They can be found in consumer products, driver's licenses, passports, and any number of other items. (See Figure 6-10.) These chips contain electronically stored information that can be read using an **RFID reader** located several yards away. They are widely used to track and locate lost pets; to monitor production and update inventory; and to record prices, product descriptions, and locations of retail items.

Some argue that these tags may one day be inserted into humans to track their locations. Even if the tags are not embedded into humans, they will likely be embedded into the clothes worn by humans. They argue that RFID tags are a serious threat to our privacy and their use needs to be carefully controlled by legislation.

Character and Mark Recognition Devices

Character and mark recognition devices are scanners that are able to recognize special characters and marks. They are specialty devices that are essential tools for certain applications. Three types are

- **Magnetic-ink character recognition (MICR)**—used by banks to automatically read those unusual numbers on the bottom of checks and deposit slips. A special-purpose machine known as a reader/sorter reads these numbers and provides input that allows banks to efficiently maintain customer account balances.
- **Optical-character recognition (OCR)**—uses special preprinted characters that can be read by a light source and changed into machine-readable code. A common OCR device is the handheld wand reader. (See Figure 6-11.) These are used in department stores to read retail price tags by reflecting light on the printed characters.
- **Optical-mark recognition (OMR)**—senses the presence or absence of a mark, such as a pencil mark. OMR is often used to score standardized multiple-choice tests.

concept check

 What is a scanner? Describe five types of scanning devices.

 List three different bar codes, and describe what they are used for.

 Describe three common character and mark recognition devices.

Standard	Pixels
HD 720	1,280 × 720
HD 1080	1,920 × 1,080
QXGA	2,048 × 1,536
WQXGA	2,560 × 1,600
QSXGA	2,560 × 2,048

Figure 6-16 **Resolution standards**

Figure 6-17 **Flat-panel monitor**

Figure 6-18 **E-book reader**

Resolution is expressed as a matrix of these dots or pixels. For example, many monitors today have a resolution of 1,920 pixel columns by 1,080 pixel rows for a total of 2,073,600 pixels. The higher a monitor's resolution (the more pixels), the clearer the image produced. See Figure 6-16 for the most common monitor resolutions.

- **Dot (pixel) pitch** is the distance between each pixel. Most newer monitors have a dot pitch of 0.30 mm (30/100th of a millimeter) or less. The lower the dot pitch (the shorter the distance between pixels), the clearer the images produced.

- **Contrast ratios** indicate a monitor's ability to display images. It compares the light intensity of the brightest white to the darkest black. The higher the ratio, the better the monitor. Good monitors typically have contrast ratios between 500:1 and 2000:1.

- **Size,** or **active display area,** is measured by the diagonal length of a monitor's viewing area. Common sizes are 15, 17, 19, 21, and 24 inches.

- **Aspect ratio** indicates the proportional relationship between a display's width and height. Typically, this relationship is expressed by two numbers separated by a colon (:). Many older, more square-shaped monitors have a 4:3 aspect ratio. Almost all newer monitors have a 16:9 aspect ratio designed to display wide-screen content.

Another important monitor feature is the ability to accept touch or gesture input such as finger movements including swiping, sliding, and pinching. While most older monitors do not support touch input, it is becoming a standard feature of newer monitors.

Flat-Panel Monitors

Flat-panel monitors are the most widely used type of monitor today. Compared to other types, they are thinner, are more portable, and require less power to operate. (See Figure 6-17.)

Almost all flat-panel displays are backlit, meaning that a common source of light is dispersed over all the pixels on the screen. There are two basic types of flat-panel monitors: LCD and LED.

- **LCD (liquid crystal display)** is widely used for older monitors and is typically less expensive.
- **LED (light-emitting diode)** monitors use similar technology with a more advanced backlighting technology. They produce better-quality images, are slimmer, and are more environmentally friendly as they require less power and use fewer toxic chemicals to manufacturer. Most new monitors are LED.

E-book Readers

E-books (electronic books) are traditional printed books in electronic format. These books are available from numerous sources including many public and private libraries, bookstore websites, and the cloud. **E-book readers (e-readers)** are dedicated mobile devices for storing and displaying e-books and other electronic media including electronic newspapers and magazines.

E-book readers have displays that are typically 6 inches and use a technology known as e-ink. **E-ink** produces images that reflect light like ordinary paper, making the display easy to read. Two well-known e-book readers are Amazon's Kindle and Barnes & Noble's Nook Simple Touch. (See Figure 6-18.)

Tablets can also display e-books. They are larger, heavier, and more expensive than e-book readers. They are also much more flexible, with displaying e-books being only one of their any number of applications. Unlike dedicated e-book readers, these tablets use LCD displays that provide crisp, colorful images, however, that are difficult to read in bright light due to their reflective nature. Two well-known traditional tablets are Apple's iPad and Samsung's Galaxy Tab.

To learn more about e-books, see Making IT Work for You: E-books, on page 150.

Other Monitors

There are several other types of monitors. Some are used for more specialized applications, such as making presentations and watching television.

- **Digital** or **interactive whiteboards** are specialized devices with a large display connected to a computer or projector. The computer's desktop is displayed on the digital whiteboard and controlled using a special pen, a finger, or some other device. Digital whiteboards are widely used in classrooms and corporate boardrooms. (See Figure 6-19.)

- **High-definition television (HDTV)** delivers a much clearer and more detailed wide-screen picture than regular television. Because the output is digital, users can readily freeze video sequences to create high-quality still images. The video and still images can then be edited and stored for later use. This technology is very useful to graphic artists, designers, and publishers. One of the most recent and dramatic advances is 3-D HDTV. (See Figure 6-20.) Using special viewing glasses, 3-D HDTV provides theater-quality three-dimensional viewing.

- **Cathode-ray tubes (CRTs)** are similar in size and technology to older televisions. They have been replaced by flat-panel monitors. Discarded CRTs, however, are a serious threat to our environment. Each color CRT contains approximately four pounds of lead and numerous other hazardous materials. Don't just throw out an obsolete CRT. Dispose of it in a responsible manner through an EPA-certified recycling program. Most large cities and manufacturers including IBM, Microsoft, and Dell have certified programs.

Figure 6-19 **Digital whiteboard**

Figure 6-20 **3-D HDTV**

E-BOOKS

Are you tired of carrying a book bag filled with textbooks? Have you ever wished you could have a reference book or text at your fingertips, instead of at home on a bookshelf? E-books are the solutions to these problems, and this guide will discuss their benefits, as well as various options on how to access and read them.

Benefits of E-books   Because e-books are digital, they offer a wide range of benefits:

1 • *Transporting.* Books can take up a large volume of space in any home (or your school bag). With e-books, you can store over a thousand books in one small device!

2 • *Searching.* Type any keyword, and you will be taken to the page(s) where that word appears. This is much faster than using an index.

3 • *Bookmarking.* Mark any number of pages as important. This is an improvement over having countless physical bookmarks or folded pages.

4 • *Adding highlights and notes.* All marks on an e-book are digital. They can be added and removed easily. The same could not be said for physical textbooks.

5 • *Purchasing.* Buying an e-book can take less than a minute, as it is downloaded instantly to your device. Prices also tend to be lower than those for physical books.

Reading E-books   Once you decide to purchase an e-book, you may be surprised by the number of devices you can use to read it.

1 • *E-book reader.* Dedicated e-book readers, such as the Amazon Kindle and the Barnes & Noble Nook, can be purchased for less than $100. If it is important for you to read in direct sunlight or areas with heavy lighting, the e-ink used by these devices will be desirable.

2 • *Smartphones and tablets.* Do you already own a smartphone or tablet that you take everywhere? If so, you may want to download the free apps from e-book sellers to avoid the cost of a separate e-book reader. The reading experience on these apps is excellent with the touch-screen interface present in these devices.

3 • *Laptop and desktop computers.* Although many e-book retailers make apps for your computer, sellers such as Google allow you to read books purchased from its Google Play store with nothing more than a web browser.

Most e-book sellers offer the synchronization of your e-books and notes with their cloud services. This allows you to start reading a book using your tablet, for example, and pick up where you left off with your smartphone.

The web is continually changing, and some of the specifics presented in this Making IT Work for You may have changed.

To learn about other ways to make information technology work for you, visit our website at www.mhhe.com/ce2015 and select Student Edition **and then** Making IT Work.

concept check

Define these monitor features: clarity, resolution, dot pitch, contrast ratios, size, and aspect ratio.

Describe flat-panel, LCD, and LED monitors.

What are e-book readers, digital whiteboards, HDTVs, and CRTs?

Printers

Even as many individuals, schools, and businesses are trying to go paperless, printers remain one of the most used output devices. You probably use a printer to print homework assignments, photographs, and web pages. **Printers** translate information that has been processed by the system unit and present the information on paper. Printer output is often called **hard copy.**

Features

There are many different types of printers. Almost all, however, have some basic distinguishing features, including resolution, color capability, speed, memory, and duplex printing.

- **Resolution** for a printer is similar to monitor resolution. It is a measure of the clarity of images produced. Printer resolution, however, is measured in **dpi (dots per inch).** (See Figure 6-21.) Most printers designed for personal use average 1,200 by 4,800 dpi. The higher the dpi, the better the quality of images produced.

- **Color** capability is provided by most printers today. Users typically have the option to print either with just black ink or with color. Because it is more expensive to print in color, most users select black ink for letters, drafts, and homework. The most common black ink selection is **grayscale,** in which images are displayed using many shades of gray. Color is used more selectively for final reports containing graphics and for photographs.

300 by
1,200 dpi

1,200 by
4,800 dpi

Figure 6-21 **DPI comparison**

Figure 6-22 **Inkjet printer**

- **Speed** is measured in the number of pages printed per minute. Typically, printers for personal use average 15 to 19 pages per minute for single-color (black) output and 13 to 15 pages per minute for color output.
- **Memory** within a printer is used to store printing instructions and documents waiting to be printed. The more memory, the faster it will be able to print large documents.
- **Duplex printing** allows automatic printing on both sides of a sheet of paper. Although not currently a standard feature for all printers, it will likely become standard in the future as a way to reduce paper waste and to protect the environment.

Inkjet Printers

Inkjet printers spray ink at high speed onto the surface of paper. This process produces high-quality images in a variety of colors, making it ideal for printing photos. (See Figure 6-22.) Inkjet printers are relatively inexpensive and are the most widely used printers. In addition, they are reliable and quiet. The most costly aspect of inkjet printers is replacing the ink cartridges. For this reason, most users specify black ink for the majority of print jobs and use the more expensive color printing for select applications. Typical inkjet printers produce 15 to 19 pages per minute of black-only output and 13 to 15 pages of color output.

Laser Printers

The **laser printer** uses a technology similar to that used in a photocopying machine. Laser printers use a laser light beam to produce images with excellent letter and graphics quality. More expensive than inkjet printers, laser printers are faster and are used in applications requiring high-quality output. (See Figure 6-23.)

Figure 6-23 **Laser printer**

There are two categories of laser printers. **Personal laser printers** are less expensive and are used by a single user. They typically can print 15 to 17 pages a minute. **Shared laser printers** typically support color, are more expensive, and are used (shared) by a group of users. Shared laser printers typically print over 50 pages a minute.

3-D Printers

3D printers, also known as **additive manufacturing,** create three-dimensional shapes by adding very thin layer after layer of material until the final shape is fully formed. (See Figure 6-24.) There are a variety of different processes and materials that can be used to create each layer. One of the most common sprays a liquid plastic or plasticlike substance through a nozzle similar to an inkjet printer.

3-D printers are controlled by data describing the shape of the object to be created. This data typically comes from a file created by a 3-D modeling program or from scanning a physical model using a 3-D scanner. Specialized

Figure 6-24 **3-D printer**

programs then take this data and further process it to create data describing hundreds or thousands of horizontal layers that when placed one on top of another form the shape of the intended object. The printer uses this data by extruding or cutting the first layer to very exact specifications. Successive layers are then created and attached to the layer below it until the product is finalized. The layers are so thin and so precise that they blend together, making a final product that shows no sign of the individual layers.

Commercial 3-D printers have been used for decades. Their cost, however, limited them to specialized manufacturing and research applications. Recently, however, their cost has dropped to as low as $400, making them available to individuals.

Other Printers

There are several other types of printers. These printers include cloud printers, thermal printers, and plotters:

- **Cloud printers** are printers connected to the Internet that provide printing services to others on the Internet. **Google Cloud Print** is a service that supports cloud printing. Once a user activates a printer using the Google Chrome OS, the user can access that printer anywhere with a smartphone or any other type of computer that is connected to the Internet. For example, you could use a smartphone from almost anywhere to send documents to be printed on a printer located at your home or school.
- **Thermal printers** use heat elements to produce images on heat-sensitive paper. These printers are widely used with ATMs and gasoline pumps to print receipts.
- **Plotters** are special-purpose printers for producing a wide range of specialized output. Using output from graphics tablets and other graphical input devices, plotters create maps, images, and architectural and engineering drawings. Plotters are typically used by graphic artists, engineers, and architects to print out designs, sketches, and drawings.

concept check

Discuss these printer features: resolution, color capability, speed, memory, and duplex printing.

Compare inkjet, laser, and 3-D printers.

Discuss cloud, thermal, and plotter printers.

Audio-Output Devices

Audio-output devices translate audio information from the computer into sounds that people can understand. The most widely used audio-output devices are **speakers** and **headsets**. (See Figure 6-25.) These devices connect to a sound card within the system unit. This connection can be by cable to an audio jack on the system unit, or the connection can be wireless. Wireless connections typically use **Bluetooth** technology. This type of connection requires special Bluetooth-enabled speakers and/or headsets. Bluetooth will be discussed further in Chapter 8. The sound card is used to capture as well as play back recorded sounds. Audio-output

Figure 6-25 **Headset**

devices are used to play music, vocalize translations from one language to another, and communicate information from the computer system to users.

Creating voice output is not anywhere near as difficult as recognizing and interpreting voice input. In fact, voice output is quite common. It is used with many smartphones, cars, and soft drink machines. It is used as a reinforcement tool for learning, such as to help students study a foreign language. It also is used in many supermarkets at the checkout counter to confirm purchases. One of its most powerful capabilities is to assist the physically challenged.

Combination Input and Output Devices

Many devices combine input and output capabilities. Sometimes this is done to save space. Other times it is done for very specialized applications. Common combination devices include multifunctional devices, Internet telephones, and virtual reality headgear and gloves.

Multifunctional Devices

Multifunctional devices (MFD) typically combine the capabilities of a scanner, printer, fax, and copy machine. These multifunctional devices offer a cost and space advantage. They cost about the same as a good printer or copy machine but require much less space than the single-function devices they replace. Their disadvantages are quality and reliability. The output quality for any one function is often not quite as good as that of the separate single-purpose devices. The reliability of multifunctional devices suffers because problems with one of the functional parts can make the entire device inoperable. Even so, multifunctional devices are widely used in home and small business offices.

Internet Telephones

Internet telephones are specialized input and output devices for receiving and sending voice communication. (See Figure 6-26.)

Voice over IP (VoIP) is a set of standards or technologies that support voice and other types of communication over the Internet. **Telephony,** also known as **Internet telephony,** is the VoIP application that uses the Internet rather than traditional telephone lines to support voice communication. To place telephone calls using Internet telephony requires a high-speed Internet connection and a service provider. Many cable service providers offer bundles including Internet, telephone, and television. While these bundles offer a price break, there are other lower-cost options for telephony from a variety of providers including Phone Power, Phone.com, and Skype.

Skype provides audio and video service that does not require any dedicated hardware. Once you subscribe to this free service, you can use your smartphone or any other type of computer to connect to any other Skype subscribers. The advantages compared to the other providers are that Skype is free for most domestic and international calls, supports video as well as audio, and does not require any special equipment. The disadvantages include that both parties must have their computers on to make or receive calls; calls can only be made between Skype subscribers, although, for an additional fee, you can place calls to non-Skype subscribers; and voice quality and reliability are not as good as traditional telephone communication. To learn more about using Skype, see Making IT Work for You: Skype, on pages 155 and 156.

Figure 6-26 **Internet telephone**

SKYPE

Do you already use a communication tool that lets you keep in touch with your friends and family? Does that tool include the ability to have face-to-face conversations, share files and screens, and make calls to those not connected to the Internet? Skype is a well-known tool that offers all these services, most of them for free. This section will help you explore some of Skype's features.

Getting Started In order to enjoy all the benefits of Skype, it is recommended that your computer have speakers, a microphone, and a webcam. If you have a laptop or tablet, these are all likely integrated. Follow these steps to create your account and install Skype on your machine:

1 Visit www.skype.com, and click the *Join us* link at the top right.

2 Enter the required information to create your Skype account. When you are finished, the software will be downloaded automatically. Do not purchase any Skype credits at the moment.

3 Run the downloaded setup file, and follow the prompts to install Skype on your machine.

4 Log in to your Skype account on the welcome screen, and follow the prompts to make sure your audio and video are working.

Adding Contacts You can find friends or other contacts manually, or you can import them from your address book on Facebook, Outlook, and several other services. To add a contact manually:

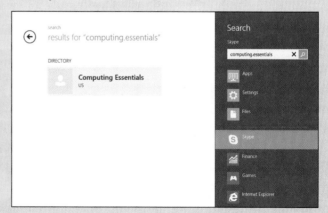

1 Right-click anywhere on the screen to bring up the options bar. Click on the *add contact* button.

2 Enter the name, Skype name, or e-mail address you know about your contact, and hit Enter.

3 Skype will display matches. Click the one that matches your contact's details, and then click the *Add* button.

Your contact must accept your request before you can see his or her online status.

Skype-to-Skype Communication When two individuals have Skype accounts, they can contact each other (for free) using a variety of methods, from voice or video calls to instant messages. They can exchange files and share screens with each other. Please note that for videoconferencing between three or more people, you must have a premium or business account.

1 From the main screen, click on *people,* then click on *available.* Click the contact you wish to communicate with.

2 Click the green video camera button to make a video call or the green handset button to make a voice call. Once your contact accepts the call, your interface will change.

3 During the call, you have the ability to send instant messages and turn audio and/or video on or off by clicking the buttons at the bottom.

4 To send files or share screens, click the *Plus* (+) button at the bottom. You could also have initiated the *Send File* feature from the contact screen without having to place a call.

5 To hang up, press the red *handset* button at the bottom.

Calling Landline or Mobile Phones (VoIP) Skype can use your Internet connection to place a call to any phone in the world. This is not a free service, but the costs are low. You can pay as you go with Skype credits, or sign up for a monthly subscription.

1 From the main screen, click the new *call* button in the top left corner of the screen.

2 Click the green *handset* button after entering the phone number.

The web is continually changing, and some of the specifics presented in this Making IT Work for You may have changed.

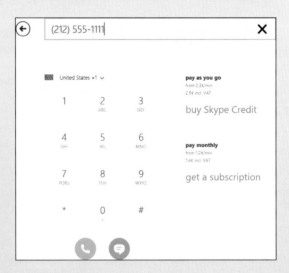

To learn about other ways to make information technology work for you, visit our website at www.mhhe.com/ce2015 and select Student Edition and then Making IT Work.

Virtual Reality Headgear and Gloves

Virtual reality (VR) is an artificial, or simulated, reality created in 3-D by computers. It strives to create a virtual or **immersive experience** by using specialized hardware that includes headgear and gloves. (See Figure 6-27.)

The **headgear** has earphones and three-dimensional stereoscopic screens. The **gloves** have sensors that collect data about your hand movements. Coupled with software, this interactive sensory equipment lets you immerse yourself in a computer-generated world.

There are any number of possible applications for virtual reality headgear and gloves. The ultimate recreational use might be something resembling a giant virtual amusement park. More serious applications can simulate important experiences or training environments, such as in aviation, surgical operations, spaceship repair, or nuclear disaster cleanup.

Figure 6-27 **Virtual reality headgear and gloves**

concept check

 What are the two most widely used audio-output devices? What is Bluetooth?

 What are multifunctional devices? Internet telephones? VoIP?

 What is virtual reality? Headgear? Gloves?

Ergonomics

People use computers to enrich their personal and private lives. There are ways, however, that computers can make people less productive and even harm their health. Anyone who frequently uses a computer can be affected. As a result, there has been great interest in a field known as ergonomics.

Ergonomics (pronounced "er-guh-nom-ix") is defined as the study of human factors related to things people use. It is concerned with fitting the task to the user rather than forcing the user to contort to do the task. For computer users and manufacturers this means designing input and output devices to increase ease of use and to avoid health risks.

Sitting in front of a screen in awkward positions for long periods may lead to physical problems such as eyestrain, headaches, and back pain. Computer users can alleviate these problems by taking frequent rest breaks and by using well-designed computer furniture. Some recommendations by ergonomics experts are illustrated in Figure 6-28.

Other recommendations to avoid physical discomfort are

- **Eyestrain and headache:** To make the computer easier on the eyes, take a 15-minute break every hour or two. Keep everything you're focusing on at about the same distance. For example, the computer screen, keyboard, and a document holder containing your work might be positioned about 20 inches away. Clean the screen of dust from time to time.

- **Back and neck pain:** To help avoid back and neck problems, make sure your equipment is adjustable. You should be able to adjust your chair for height and angle, and the chair should have good back support. The monitor should be at eye level or slightly below eye level. Use a footrest, if necessary, to reduce leg fatigue.

Good lighting

Adjustable-height document table

Wrist rest

Adjustable backrest

Adjustable tilt-and-swivel monitor

Adjustable bilevel table

Table height 25–29 inches

Footrest, if needed

Figure 6-28 Ergonomic recommendations

- **Repetitive strain injury: Repetitive strain injury (RSI)** is any injury that is caused by fast, repetitive work that can generate neck, wrist, hand, and arm pain. RSI is by far the greatest cause of workplace illnesses, resulting in compensation claims totaling billions of dollars and lost productivity every year. One particular type of RSI, **carpal tunnel syndrome,** found among heavy computer users, consists of damage to nerves and tendons in the hands. Some victims report the pain is so intense that they cannot open doors or shake hands and that they require corrective surgery. Ergonomically correct keyboards have been developed to help prevent injury from heavy computer use. (See Figure 6-29.) In addition to using ergonomic keyboards, you should take frequent short rest breaks and gently massage your hands.

Portable Computers

While the above recommendations apply to all personal computers, the design of portable computers including laptops, tablets, and smartphones presents some specific ergonomic challenges.

Figure 6-29 Ergonomic keyboard

- **Laptops:** Almost all laptops have attached keyboards and screens. Unfortunately, it is impossible to optimally position either for safe ergonomic use. When the screen is positioned appropriately at eye level, the keyboard is too high. When the keyboard is appropriately positioned, the screen is too low. To minimize the negative impact, raise the level of the screen by using books or reams of paper under the laptop and attach an external keyboard to be used at waist level.

- **Tablets:** Almost all tablets use a virtual keyboard and are designed to be held in your hands, flat on a table, or slightly angled. These design features cause the user to improperly align his or her head to the viewing surface, often causing neck and back pain. This problem, sometimes referred to as *tablet hunch,* can be minimized by taking frequent breaks, moving around while working, using a tablet cover or stand that allows the screen to be tipped at various angles, and using an external keyboard.

- **Smartphones:** Today, smartphones are more likely to be used for texting than talking. As a result, thumbs are often used to type on a tiny keyboard. The result can be a pain at the base or in the muscles of the thumb or wrist. This problem, sometimes referred to as *Blackberry thumb,* can be minimized by keeping wrists straight (not bent), head up, and shoulders straight and frequently resting thumbs by using other fingers.

In today's world, it is important to protect yourself by using computers appropriately.

concept check

What is ergonomics? How does it relate to input and output devices?

What can be done to minimize eyestrain, headache, back pain, and neck pain?

What is RSI? What is carpal tunnel syndrome?

Careers in IT

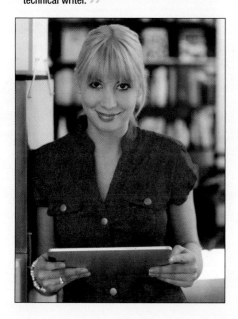

Now that you've learned about input and output devices, I'd like to tell you about my career as a technical writer.

Technical writers prepare instruction manuals, technical reports, and other scientific or technical documents. Most technical writers work for computer software firms, government agencies, or research institutions. They translate technical information into easily understandable instructions or summaries. As new technology continues to develop and expand, the need for technical writers who can communicate technical expertise to others is expected to increase.

Technical writing positions typically require an associate's or a bachelor's degree in communications, journalism, or English and a specialization in, or familiarity with, a technical field. However, individuals with strong writing skills sometimes transfer from jobs in the sciences to positions in technical writing.

Technical writers can expect to earn an annual salary in the range of $41,000 to $78,000. Advancement opportunities can be limited within a firm or company, but there are additional opportunities in consulting. To learn about other careers in information technology, visit us at www.mhhe.com/ce2015 and select Student Edition and then Careers.

A LOOK TO THE FUTURE

Augmented Reality Displays

Have you ever run into someone who looks familiar, but you cannot remember her name or where you know her from? What about finding yourself in an unfamiliar town, constantly having to look at your smartphone or GPS to get directions? Don't you wish the information would appear instantly, right before your eyes? With wearable augmented reality displays, this wish will become a reality. Data from your computer and the Internet will become instantly accessible and viewable without having to access another device. The reality you see in front of you is improved, or augmented, with additional visual information using projected images.

Bringing up information about a visual image is not new. Several search engines already have the ability to identify an image simply by looking for similar images in their databases. In addition, many types of software can do the same with faces, looking at key points in the image in order identify that individual. These augmented reality displays will take that technology one step further by integrating it with wearable glasses or contact lenses. Whether you look at a landmark, textbook, or person, the computer connected to that display will be able to retrieve the information you need and place it in your field of vision. So if you forgot the name of the person greeting you in the coffee shop, do not worry. Her name and brief biography will be retrieved from her social networking account and be displayed in front of you in time to properly return the greeting.

Identification of people and objects is not the only use of augmented reality. As technology continues to shrink in size, the device will be able to perform all the tasks of your smartphone. You will be able to look at the sky and see information

about today's weather. Text message and incoming call notifications can appear in front of you. Prices from various online stores will appear by the time you ask your friend where he got that new T-shirt. And, of course, integrated GPS will display arrows in front of you and guide you as you walk through unfamiliar city streets.

Although this technology will likely be available in the next few years, there are some challenges. First, you have the issue of powering the device. Something as small as a pair of glasses or contact lenses may not have room for a battery large enough to power it all day. Another issue involves limitations of human vision. Normally, our eyes find it difficult to focus on objects that are placed very close to them. Researchers have come up with various solutions to fix this problem, but they need to make it comfortable for the eyes to shift focus between the information being projected up close and the real-world object that could be far away. Lastly, there is the issue of comfort. Will these glasses or contact lenses be comfortable to wear all day? Will they make you look strange to those that do not know about augmented reality?

Many companies and universities are working on various types of augmented reality displays. There are a few that have received funding from the military in order to assist soldiers and pilots. The ones that seem closest to release for the general public are from Google. Prototype eyeglasses from its "Project Glass" division are already being tested by various Google employees.

Now that you have learned more about augmented reality, do you see yourself wearing these sorts of eyeglasses when they become affordable? Do you think that they can end up being a dangerous distraction?

KEYBOARDS

Input is any data or instructions that are used by a computer. **Input devices** translate words, numbers, sounds, images, and gestures that people understand into a form that the system unit can process. These include keyboards and pointing, scanning, image capturing, and audio-input devices.

Keyboards convert numbers, letters, and special characters that people understand into electrical signals. These signals are sent to, and processed by, the system unit.

Keyboards

There are four basic categories of keyboards: traditional, laptop, virtual, and thumb.

- **Traditional keyboards,** used on desktop and larger computers. Standard keyboard has 101 keys. **Toggle keys** turn features on and off. **Combination keys** perform actions when combinations of keys are held down.
- **Laptop keyboards,** used on laptop computers. Smaller than traditional keyboard with fewer keys. Typically does not have numeric keypad or standard location for function and navigation keys.
- **Virtual keyboard,** primarily used on mobile devices and tablets. Does not have a physical keyboard. Keys displayed on screen and selected by pressing a key's image.
- **Thumb keyboard,** used on smartphones and other small mobile devices. Designed primarily for communicating via texting and connecting to the web.

POINTING DEVICES

Pointing devices provide an intuitive interface with the system unit by accepting physical movements or gestures and converting them into machine-readable input.

Mouse

A **mouse** controls a pointer that is displayed on the monitor. The **mouse pointer** usually appears in the shape of an arrow. Some mice have a **wheel button** that rotates to scroll through information on the monitor. **Optical mouse** is the most widely used. A **cordless** or **wireless mouse** uses radio waves or infrared light waves. A **touch pad** operates by touching or tapping a surface. Widely used instead of a mouse with laptops and some types of mobile devices.

Touch Screens

Touch screens allow users to select actions by touching the screen with a finger or penlike device. **Multitouch screens** accept multiple-finger commands.

Game Controllers

Game controllers provide input to computer games. Widely used controllers include **joysticks, dance pads, gamepads,** and **motion-sensing devices.**

Stylus

A **stylus** is typically used with tablets and mobile devices. Often, a stylus interacts with **handwriting recognition software** to translate handwritten notes into a form that the system unit can process.

To efficiently and effectively use computers, you need to be aware of the most commonly used input and output devices. These devices are translators for information into and out of the system unit. Input devices translate words, sounds, and actions into symbols the system unit can process. Output devices translate symbols from the system unit into words, images, and sounds that people can understand.

SCANNING DEVICES

Scanning devices move across text and images to convert them into a form that the system unit can process.

Optical Scanners

An **optical scanner (scanner)** converts documents into machine-readable form. The three basic types are **flatbed**, **document**, and **portable**.

Card Readers

Card readers interpret encoded information located on a variety of cards. The most common is the **magnetic card reader** that reads information from a thin magnetic strip on the back of a card.

Bar Code Readers

Bar code readers or **scanners** (either handheld **wand readers** or **platform scanners**) read **bar codes** on products. There are a variety of different codes including the **UPC**, **MaxiCode**, and **QR codes**.

RFID Readers

RFID readers read **RFID (radio-frequency identification) tags**. These tags are widely used for tracking lost pets, production, and inventory and for recording prices and product descriptions.

Character and Mark Recognition Devices

Character and mark recognition devices are scanners that are able to recognize special characters and marks. Three types are **magnetic-ink character recognition (MICR)**, **optical-character recognition (OCR)**, and **optical-mark recognition (OMR)**.

IMAGE CAPTURING DEVICES

Image capturing devices create or capture original images. These devices include digital cameras and webcams.

Digital Cameras

Digital cameras record images digitally and store them on a memory card or in the camera's memory. Most digital cameras record video too.

Webcams

Webcams are specialized digital video cameras that capture images and send them to a computer for broadcast over the Internet. Webcams are built into many smartphones and tablets, while others are attached to the computer monitor.

AUDIO-INPUT DEVICES

Audio-input devices convert sounds into a form that can be processed by the system unit. By far the most widely used audio-input device is the microphone.

Voice Recognition Systems

Voice recognition systems use a microphone, a sound card, and special software. These systems allow users to operate computers and other devices as well as create documents by using voice commands. Specialized portable voice recorders are widely used by doctors, lawyers, and others to record dictation. Some systems are able to translate dictation from one language to another, such as from English to Japanese.

MONITORS

Output is processed data or information. **Output devices** are hardware to provide or create output.

Monitors (display screens) are the most-used output device. Output is often referred to as **soft copy**. Monitors vary in size, shape, and cost. Almost all, however, have some basic distinguishing features.

Features

The most important characteristic of a monitor is its **clarity**, which relates to the quality and sharpness of images. It is a function of several monitor features, including **resolution** (matrix of **pixels** or **picture elements**), **dot pitch**, **contrast ratio**, **size (active display area)**, and **aspect ratio**. New monitors support gesture input.

Flat Panel

Flat-panel monitors are the most widely used monitor. Two basic types are **LCD (liquid crystal display)**, typically used for older monitors, and **LED (light-emitting diode)**, slimmer and more environmentally friendly.

E-book Readers

E-books (electronic books) are traditional printed books in electronic format. **E-book readers (e-readers)** store and display e-books and other electronic media. They use **e-ink** technology. Tablets can display e-books and have a larger display area but are heavier, more expensive, and more difficult to read in bright light.

Other Monitors

Other types of monitors include **digital (interactive) whiteboards** to project output; **high-definition television (HDTV)** to display clear detailed images; and older monitors using **cathode-ray tubes (CRTs).**

PRINTERS

Printers translate information processed by the system unit and present the information on paper. Printer output is often called **hard copy**.

Features

Basic features include **resolution** measured in **dpi (dots per inch)**, color capability (most common black ink selection is **grayscale**), speed, memory, and **duplex** (both sides of paper) **printing.**

Inkjet

Inkjet printers spray ink at high speed onto the surface of paper. Most widely used type of printer, reliable, quiet, and inexpensive. The most costly aspect of inkjet printers is replacing the ink cartridges.

Laser

Laser printers use technology similar to photocopying machine. There are two categories: **personal** and **shared**.

3-D Printer

3-D printers (additive manufacturing) create objects by adding layers of material onto one another. Available for decades; however, recent price reductions have increased their popularity.

Other Printers

There are several other types of printers. These printers include **cloud printers (Google Cloud Print** is a cloud printing service), **thermal printers** (use heat elements to produce images on heat-sensitive paper), and **plotters** (using data from graphics tablets and other graphical devices).

AUDIO-OUTPUT DEVICES

Audio-output devices translate audio information from the computer into sounds that people can understand. The most widely used are **speakers** and **headsets**. These devices connect either by cable to an audio jack on the system unit or by a wireless connection. **Bluetooth** technology is widely used to connect wireless devices.

COMBINATION INPUT AND OUTPUT DEVICES

Many devices combine input and output capabilities.

Multifunctional Devices
Multifunctional devices (MFD) typically combine the capabilities of a scanner, printer, fax, and copy machine.

Internet Telephones
Internet telephones send and receive voice communication over computer networks. **Voice over IP (VoIP)** is a set of standards for communications over the Internet. **Telephony (Internet telephony)** is a VoIP application. **Skype** is a widely used VoIP service provider.

Virtual Reality Headgear and Gloves
Virtual reality (VR) creates 3-D simulated **immersive experiences**. Virtual reality hardware includes **headgear** and **gloves**. Applications include training environments, such as in aviation, surgery, spaceship repair, or nuclear disaster cleanup.

ERGONOMICS

Ergonomics is the study of human factors related to things people use.

Recommendations
Some recommendations to avoid physical discomfort associated with heavy computer use:

- To avoid eyestrain and headache, take 15-minute break every hour; keep everything you're focusing on at same distance; and clean screen periodically.
- To avoid back and neck pain, use adjustable equipment; chairs adjust for height, angle, and back support; monitors at eye level or slightly below. Use footrest, if necessary, to reduce leg fatigue.
- To avoid **repetitive strain injury (RSI)** and **carpal tunnel syndrome**, use ergonomically correct keyboards; take frequent, short rest breaks; and gently massage hands.

Portable Computers
Design of portable computers presents ergonomic challenges.

- Laptops do not allow correct positioning of keyboard and screen; raise level of laptop and use external keyboard.
- Tablets with virtual keyboards cause improper alignment of user's head; take frequent breaks, move while working, use cover or stand, use external keyboard.
- Smartphones require extensive use of thumbs; keep wrists straight, head up, and shoulders straight and use other fingers.

CAREERS IN IT

Technical writers prepare instruction manuals, technical reports, and other documents. An associate's or a bachelor's degree in communication, journalism, or English and a specialization in, or familiarity with, a technical field are required. Salary range is $41,000 to $78,000.

KEY TERMS

3-D printers (152)
active display area (148)
additive manufacturing (152)
aspect ratio (148)
bar code (144)
bar code reader (144)
bar code scanner (144)
Bluetooth (153)
card reader (144)
carpal tunnel syndrome (158)
cathode-ray tube (CRT) (150)
clarity (147)
cloud printer (153)
combination key (141)
contrast ratio (148)
cordless mouse (142)
dance pad (143)
digital camera (146)
digital whiteboard (150)
display screen (147)
document scanner (144)
dot pitch (148)
dots per inch (dpi) (151)
duplex printing (152)
e-book reader (148)
e-books (148)
e-ink (148)
e-reader (148)
electronic books (148)
ergonomics (157)
flat-panel monitor (148)
flatbed scanner (144)
game controller (142)
gamepads (143)
gloves (157)
Google Cloud Print (153)
grayscale (151)
handwriting recognition software (143)
hard copy (151)

headgear (157)
headsets (153)
high-definition television (HDTV) (150)
immersive experience (157)
inkjet printer (152)
input (140)
input device (140)
interactive whiteboard (150)
Internet telephone (154)
Internet telephony (154)
joystick (143)
keyboard (140)
laptop keyboard (141)
laser printer (152)
light-emitting diode (LED) (148)
liquid crystal display (LCD) (148)
magnetic card reader (144)
magnetic-ink character recognition (MICR) (145)
MaxiCode (145)
monitor (147)
motion-sensing device (143)
mouse (142)
mouse pointer (142)
multifunctional device (MFD) (154)
multitouch screen (142)
optical-character recognition (OCR) (145)
optical-mark recognition (OMR) (145)
optical mouse (142)
optical scanner (144)
output (147)
output device (147)
personal laser printer (152)

picture element (147)
pixel (147)
pixel pitch (148)
platform scanner (144)
plotter (153)
pointing device (142)
portable scanner (144)
printer (151)
QR codes (145)
repetitive strain injury (RSI) (158)
resolution (147)
RFID reader (145)
RFID (radio-frequency identification) tag (145)
scanner (144)
scanning devices (144)
shared laser printer (152)
Skype (154)
soft copy (147)
speakers (153)
stylus (143)
technical writer (159)
telephony (154)
thermal printer (153)
thumb keyboard (141)
toggle key (141)
touch pad (142)
touch screen (142)
traditional keyboard (141)
Universal Product Code (UPC) (145)
virtual keyboard (141)
virtual reality (VR) (157)
voice over IP (VoIP) (154)
voice recognition system (146)
wand reader (144)
webcam (146)
wheel button (142)
wireless mouse (142)

To test your knowledge of these key terms with animated flash cards, visit our website at www.mhhe.com/ce2015, select Student Edition, and choose Chapter 6 and then Flashcards.

MULTIPLE CHOICE

Circle the correct answer.

1. Most keyboards use an arrangement of keys known as:
    a. Alpha
    b. Daisy
    c. OptiKey
    d. QWERTY

2. The device that controls a pointer displayed on the monitor.
    a. cord
    b. mouse
    c. printer
    d. scanner

3. The type of screen that can be touched with more than one finger and supports zooming in and out by pinching and stretching your fingers.
    a. digital
    b. dynamic
    c. multitouch
    d. AMOLED

4. Flatbed and document are types of:
    a. headsets
    b. HDTVs
    c. monitors
    d. scanners

5. Device used by banks to automatically read those unusual numbers on the bottom of checks and deposit slips.
    a. MICR
    b. FDIC
    c. OMR
    d. UPC

6. The most widely used audio-input device.
    a. mouse
    b. VR
    c. microphone
    d. TFT

7. The monitor feature that indicates the ability to display colors.
    a. aspect ratio
    b. contrast ratio
    c. dot pitch
    d. resolution rate

8. Mobile devices able to store and display electronic media.
    a. e-book readers
    b. HDTV
    c. lasers
    d. whiteboards

9. Virtual reality strives to create this type of experience.
    a. electronic
    b. immersive
    c. LCD
    d. VoIP

10. The study of human factors related to things people use is:
    a. ergonomics
    b. RFID
    c. RSI
    d. telephony

For an interactive multiple-choice practice test, visit our website at www.mhhe.com/ce2015, select Student Edition, and choose Chapter 6 and then Multiple Choice.

MATCHING

Match each numbered item with the most closely related lettered item. Write your answers in the spaces provided.

a. active display area
b. digital camera
c. dot pitch
d. mouse
e. plotters
f. scanners
g. Skype
h. stylus
i. toggle key
j. UPC

_____ 1. Pressing this key turns a feature on or off.

_____ 2. Input device that controls a pointer that is displayed on the monitor.

_____ 3. A penlike device commonly used with tablet PCs and PDAs.

_____ 4. Bar code readers use either handheld wand readers or platform _____.

_____ 5. Bar code system used by many electronic cash registers.

_____ 6. Records images digitally on a memory card or in its memory.

_____ 7. The distance between each pixel.

_____ 8. A monitor feature that is measured by the diagonal length of the viewing area.

_____ 9. Special-purpose printers for creating maps, images, and architectural and engineering drawings.

_____10. A provider of lower-cost options for telephony.

For an interactive matching practice test, visit our website at www.mhhe.com/ce2015, select Student Edition, and choose Chapter 6 and then Matching.

OPEN-ENDED

On a separate sheet of paper, respond to each question or statement.

1. Define input and input devices.
2. Describe the different types of keyboard, pointing, scanning, image capturing, and audio-input devices.
3. Define output and output devices.
4. Describe the features and different types of monitors and printers.
5. Describe audio-output devices including Bluetooth technology.
6. Discuss combination input and output devices, including multifunctional devices, Internet telephones, and virtual reality headgear and gloves.
7. Define ergonomics, describe ways to minimize physical discomfort, and discuss design issues with portable computers.

DISCUSSION

Respond to each of the following questions.

1 Making IT Work for You: E-BOOKS

Are you tired of carrying a book bag filled with textbooks? Review the Making IT Work for You: E-books on page 149, and then respond to the following: (a) Have you ever purchased or read an e-book? If so, what was your most recent one? If not, have you considered it? Why or why not?

(b) Download and install an e-book app (desktop, tablet, or smartphone version), and then download a free e-book for that particular service. Identify the e-book you selected, and describe your experience with that e-book service, as well as some of the in-book features of its app. (c) Based on your experience, will you be purchasing more e-books in the future? Why or why not? (d) Would you consider buying future textbooks as e-books? Discuss the advantages and disadvantages of e-book textbooks.

2 Making IT Work for You: SKYPE

Do you already use a communication tool that lets you keep in touch with your friends and family? Review the Making IT Work for You: Skype on pages 155 and 156, and then respond to the following: (a) Have you ever used Skype or a similar service? If so, what service have you used, and what do you typically use it for? If you have not used Skype or a similar service, do you expect to in the future? Why or why not? (b) If you do not have a Skype account, create a free one, and add one of your classmates as a contact. Try a few of Skype's features after connecting with your classmate, and then describe your experience with those features. (c) Discuss the advantages and disadvantages of using Skype or a similar service for communication. (d) Do you currently use VoIP with your Internet provider or any other online service? Why or why not?

3 Privacy: PRINTERS AND ANONYMITY

Did you know that your printer may print personally identifying information on every document you print without your knowledge or consent? Review the Privacy box on page 153, and respond to the following: (a) It's one thing that these codes can be used to identify a specific printer. But do you think the codes can lead to identifying the person who owns the printer? Why or why not? (b) Do you think the hidden codes are a violation of privacy? Explain your position. (c) Does a printer manufacturer have a duty to assist the government in criminal investigations? Justify your position. (d) Does a printer manufacturer have a duty to protect the privacy of its customers? Why or why not?

4 Ethics: WEBCAMS

Webcams can be set up almost anywhere by anyone. Once in place, these webcams can continuously broadcast images to the Internet. Some images can be very embarrassing to the individuals who were recorded. Review the Ethics box on page 146, and respond to the following: (a) Would you feel uncomfortable if a hidden webcam was recording you when you entered a private home or business? What if the video was broadcast online? Why or why not? (b) Do you think recording and broadcasting images without permission is an ethical or a privacy concern? What if that person is in a public place at the moment the recording took place? In your response, consider whether such ethical concerns are significant enough to warrant new laws and regulations. (c) Many cities use webcams or video cameras for traffic control purposes. If those cameras record a person engaged in an illegal or questionable activity that is not related to traffic, should law enforcement be able to use the video in court? Should a concerned parent or jealous spouse be able to access that video? Defend your responses.

5 Environment: INKJET PRINTERS

Have you considered the environmental impact of using your inkjet printer? Review the Environment box on page 151, and then respond to the following: (a) How often do you use your printer at home? What sort of items do you typically print? (b) Have you considered any alternatives to printing? If so, what are those alternatives? Why would or wouldn't you use these alternatives? (c) Does the manufacturer of your ink cartridges use recycled plastic? Support your answer with details from the manufacturer's website. (d) Find a store near you that accepts used ink cartridges. Name the store, and provide details on the benefits it gives you for turning in cartridges.

chapter 7　Secondary Storage

Learning Objectives

After you have read this chapter, you should be able to:

1 Distinguish between primary and secondary storage.

2 Identify the important characteristics of secondary storage including media, capacity, storage devices, and access speed.

3 Describe hard-disk platters, tracks, sectors, cylinders, and head crashes.

4 Compare internal and external hard drives.

5 Compare performance enhancements including disk caching, RAID, file compression, and file decompression.

6 Define optical storage including compact discs, digital versatile discs, and Blu-ray discs.

7 Define solid-state storage including solid-state drives, flash memory cards, and USB drives.

8 Define cloud storage and cloud storage services.

9 Describe mass storage, mass storage devices, enterprise storage systems, and storage area networks.

Why should I read this chapter?

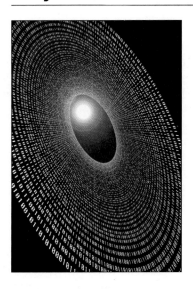

If you don't have the right secondary storage your computer will slow to a crawl, your digital camera won't take pictures, and your phone won't be able run apps. In the future, that will likely not be a problem as we will see storage types that can hold the entire U.S. Library of Congress on a single disk the size of a coin and store information in holograms or even organic molecules.

This chapter covers the things you need to know to be prepared for this ever changing digital world, including:

- Hard drives—get the right hard drive on your computer to meet all your needs.
- Optical discs—share digital information on Blu-ray, CD, or DVD.
- Solid state storage—make your portable electronics faster and use less power.
- Cloud storage—store your information safely and securely on the Internet.

Introduction

"Hi, I'm James, and I'm a disaster recovery specialist. I'd like to talk with you about secondary storage, one of the most critical parts of any computer system. I'd also like to talk about various cloud storage services."

Secondary storage devices are used to save, back up, and even transport files consisting of data or programs from one location or computer to another. At one time, almost all files contained only numbers and letters. The demands for saving these files were easily met with low-capacity storage devices.

Data storage has expanded from text and numeric files to include digital music files, photographic files, video files, and much more. These new types of files require secondary storage devices that have much greater capacity.

Secondary storage devices have always been an indispensable element in any computer system. They have similarities to output and input devices. Like output devices, secondary storage devices receive information from the system unit in the form of the machine language of 0s and 1s. Rather than translating the information, however, secondary storage devices save the information in machine language for later use. Like input devices, secondary storage devices send information to the system unit for processing. However, the information, since it is already in machine form, does not need to be translated. It is sent directly to memory (RAM), where it can be accessed and processed by the CPU.

To efficiently and effectively use computers, you need to be aware of the different types of secondary storage. You need to know the capabilities, limitations, and uses of hard disks, solid-state drives, optical discs, cloud storage, and other types of secondary storage. Additionally, you need to be aware of specialty storage devices for portable computers and to be knowledgeable about how large organizations manage their extensive data resources.

Storage

An essential feature of every computer is the ability to save, or store, information. As discussed in Chapter 5, random-access memory (RAM) holds or stores data and programs that the CPU is presently processing. Before data can be processed or a program can be run, it must be in RAM. For this reason, RAM is sometimes referred to as **primary storage.**

Unfortunately, most RAM provides only temporary or volatile storage. That is, it loses all of its contents as soon as the computer is turned off. Its contents also are lost if there is a power failure that disrupts the electric current going into the system unit. This volatility results in a need for more permanent or nonvolatile storage for data and programs. We also need external storage because users need much more storage capacity than is typically available in a computer's primary or RAM memory.

Secondary storage provides permanent or nonvolatile storage. Using **secondary storage devices** such as a hard-disk drive, data and programs can be retained after the computer has been shut off. This is accomplished by *writing* files to and *reading* files from secondary storage devices. Writing is the process of saving information *to* the secondary storage device. Reading is the process of accessing information *from* secondary storage. This chapter focuses on secondary storage devices.

Some important characteristics of secondary storage include

- **Media** are the physical material that holds the data and programs. (See Figure 7-1.)
- **Capacity** measures how much a particular storage medium can hold.
- **Storage devices** are hardware that reads data and programs from storage media. Most also write to storage media.
- **Access speed** measures the amount of time required by the storage device to retrieve data and programs.

Most desktop personal computer systems have hard-disk and optical disc drives, as well as ports where additional storage devices can be connected.

Hard Disks

Hard disks save files by altering the magnetic charges of the disk's surface to represent 1s and 0s. Hard disks retrieve data and programs by reading these charges from the magnetic disk. Characters are represented by positive (+) and negative (−) charges using the ASCII, EBCDIC, or Unicode binary codes. For example, the letter A would require a series of 8 charges. (See Figure 7-2.) **Density** refers to how tightly these charges can be packed next to one another on the disk.

Hard disks use rigid metallic **platters** that are stacked one on top of another. Hard disks store and organize files using tracks, sectors, and cylinders. **Tracks** are rings of concentric circles on the platter. Each track is divided into invisible wedge-shaped sections called **sectors.** (See Figure 7-3.) A **cylinder** runs through each track of a stack of platters. Cylinders are necessary to differentiate files stored on the same track and sector of different platters. When a hard disk is formatted, tracks, sectors, and cylinders are assigned.

Figure 7-1 Secondary storage media

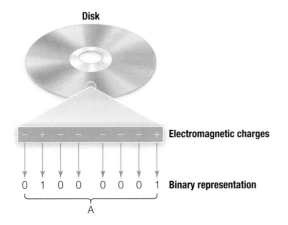

Figure 7-2 How charges on a disk surface store the letter A

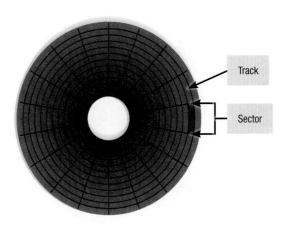

Figure 7-3 Tracks and sectors

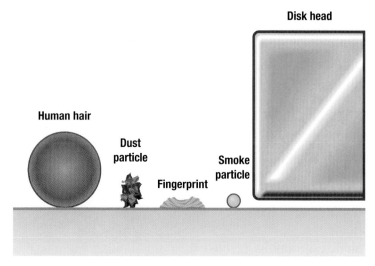

Human hair

Dust
particle

Fingerprint

Smoke
particle

Disk head

Hard disks are sensitive instruments. Their read/write heads ride on a cushion of air about 0.000001 inch thick. It is so thin that a smoke particle, fingerprint, dust, or human hair could cause what is known as a head crash. (See Figure 7-4.)

A **head crash** occurs when a read/write head makes contact with the hard disk's surface or with particles on its surface. A head crash is a disaster for a hard disk. The disk surface is scratched, and some or all of the data is destroyed. At one time, head crashes were commonplace. Now, fortunately, they are rare.

There are two basic types of hard disks: internal and external.

Figure 7-4 **Materials that can cause a head crash**

Internal Hard Disk

An **internal hard disk** is located inside the system unit. These hard disks are able to store and retrieve large quantities of information quickly. They are used to store programs and data files. For example, nearly every personal computer uses its internal hard disk to store its operating system and major applications such as Word and Excel.

To see how a hard disk works, visit our website at www.mhhe.com/ce2015 and select Student Edition, then Explore, and then Disk.

To ensure adequate performance of your internal hard disk and the safety of your data, you should perform routine maintenance and periodically make backup copies of all important files. For hard-disk maintenance and backup procedures, refer to Chapter 4's coverage of the Windows utilities File History, Disk Cleanup, and Optimize Drives.

External Hard Drives

While internal hard disks provide fast access, they have a fixed amount of storage and cannot be easily removed from the system unit. External hard disks provide slower access and are typically connected to a USB or Thunderbolt port on the system unit and are easily removed. Like an internal hard disk, external hard disks have a fixed amount of storage. However, since each removable hard disk can be easily replaced by another removable hard disk, a single port on the system unit can provide access to an unlimited amount of storage. (See Figure 7-5.)

External hard drives use the same basic technology as internal hard disks and are used primarily to complement an internal hard disk. Because they are easily removed, they are particularly useful to protect or secure sensitive information. Other uses for external drives include backing up the contents of the internal hard disk and providing additional hard-disk capacity.

Figure 7-5 **External hard drive**

Performance Enhancements

Three ways to improve the performance of hard disks are disk caching, redundant arrays of inexpensive disks, and file compression/decompression.

Disk caching improves hard-disk performance by anticipating data needs. It performs a function similar to cache memory discussed in Chapter 5. While cache memory improves processing by acting as a temporary high-speed holding area between memory and the CPU, disk caching improves processing by acting as a temporary high-speed holding area between a secondary storage device and the CPU. Disk caching requires a combination of hardware and software. During idle processing time, frequently used data is automatically identified and read from the hard disk into

Figure 7-6 **RAID storage device**

the disk cache. When needed, the data is then accessed directly from memory. The transfer rate from memory is much faster than from the hard disk. As a result, overall system performance is often increased by as much as 30 percent.

Redundant arrays of inexpensive disks (RAID) improve performance by expanding external storage, improving access speed, and providing reliable storage. Several inexpensive hard-disk drives are connected to one another. These connections can be by a network or within specialized RAID devices. (See Figure 7-6.) The connected hard-disk drives are related or grouped together, and the computer system interacts with the RAID system as though it were a single large-capacity hard-disk drive. The result is expanded storage capability, fast access speed, and high reliability. For these reasons, RAID is often used by Internet servers and large organizations.

File compression and **file decompression** increase storage capacity by reducing the amount of space required to store data and programs. File compression is not limited to hard-disk systems. It is frequently used to compress files on DVDs, CDs, and flash drives as well. File compression also helps to speed up transmission of files from one computer system to another. Sending and receiving compressed files across the Internet is a common activity.

File compression programs scan files for ways to reduce the amount of required storage. One way is to search for repeating patterns. The repeating patterns are replaced with a token, leaving enough tokens so that the original can be rebuilt or decompressed. These programs often shrink files to a quarter of their original size. To learn more about file compression, visit our website at www.mhhe.com/ce2015 and select Student Edition, then Explore, and then Compression.

Windows and Mac operating systems provide compression and decompression utilities. For more advanced compression schemes, you can use specialized utilities such as WinZip. For a summary of performance enhancement techniques, see Figure 7-7.

privacy

Did you know that when you sell your computer, you might be selling all your data as well. When you delete a file, the computer does not remove the data. It simply makes that hard disk space available to be written on in the future. If you accidentally delete a file, file recovery software is available to check the hard disk to see if the data is still there and has not been overwritten yet. In the same way that data can be recovered when accidentally deleted, thieves can recover data that was intentionally deleted. To confidently delete files, use a secure deletion utility before selling a computer. **To see more privacy facts, visit our website at www.mhhe. com/ce2015 and select** Student Edition **and then** Privacy.

Technique	Description
Disk caching	Uses cache and anticipates data needs
RAID	Linked, inexpensive hard-disk drives
File compression	Reduces file size
File decompression	Expands compressed files

Figure 7-7 **Performance enhancement techniques**

STORAGE

RAM is **primary storage**. Most RAM is volatile, meaning that it loses its contents whenever power is disrupted. **Secondary storage** provides nonvolatile storage. Secondary storage retains data and information after the computer system is turned off.

Writing is the process of saving information to **secondary storage devices**. Reading is the process of accessing information.

Important characteristics include

- **Media**—actual physical material that retains data and programs.
- **Capacity**—how much a particular storage medium can hold.
- **Storage devices**—hardware that reads and writes to storage media.
- **Access speed**—time required to retrieve data from a secondary storage device.

HARD DISKS

Hard disks use rigid metallic **platters** that provide a large amount of capacity. They store data and programs by altering the electromagnetic charges on the platter's surface. Files are organized according to

- **Tracks**—concentric rings on the platter.
- **Sectors**—wedge-shaped sections.
- **Cylinders**—run through each track of a stack of platters.

Density refers to how tightly electromagnetic charges can be packed next to one another on the disk.

A **head crash** occurs when the hard disk makes contact with the drive's read/write heads.

Two types are internal and external hard disks.

Internal Hard Disk

Internal hard disks are located within the system unit. Used to store programs and data files.

To efficiently and effectively use computers, you need to be aware of the different types of secondary storage. You need to know their capabilities, limitations, and uses. There are four widely used storage media: hard disk, optical disc, solid-state, and cloud storage.

HARD DISKS

External Hard Drives

Unlike internal hard disks, **external hard drives** are removable. External drives use the same basic technology as internal disks.

Performance Enhancements

Three ways to improve hard-disk performance are disk caching, RAID, and file compression and decompression.

- **Disk caching**—provides a temporary high-speed holding area between a secondary storage device and the CPU; improves performance by anticipating data needs and reducing time to access data from secondary storage.
- **RAID (redundant array of inexpensive disks)**—several inexpensive hard-disk drives are connected together; improves performance by providing expanded storage, fast access, and high reliability.
- **File compression and decompression**—files are compressed before storing and then decompressed before being used again; improves performance through efficient storage.

OPTICAL DISCS

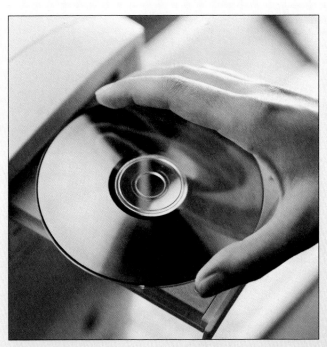

Optical discs use laser technology. 1s and 0s are represented by **pits** and **lands**. **Optical disc drives** project light and measure the reflected light.

Compact Disc

Compact discs (CDs) have typical capacity of 700 MB on one side. Three types are **CD-ROM (compact disc–read-only memory)**, **CD-R (CD-recordable; CD-R** drives are also known as CD burners), and **CD-RW (compact disc rewritable, erasable optical discs)**.

Digital Versatile Disc

DVDs (digital versatile discs, digital video discs) have far greater capacity than CDs with a typical capacity of 4.7 GB on one side. Three types are **DVD-ROM (digital versatile disc–read-only memory; DVD** players are drives), write once (**DVD+R, DVD-R**), and rewritable (**DVD+RW, DVD-RW, DVD-RAM**).

Blu-ray Disc

Hi-def (high-definition) Blu-ray discs are the next standard optical disc. **Blu-ray discs (BDs)** have a capacity of 50 GB on one side. Same size as other optical media but much greater capacity and requires special drives. Three basic types: read only, write once, and rewritable.

SOLID-STATE STORAGE

Solid-state storage devices have no moving parts and are more reliable and require less power than hard disks.

Solid-State Drives

Solid-state drives (SSDs) are similar to internal hard-disk drives except they use solid-state memory; are faster, more durable, and more expensive; and generally provide less capacity. Hybrid systems contain SSD and magnetic disks.

Flash Memory Cards

Flash memory cards are small solid-state storage devices that are widely used with portable devices. They are used with a variety of specialized input devices including digital cameras to store and transfer images and digital media players like the iPod to store and transfer music and video files.

USB Drives

USB drives (flash drives) are so small that they fit onto a key ring. These drives connect to a computer's USB port and are widely used to transfer data and information between computers, specialty devices, and the Internet.

CLOUD STORAGE

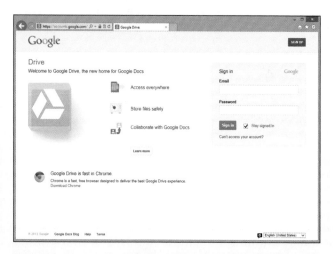

With cloud computing, the Internet acts as a "cloud" of servers. Cloud storage (online storage) is supplied by these servers.

- Cloud servers provide storage, processing, and memory.
- Advantages for users include less maintenance, fewer hardware upgrades, and easy file sharing and collaboration.
- Disadvantages for users include slower access speed and less control over file security.

MASS STORAGE DEVICES

Mass storage refers to the tremendous amount of secondary storage required by large organizations. Mass storage devices are specialized high-capacity secondary storage devices.

Most large organizations have established a strategy called an enterprise storage system to promote efficient and safe use of data.

Mass storage devices that support this strategy are file servers, network attached storage (NAS), RAID systems, and organizational cloud storage. A storage area network (SAN) is a method of using enterprise-level remote storage systems as if they were local to your computer.

CAREERS IN IT

Disaster recovery specialists are responsible for recovering systems and data after a disaster strikes an organization. Bachelor's or associate's degree in information systems or computer science, experience, and additional skills in the areas of networking, security, and database administration are desirable. Salary range is $70,000 to $103,000.

KEY TERMS

access speed (173)
Blu-ray disc (BD) (177)
capacity (173)
CD (compact disc) (176)
CD-R (CD-recordable) (177)
CD-ROM (compact disc–read-only memory) (176)
CD-RW (compact disc rewritable) (177)
cloud computing (180)
cloud storage (180)
cylinder (173)
density (173)
disaster recovery specialist (184)
disk caching (175)
DVD (digital versatile disc or digital video disc) (177)
DVD player (177)
DVD-R (DVD recordable) (177)
DVD+R (DVD recordable) (177)
DVD-RAM (DVD random-access memory) (177)
DVD-ROM (DVD–read-only memory) (177)
DVD-RW (DVD rewritable) (177)
DVD+RW (DVD rewritable) (177)
enterprise storage system (183)
erasable optical disc (177)
external hard drive (174)
file compression (175)
file decompression (175)
file server (184)

flash drive (179)
flash memory card (179)
hard disk (173)
head crash (174)
hi def (high definition) (177)
internal hard disk (174)
land (176)
mass storage (183)
mass storage devices (183)
media (173)
network attached storage (NAS) (184)
online storage (180)
optical disc (176)
optical disc drive (176)
organizational cloud storage (184)
pit (176)
platter (173)
primary storage (172)
RAID system (184)
redundant array of inexpensive disks (RAID) (175)
secondary storage (172)
secondary storage device (172)
sector (173)
solid-state drive (SSD) (178)
solid-state storage (178)
storage area network (SAN) (184)
storage device (173)
track (173)
USB drive (179)

To test your knowledge of these key terms with animated flash cards, visit our website at www.mhhe.com/ce2015, select Student Edition, and choose Chapter 7 and then Flashcards.

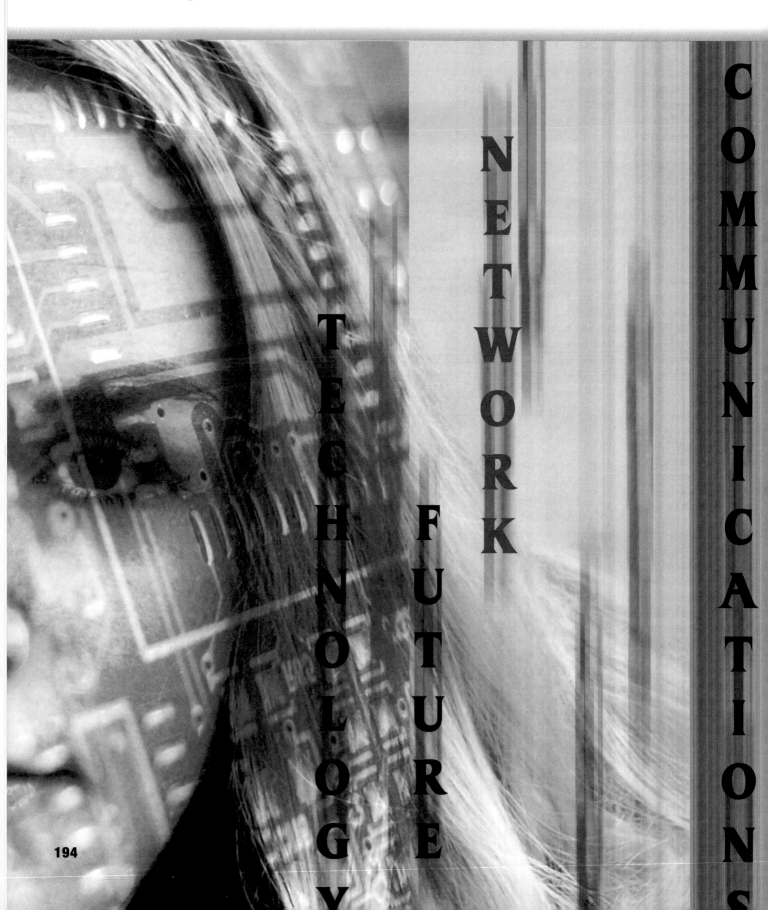

chapter 8

Communications and Networks

Learning Objectives

After you have read this chapter, you should be able to:

1. Explain connectivity, the wireless revolution, and communication systems.

2. Describe physical and wireless communication channels.

3. Differentiate between connection devices and services including dial-up, DSL, cable, satellite, and cellular.

4. Describe data transmission factors, including bandwidth and protocols.

5. Define networks and key network terminology including network interface cards and network operating systems.

6. Describe different types of networks, including local, home, wireless, personal, metropolitan, and wide area networks.

7. Describe network architectures, including topologies and strategies.

8. Explain the organization issues related to Internet technologies and network security.

Why should I read this chapter?

Communication networks are the backbone of nearly every aspect of modern digital life. In the future, telepresence (the ability to fully experience the reality of a different place without actually being there) will be common place. For example, doctors will routinely perform surgery on patients located halfway around the world!

This chapter covers the things you need to know to be prepared for this ever changing digital world, including:

- Wired networks—learn about coaxial and fiber-optic cables so you can make smart decisions about home Internet connections.
- Wireless networks—use your digital devices smarter and safer by understanding Wi-Fi, satellites and Bluetooth.
- Mobile computing—become a digital road warrior using 4G data networks and GPS.

Introduction

"Hi, I'm Michael, and I'm a network administrator. I'd like to talk with you about computer communications and networks. I'd also like to talk about technologies that support mobile computing including global positioning systems, Wi-Fi, and 3G and 4G networks."

We live in a truly connected society. We can communicate almost instantaneously with others worldwide; changing events from the smallest of countries and places are immediately broadcast to the world; our e-mail messages are delivered to handheld devices; cars access the Internet to receive driving instructions and solve mechanical problems. Even household appliances can connect to the Internet and be remotely controlled. The communications and information options we have at our fingertips have changed how we react and relate to the world around us.

As the power and flexibility of our communication systems have expanded, the sophistication of the networks that support these systems has become increasingly critical and complex. The network technologies that handle our cellular, business, and Internet communications come in many different forms. Satellites, broadcast towers, telephone lines, even buried cables and fiber optics carry our telephone messages, e-mail, and text messages. These different networks must be able to efficiently and effectively integrate with one another.

To efficiently and effectively use computers, you need to understand the concept of connectivity, wireless networking, and the elements that make up network and communications systems. Additionally, you need to understand the basics of communications channels, connection devices, data transmission, network types, network architectures, and organizational networks.

Communications

Computer communications is the process of sharing data, programs, and information between two or more computers. We have discussed numerous applications that depend on communication systems, including

- **E-mail**—provides a fast, efficient alternative to traditional mail by sending and receiving electronic documents.
- **Texting**—provides very efficient direct text communication between individuals using short electronic messages.
- **Videoconferencing**—provides a very low-cost alternative to long-distance telephone calls using electronic voice and video delivery.
- **Electronic commerce**—buying and selling goods electronically.

In this chapter, we will focus on the communication systems that support these and many other applications. Connectivity, the wireless revolution, and communication systems are key concepts and technologies for the 21st century.

Connectivity

Connectivity is a concept related to using computer networks to link people and resources. For example, connectivity means that you can connect your personal computer to other computers and information sources almost anywhere. With this connection, you are linked to the world of larger computers and the Internet. This includes hundreds of thousands of web servers and their extensive information resources. Thus, being able to efficiently and effectively use computers becomes a matter of knowing not only about connectivity through networks to personal computers but also about larger computer systems and their information resources.

The Wireless Revolution

The single most dramatic change in connectivity and communications in the past decade has been the widespread use of mobile devices like smartphones and tablets with wireless Internet connectivity. Students, parents, teachers, businesspeople, and others routinely talk and communicate with these devices. It is estimated that over 1.5 billion smartphones are in use worldwide. This wireless technology allows individuals to stay connected with one another from almost anywhere at any time.

Figure 8-1 **Wireless revolution**

So what's the revolution? While wireless technology was originally used primarily for voice communications, today's mobile computers support e-mail, web access, social networking, and a variety of Internet applications. In addition, wireless technology allows a wide variety of nearby devices to communicate with one another without any physical connection. Wireless communications allows you to share a high-speed printer, share data files, and collaborate on working documents with a nearby co-worker without having your computers connected by cables or telephone. High-speed Internet wireless technology allows individuals to connect to the Internet and share information from almost anywhere in the world. (See Figure 8-1.) But is it a revolution? Most experts say yes and that the revolution is just beginning.

Communication Systems

Communication systems are electronic systems that transmit data from one location to another. Whether wired or wireless, every communication system has four basic elements. (See Figure 8-2.)

- **Sending and receiving devices.** These are often a computer or specialized communication device. They originate (send) as well as accept (receive) messages in the form of data, information, and/or instructions.
- **Connection devices.** These devices act as an interface between the sending and receiving devices and the communication channel. They convert outgoing messages into packets that can travel across the communication channel. They also reverse the process for incoming messages.

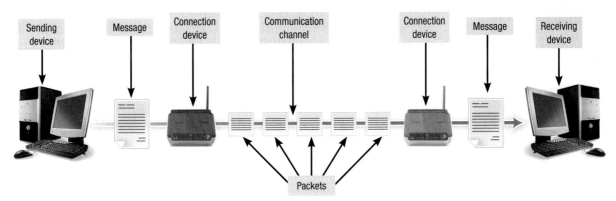

Figure 8-2 **Basic elements of a communication system**

Unlike radio waves, **infrared** uses infrared light waves to communicate over short distances. Like microwave transmissions, infrared is a line-of-sight communication. Because light waves can only travel in a straight line, sending and receiving devices must be in clear view of one another without any obstructions blocking that view. One of the most common infrared devices is the TV remote control.

concept check

What are communication channels? List three physical connections.

What is Bluetooth? Wi-Fi? Microwave communication? WiMax?

What is LTE? Satellite communications? GPS? Infrared?

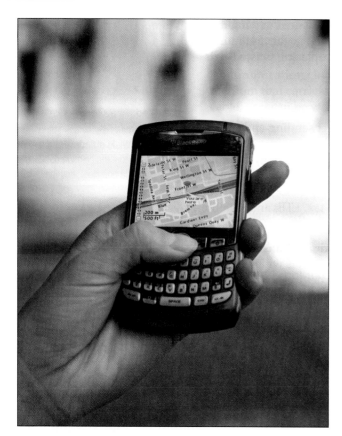

Figure 8-8 **GPS navigation**

Connection Devices

At one time nearly all computer communication used telephone lines. However, because the telephone was originally designed for voice transmission, telephones typically send and receive **analog signals,** which are continuous electronic waves. Computers, in contrast, send and receive **digital signals**. (See Figure 8-9.) These represent the presence or absence of an electronic pulse—the on/off binary signals we mentioned in Chapter 5. To convert the digital signals to analog signals and vice versa, you need a modem.

Analog

Digital

Figure 8-9 **Analog and digital signals**

Unit	Speed
Mbps	Million bits per second
Gbps	Billion bits per second
Tbps	Trillion bits per second

Figure 8-10 **Typical transfer rates**

Modems

The word **modem** is short for *modulator-demodulator.* **Modulation** is the name of the process of converting from digital to analog. **Demodulation** is the process of converting from analog to digital. The modem enables digital personal computers to communicate across different media, including telephone wires, cable lines, and radio waves.

The speed with which modems transmit data varies. This speed, called **transfer rate,** is typically measured in millions of bits **(megabits) per second (Mbps).** (See Figure 8-10.) The higher the speed, the faster you can send and receive information. For example, to download a complete full-length motion picture (700 MB) on a 1.5-Mbps modem would take about 1 hour. Using a 6.0-Mbps modem would take about 15 minutes. To learn more about transfer rates, visit our website at www.mhhe.com/ce2015 and select Student Edition, then Explore, and then Rate.

There are four commonly used types of modems: telephone, DSL, cable, and wireless. (See Figure 8-11.)

- A **telephone modem** is used to connect a computer directly to a telephone line. These modems can be either internal or external. Internal modems are on an expansion card that plugs into a slot on the system board. An external modem is typically connected to the system unit through a USB port. Of the four types of modems, the telephone modem is the slowest and least used.

- A **DSL (digital subscriber line)** modem uses standard phone lines to create a high-speed connection directly to your phone company's offices. These devices are usually external and connect to the system unit using either a USB or an Ethernet port.

Telephone   DSL   Cable   Wireless

Figure 8-11 Basic types of modems

- A **cable modem** uses the same coaxial cable as your television. Like a DSL modem, a cable modem creates high-speed connections using the system unit's USB or Ethernet port.
- A **wireless modem** is also known as a **WWAN (wireless wide area network) modem.** It is usually a small plug-in USB or ExpressCard device that provides very portable high-speed connectivity from virtually anywhere.

Connection Service

For years, large corporations have been leasing special high-speed lines from telephone companies. Originally, these were copper lines, known as **T1** lines, that could be combined to form higher-capacity options known as **T3** or **DS3** lines. These lines have largely been replaced by faster **optical carrier (OC)** lines.

While the special high-speed lines are too costly for most individuals, Internet service providers (as discussed in Chapter 2) do provide affordable connections. For years, individuals relied on **dial-up services** using existing telephones and telephone modems to connect to the Internet. This type of service has been replaced by higher-speed connection services including DSL, cable, satellite, and cellular services.

- **Digital subscriber line (DSL) service** is provided by telephone companies using existing telephone lines to provide high-speed connections. **ADSL (asymmetric digital subscriber line)** is one of the most widely used types of DSL. DSL is much faster than dial-up.
- **Cable service** is provided by cable television companies using their existing television cables. These connections are usually faster than DSL.
- **Fiber-optic service (FiOS)** is showing up in some areas, but it is a new technology and not widely available. Current providers of FiOS include Google and Verizon with speeds faster than cable or DSL connections.

- **Satellite connection services** use satellites to provide wireless connections. While slower than DSL and cable modem, satellite connections are available almost anywhere using a satellite-receiving disk.
- **Cellular service providers,** including Verizon, AT&T, Sprint, and T-Mobile, support voice and data transmission to wireless devices. Cellular services have gone through different generations. **First-generation mobile telecommunications (1G)** started in the 1980s using analog radio signals to provide analog voice transmission service. **Second-generation mobile telecommunications (2G)** stared in the 1990s using digital radio signals. **Third-generation mobile telecommunications (3G)** started in the 2000s and provided services capable of effective connectivity to the Internet, marking the beginning of smartphones.

  The **fourth-generation mobile telecommunications (4G)** has begun to replace 3G networks in some areas with providers using WiMax and LTE connections to provide faster transmission speeds. While a user's experience with 4G will depend on several factors, including carrier, geography, and proximity to cell towers, 4G technologies can provide speeds up to 10 times faster than 3G.

  To learn more about how you can use mobile communications, see Making IT Work for You: Mobile Internet on page 203.

concept check

 What is the function of a modem? Compare the four types of modems.

 What is a connection service? Compare the five high-speed connection services.

Describe the four generations of mobile communications.

Data Transmission

Several factors affect how data is transmitted. These factors include bandwidth and protocols.

Bandwidth

Bandwidth is a measurement of the width or capacity of the communication channel. Effectively, it means how much information can move across the communication channel in a given amount of time. For example, to transmit text documents, a slow bandwidth would be acceptable. However, to effectively transmit video and audio, a wider bandwidth is required. There are four categories of bandwidth.

- **Voiceband,** also known as **low bandwidth,** is used for standard telephone communication. Personal computers with telephone modems and dial-up service use this bandwidth. While effective for transmitting text documents, it is too slow for many types of transmission, including high-quality audio and video.
- **Medium band** is used in special leased lines to connect midrange computers and mainframes as well as to transmit data over long distances. This bandwidth is capable of very-high-speed data transfer.
- **Broadband** is widely used for DSL, cable, and satellite connections to the Internet. Several users can simultaneously use a single broadband connection for high-speed data transfer.
- **Baseband** is widely used to connect individual computers that are located close to one another. Like broadband, it is able to support high-speed transmission. Unlike broadband, however, baseband can only carry a single signal at one time.

MOBILE INTERNET

Is your smartphone or tablet always connected to the Internet? Millions have this always-on connection to access their e-mail, favorite websites, cloud services, and apps from anywhere at any time. What can be confusing to many is the variety of connection devices, data plans, and penalties for exceeding usage limits.

Devices   There are many devices that can help you get Internet access from wherever you are.

1 ● *Smartphones.* **Most modern smartphones are capable of accessing the Internet via Wi-Fi and 3G or 4G networks.**

2 ● *Tablets.* **Most tablets will provide Wi-Fi access, but to get 3G or 4G capabilities, you will generally have to purchase a higher-priced model.**

3 ● *Laptops.* **By inserting a USB modem, almost all laptops can access the Internet through a 3G or 4G network.**

4 ● *Mobile hotspot device.* **This is a stand-alone device that connects to a 3G or 4G network. It will then allow multiple devices near it to access the Internet via a Wi-Fi connection.**

Many smartphones can provide Wi-Fi sharing, or tethering, like a mobile hotspot device. However, you may have to pay an additional monthly fee.

Data Plans   A data plan defines how much data you can download using your 3G or 4G connection. These plans can be very confusing, but for most individuals, the plan that gives you a few gigabytes per month is best. Although a few providers have unlimited data plans, they may slow down, or throttle, your connection speed significantly if they deem that your usage is excessive.

Overage Charges   If you exceed the monthly data limit, wireless providers will start charging overage fees. For example, one provider charges $10 for every extra gigabyte used. To minimize overage charges, consider the following:

1 ● *Wi-Fi access points.* **Whenever possible, use a Wi-Fi connection. These connections are not subject to your data plan limits. So if you are in a coffee shop that offers free Wi-Fi, use it!**

2 ● *Streaming music/video.* **Streaming too much of any media can quickly become a problem. The solution: Be selective when watching TV shows, movies, and YouTube videos, and try to store some of your music on your device.**

3 ● *Downloading.* **Limit your downloading of new apps and music to Wi-Fi connections only. Many programs and MP3 files can reach (or even exceed) a size of 10 MB.**

4 ● *Monitor your data usage.* **Most wireless companies provide a free app that helps you monitor your minutes, text messages, and data. Keep an eye on this.**

The web is continually changing, and some of the specifics presented in this Making IT Work for You may have changed.

To learn about other ways to make information technology work for you, visit our website at www.mhhe.com/ce2015 and select Student Edition **and then** Making IT Work.

URL

www.mhhe.com

DNS

IP Address

65.39.69.50

Figure 8-12 DNS converts text-based addresses to numeric IP addresses

Protocols

For data transmission to be successful, sending and receiving devices must follow a set of communication rules for the exchange of information. These rules for exchanging data between computers are known as **protocols.**

As discussed in Chapter 2, **http,** or **hypertext transfer protocol,** is a widely used protocol used for web traffic. Another protocol, **https,** or **hypertext transfer protocol secure,** is becoming widely used to protect the transfer of sensitive information. Another widely used Internet protocol is **TCP/IP (transmission control protocol/Internet protocol).** The essential features of this protocol involve (1) identifying sending and receiving devices and (2) breaking information into small parts, or packets, for transmission across the Internet.

- **Identification:** Every computer on the Internet has a unique numeric address called an **IP address (Internet protocol address).** Similar to the way a postal service uses addresses to deliver mail, the Internet uses IP addresses to deliver e-mail and to locate websites. Because these numeric addresses are difficult for people to remember and use, a system was developed to automatically convert text-based addresses to numeric IP addresses. This system uses a **domain name server (DNS)** that converts text-based addresses to IP addresses. For example, whenever you enter a URL, say www.mhhe.com, a DNS converts this to an IP address before a connection can be made. (See Figure 8-12.)
- **Packetization:** Information sent or transmitted across the Internet usually travels through numerous interconnected networks. Before the message is sent, it is reformatted or broken down into small parts called **packets.** Each packet is then sent separately over the Internet, possibly traveling different routes to one common destination. At the receiving end, the packets are reassembled into the correct order.

concept check

What is bandwidth? Describe the four categories.

What are protocols? What is the standard protocol for the Internet?

Define TCP/IP, IP address, and packets.

Networks

A **computer network** is a communication system that connects two or more computers so that they can exchange information and share resources. Networks can be set up in different arrangements to suit users' needs. (See Figure 8-13.)

Terms

There are a number of specialized terms that describe computer networks. These terms include

- **Node**—any device that is connected to a network. It could be a computer, printer, or data storage device.
- **Client**—a node that requests and uses resources available from other nodes. Typically, a client is a user's personal computer.
- **Server**—a node that shares resources with other nodes. Dedicated servers specialize in performing specific tasks. Depending on the specific task, they may be called an application server, communication server, database server, file server, printer server, or web server.

Figure 8-13 Computer network

- **Directory server**—a specialized server that manages resources, such as user accounts, for an entire network.
- **Host**—any computer system that can be accessed over a network.
- **Router**—a node that forwards or routes data packets from one network to their destination in another network.
- **Switch**—central node that coordinates the flow of data by sending messages directly between sender and receiver nodes. A **hub** previously filled this purpose by sending a received message to all connected nodes, rather than just the intended node.
- **Network interface cards (NIC)**—as discussed in Chapter 5, these are expansion cards located within the system unit that connect the computer to a network. Sometimes referred to as a LAN adapter.
- **Network operating systems (NOS)**—control and coordinate the activities of all computers and other devices on a network. These activities include electronic communication and the sharing of information and resources.
- **Network administrator**—a computer specialist responsible for efficient network operations and implementation of new networks.

A network may consist only of personal computers, or it may integrate personal computers or other devices with larger computers. Networks can be controlled by all nodes working together equally or by specialized nodes coordinating and supplying all resources. Networks may be simple or complex, self-contained or dispersed over a large geographic area.

concept check

 What is a computer network? What are nodes, clients, servers, directory servers, hosts, routers, and switches?

 What is the function of an NIC and an NOS?

 What is a network administrator?

Network Types

Clearly, different types of channels—wired or wireless—allow different kinds of networks to be formed. Telephone lines, for instance, may connect communications equipment within the same building or within a home. Networks also may be citywide and even international, using both cable and wireless connections. Local area, metropolitan area, and wide area networks are distinguished by the size of the geographic area they serve.

Local Area Networks

Networks with nodes that are in close physical proximity—within the same building, for instance—are called **local area networks (LANs).** Typically, LANs span distances less than a mile and are owned and operated by individual organizations. LANs are widely used by colleges, universities, and other types of organizations to link personal computers and to share printers and other resources. For a simple LAN, see Figure 8-14.

Figure 8-14 **Local area network**

The LAN represented in Figure 8-14 is a typical arrangement and provides two benefits: economy and flexibility. People can share costly equipment. For instance, the four personal computers share the high speed laser printer and the file server, which are expensive pieces of hardware. Other equipment or nodes also may be added to the LAN—for instance, more personal computers, a mainframe computer, or optical disc storage devices. Additionally, the **network gateway** is a device that allows one LAN to be linked to other LANs or to larger networks. For example, the LAN of one office group may be connected to the LAN of another office group.

There are a variety of different standards or ways in which nodes can be connected to one another and ways in which their communications are controlled in a LAN. The most common standard is known as **Ethernet.** LANs using this standard are sometimes referred to as Ethernet LANs.

Home Networks

While LANs have been widely used within organizations for years, they are now being commonly used by individuals in their homes and apartments. These LANs, called **home networks,** allow different computers to share resources, including a common Internet connection. Computers can be connected in a variety of ways, including electrical wiring, telephone wiring, and special cables. One of the simplest ways, however, is without cables, or wireless.

Wireless LAN

A wireless local area network is typically referred to as a **wireless LAN (WLAN).** It uses radio frequencies to connect computers and other devices. All communications pass through the network's centrally located **wireless access point** or **base station.** This access point interprets incoming radio frequencies and routes communications to the appropriate devices. To see how wireless home networks work, visit our website at www.mhhe.com/ce2015 and select Student Edition, then Explore, and then Network.

Figure 8-15 Wireless adapter

Wireless access points that provide Internet access are widely available in public places such as coffee shops, libraries, bookstores, colleges, and universities. These access points are known as **hotspots** and typically use Wi-Fi technology. Many of these services are free and easy to find using free locator sites such as www.hotspot-locations.com. Most mobile computing devices have an internal wireless network card to connect to hotspots. If your mobile device does not have an internal wireless network card, you can use an external wireless adapter (see Figure 8-15) that plugs into your computer's USB port or PC card slot.

Personal Area Network

A **personal area network (PAN)** is a type of wireless network that works within a very small area—your immediate surroundings. PANs connect cell phones to headsets, PDAs to other PDAs, keyboards to cell phones, and so on. These networks make it possible for wireless devices to interact with each other. The most popular PAN technology is Bluetooth, with a maximum range of around 33 feet. Virtually all wireless peripheral devices available today use Bluetooth, including the controllers on popular game systems like the PlayStation and Wii.

Metropolitan Area Networks

Metropolitan area networks (MAN) span distances up to 100 miles. These networks are frequently used as links between office buildings that are located throughout a city.

Unlike a LAN, a MAN is typically not owned by a single organization. Rather, it is owned either by a group of organizations or by a single network service provider that provides network services for a fee.

Wide Area Networks

Wide area networks (WANs) are countrywide and worldwide networks. These networks provide access to regional service (MAN) providers and typically span distances greater than 100 miles. They use microwave relays and satellites to reach users over long distances—for example, from Los Angeles to Paris. Of course, the widest of all WANs is the Internet, which spans the entire globe.

The primary difference between a PAN, LAN, MAN, and WAN is the geographic range. Each may have various combinations of hardware, such as personal computers, midrange computers, mainframes, and various peripheral devices.

For a summary of network types, see Figure 8-16.

concept check

What is a LAN? Network gateway? Ethernet? Home network?

What is a wireless network? Wireless access point? Hotspot?

What is a PAN? MAN? WAN?

Type	Description
LAN	Local area network; located within close proximity
Home	Local area network for home and apartment use; typically wireless
WLAN	Wireless local area network; all communication passes through access point
PAN	Personal area network; connects digital devices, such as PDAs
MAN	Metropolitan area network; typically spans cities with coverage up to 100 miles
WAN	Wide area network for countrywide or worldwide coverage

Figure 8-16 **Types of networks**

Network Architecture

Network architecture describes how a network is arranged and how resources are coordinated and shared. It encompasses a variety of different network specifics, including network topologies and strategies. Network topology describes the physical arrangement of the network. Network strategies define how information and resources are shared.

Topologies

A network can be arranged or configured in several different ways. This arrangement is called the network's **topology.** The most common topologies are

- **Bus network**—each device is connected to a common cable called a **bus** or **backbone,** and all communications travel along this bus.
- **Ring network**—each device is connected to two other devices, forming a ring. (See Figure 8-17.) When a message is sent, it is passed around the ring until it reaches the intended destination.
- **Star network**—each device is connected directly to a central network switch. (See Figure 8-18.) Whenever a node sends a message, it is routed to the switch,

Figure 8-17 **Ring network**

Figure 8-18 **Star network**

Figure 8-19 Tree network

Figure 8-20 Mesh network

which then passes the message along to the intended recipient. The star network is the most widely used network topology today. It is applied to a broad range of applications from small networks in the home to very large networks in major corporations.

- **Tree network**—each device is connected to a central node, either directly or through one or more other devices. The central node is connected to two or more subordinate nodes that in turn are connected to other subordinate nodes, and so forth, forming a treelike structure. (See Figure 8-19.) This network, also known as a **hierarchical network,** is often used to share corporatewide data.

- **Mesh network**—this topology is the newest type and does not use a specific physical layout (such as a star or a tree). Rather, the mesh network requires that each node have more than one connection to the other nodes. (See Figure 8-20.) The resulting pattern forms the appearance of a mesh. If a path between two nodes is somehow disrupted, data can be automatically rerouted around the failure using another path. Wireless technologies are frequently used to build mesh networks.

Strategies

Every network has a **strategy,** or way of coordinating the sharing of information and resources. Two of the most common network strategies are client/server and peer-to-peer.

Client/server networks use central servers to coordinate and supply services to other nodes on the network. The server provides access to resources such as web pages, databases, application software, and hardware. (See Figure 8-21.) This strategy is based on specialization. Server nodes coordinate and supply specialized services, and client nodes request the services. Commonly used server operating systems are Windows Server, Mac OS X Server, Linux, and Solaris.

Client/server networks are widely used on the Internet. For example, each time you open a web browser, your computer (the client) sends out a request for a specific web page. This request is routed over the Internet to a server. This server locates and sends the requested material back to your computer.

Figure 8-21 Client/server network

One advantage of the client/server network strategy is the ability to handle very large networks efficiently. Another advantage is the availability of powerful network management software to monitor and control network activities. The major disadvantages are the cost of installation and maintenance.

In a **peer-to-peer (P2P) network,** nodes have equal authority and can act as both clients and servers. The most common way to share games, movies, and music over the Internet is to use a P2P network. For example, special file-sharing software such as BitTorrent can be used to obtain files located on another personal computer and also can provide files to other personal computers.

P2P networks are rapidly growing in popularity as people continue to share information with others around the world. The primary advantage is that they are easy and inexpensive (often free) to set up and use. One disadvantage of P2P networks is the lack of security controls or other common management functions. For this reason, few businesses use this type of network to communicate sensitive information.

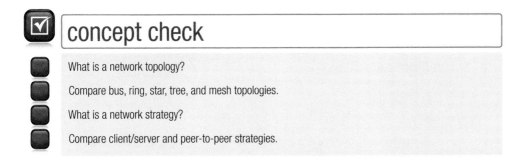

concept check

What is a network topology?

Compare bus, ring, star, tree, and mesh topologies.

What is a network strategy?

Compare client/server and peer-to-peer strategies.

Organizational Networks

Computer networks in organizations have evolved over time. Most large organizations have a complex and wide range of different network configurations, operating systems, and strategies. These organizations face the challenge of making these networks work together effectively and securely.

Internet Technologies

Many organizations today employ Internet technologies to support effective communication within and between organizations using intranets and extranets.

- An **intranet** is a *private* network within an organization that resembles the Internet. Like the *public* Internet, intranets use browsers, websites, and web pages. Typical applications include electronic telephone directories, e-mail addresses, employee benefit information, internal job openings, and much more. Employees find surfing their organizational intranets to be as easy and as intuitive as surfing the Internet.

- An **extranet** is a *private* network that connects *more than one* organization. Many organizations use Internet technologies to allow suppliers and others limited access to their networks. The purpose is to increase efficiency and reduce costs. For example, an automobile manufacturer has hundreds of suppliers for the parts that go into making a car. By having access to the car production schedules, suppliers can schedule and deliver parts as they are needed at the assembly plants. In this way, operational efficiency is maintained by both the manufacturer and the suppliers.

Network Security

Large organizations face the challenge of ensuring that only authorized users have access to network resources, sometimes from multiple geographic locations or across the Internet. Securing large computer networks requires specialized technology. Three technologies commonly used to ensure network security are firewalls, intrusion detection systems, and virtual private networks.

- A **firewall** consists of hardware and software that control access to a company's intranet and other internal networks. Most use software or a special computer called a **proxy server.** All communications between the company's internal networks and the outside world pass through this server. By evaluating the source and the content of each communication, the proxy server decides whether it is safe to let a particular message or file pass into or out of the organization's network. (See Figure 8-22.)

- **Intrusion detection systems (IDS)** work with firewalls to protect an organization's network. These systems use sophisticated statistical techniques to analyze all incoming and outgoing network traffic. Using advanced pattern matching and heuristics, an IDS can recognize signs of a network attack and disable access before an intruder can do damage.

Figure 8-22 **Intranets, extranets, firewalls, and proxy servers**

- **Virtual private networks (VPN)** create a secure private connection between a remote user and an organization's internal network. Special VPN protocols create the equivalent of a dedicated line between a user's home or laptop computer and a company server. The connection is heavily encrypted, and, from the perspective of the user, it appears that the workstation is actually located on the corporate network.

Like organizations, end users have security challenges and concerns. We need to be concerned about the privacy of our personal information. In the next chapter, we will discuss personal firewalls and other ways to protect personal privacy and security.

concept check

 What are Internet technologies? Compare intranets and extranets.

 What is a firewall? What is a proxy server?

 What are intrusion detection systems?

 What are virtual private networks?

Careers in IT

Now that you have learned about computer communications and networks, let me tell you about my career as a network administrator.

Network administrators manage a company's LAN and WAN networks. They may be responsible for design, implementation, and maintenance of networks. Duties usually include maintenance of both hardware and software related to a company's intranet and Internet networks. Network administrators are typically responsible for diagnosing and repairing problems with these networks. Some network administrators' duties include planning and implementation of network security as well.

Employers typically look for candidates with a bachelor's or an associate's degree in computer science, computer technology, or information systems as well as practical networking experience. Experience with network security and maintenance is preferred. Also technical certification may be helpful in obtaining this position. Because network administrators are involved directly with people in many departments, good communication skills are essential.

Network administrators can expect to earn an annual salary of $46,000 to $84,000. Opportunities for advancement typically include upper-management positions. This position is expected to be among the fastest-growing jobs in the near future. To learn about other careers in information technology, visit us at www.mhhe.com/ce2015 and select Student Edition and then Careers.

A LOOK TO THE FUTURE

Telepresence Lets You Be There without Actually Being There

How would you like to speak with distant friends or family as though they were in the same room at the touch of a button? Can you imagine receiving a physical examination from a doctor thousands of miles away? All this and more could be possible in the future thanks to the emerging technology known as telepresence.

Telepresence seeks to create the illusion that you are actually at a remote location, seeing, hearing, and, someday maybe, even feeling as though you were really there. Today's early implementations, such as Cisco TelePresence, mainly focus on an extension of video-conferencing, allowing people in different locations to conduct meetings as though they are sitting across a table from one another. This illusion is created with very high definition video, acoustically tuned audio systems, and high-speed networks. However, telepresence could someday go beyond the simple voice and videoconferencing available today, and the applications seem endless.

Robots are quickly becoming a key part of many telepresence applications. In addition to audio and video feeds from another location, robots will bring you the ability to manipulate objects at the remote location. Such robots are already

being used in the medical field. In one system, a surgeon uses special controls and screens in one room to control robotic arms that operate on the patient in another room. This type of system could be used to allow expert surgeons to perform several procedures on various patients located throughout the world in just one day!

In addition to manipulating objects, users may one day wear special gloves and other sensors that permit them to feel the objects being touched by the robot. This technology might be used to allow people to work in hazardous areas or perform search and rescue operations from a safe, remote location. A more casual application may see individuals using telepresence as a substitute for traditional vacations. Imagine touring remote cities or touching objects from a shipwreck on a deep-sea diving expedition without the expense, hassle, or risk of travel.

Various research institutions are currently experiencing breakthroughs in the areas of holography, which is technology that creates 3-D images called holograms that might pave the way to advanced telepresence. In the coming decade, you might be able to interact virtually with others via a projected, 3-D hologram of yourself.

How would you use telepresence? What benefits do you see from this technology? How might telepresence affect traveling? Do you see any disadvantages?

COMMUNICATIONS

Communications is the process of sharing data, programs, and information between two or more computers. Applications include e-mail, texting, videoconferencing, and electronic commerce.

Connectivity

Connectivity is a concept related to using computer networks to link people and resources. You can link or connect to large computers and the Internet, providing access to extensive information resources.

The Wireless Revolution

Mobile devices like smartphones and tablets have brought dramatic changes in connectivity and communications. These wireless devices are becoming widely used for computer communication.

Communication Systems

Communication systems transmit data from one location to another. Four basic elements are

- Sending and receiving devices originate or accept messages.
- Connection devices act as an interface between sending and receiving devices and the communication channel.
- Data transmission specifications are rules and procedures for sending and receiving data.
- Communication channel is the actual connecting or transmission medium for messages.

COMMUNICATION CHANNELS

Communication channels carry data from one computer to another.

Physical Connections

Physical connections use a solid medium to connect sending and receiving devices. Connections include **twisted-pair cable (telephone lines and Ethernet cables), coaxial cable,** and **fiber-optic cable.**

Wireless Connections

Wireless connections do not use a solid substance to connect devices. Most use radio waves.

- **Bluetooth**—transmits data over short distances; widely used for a variety of wireless devices.
- **Wi-Fi (wireless fidelity)**—uses high-frequency radio signals; most home and business wireless networks use Wi-Fi.
- **Microwave**—line-of-sight communication; used to send data between buildings; longer distances require microwave stations.
- **WiMax (Worldwide Interoperability for Microwave Access)**—extends the range of Wi-Fi networks using microwave connections.
- **LTE (Long Term Evolution)**—currently has similar performance to WiMax; promises to provide greater speed and quality transmissions in the near future.
- **Satellite**—uses microwave relay stations; **GPS (global positioning system)** tracks geographic locations.
- **Infrared**—uses light waves over a short distance; line-of-sight communication.

To efficiently and effectively use computers, you need to understand the concepts of connectivity, the wireless revolution, and communication systems. Additionally, you need to know the essential parts of communication technology, including channels, connection devices, data transmission, networks, network architectures, and network types.

CONNECTION DEVICES

Many communication systems use standard telephone lines and **analog signals**. Computers use **digital signals**.

Modems

Modems modulate and demodulate. Transfer rate is measured in **megabits per second**. Four types are telephone, DSL, cable, and wireless (wireless wide area network, WWAN).

Connection Service

T1, T3 (DS3), and **OC (optical carrier)** lines provide support for very-high-speed, all-digital transmission for large corporations. More affordable technologies include **dial-up, DSL (digital subscriber line), ADSL** (widely used), **cable, fiber-optic service (FiOS),** satellite, and **cellular** services. **4G (fourth-generation mobile telecommunications)** can provide 10 times faster speeds than 3G.

DATA TRANSMISSION

Bandwidth measures a communication channel's width or capacity. Four bandwidths are **voiceband** (low bandwidth), **medium band, broadband** (high-capacity transmissions), and **baseband**. Protocols are rules for exchanging data. Widely used Internet protocols include **http, https,** and **TCP/IP. IP addresses (Internet protocol addresses)** are unique numeric Internet addresses. **DNS (domain name server)** converts text-based addresses to and from numeric IP addresses. **Packets** are small parts of messages.

NETWORKS

Computer networks connect two or more computers. Some specialized network terms include

- **Node**—any device connected to a network.
- **Client**—node requesting resources.
- **Server**—node providing resources.
- **Directory server**—specialized node that manages resources.
- **Host**—any computer system that can be accessed over a network.
- **Router**—a node that forwards data packets from one network to another network.
- **Switch**—node that coordinates direct flow of data between other nodes. **Hub** is an older device that directed flow to all nodes.
- **NIC (network interface card)**—LAN adapter card for connecting to a network.
- **NOS (network operating system)**—controls and coordinates network operations.
- **Network administrator**—network specialist responsible for network operations.

NETWORK TYPES

Networks can be citywide or even international, using both wired and wireless connections.

- **Local area networks (LANs)** connect nearby devices. **Network gateways** connect networks to one another. **Ethernet** is a LAN standard. These LANs are called Ethernet LANs.
- **Home networks** are LANs used in homes.
- **Wireless LANs (WLANs)** use a **wireless access point (base station)** as a hub. Hotspots provide Internet access in public places.
- **Personal area networks (PANs)** are wireless networks for PDAs, cell phones, and other wireless devices.
- **Metropolitan area networks (MANs)** link office buildings within a city, spanning up to 100 miles.
- **Wide area networks or WANs** are the largest type. They span states and countries or form worldwide networks. The Internet is the largest wide area network in the world.

Network architecture describes how networks are arranged and resources are shared.

Topologies

A network's **topology** describes the physical arrangement of a network.

- **Bus network**—each device is connected to a common cable called a **bus** or **backbone.**
- **Ring network**—each device is connected to two other devices, forming a ring.
- **Star network**—each device is connected directly to a central network switch; most common type today.
- **Tree (hierarchical) network**—a central node is connected to subordinate nodes forming a treelike structure.
- **Mesh network**—newest; each node has two or more connecting nodes.

Strategies

Every network has a **strategy**, or way of sharing information and resources. Common network strategies include client/server and peer-to-peer.

- **Client/server (hierarchical) network**—central computers coordinate and supply services to other nodes; based on specialization of nodes; widely used on the Internet; able to handle very large networks efficiently; powerful network management software available.
- **Peer-to-peer network**—nodes have equal authority and act as both clients and servers; widely used to share games, movies, and music over the Internet; easy to set up and use; lacks security controls.

Internet Technologies

Internet technologies support effective communication using intranets and extranets.

- **Intranet**—private network within an organization; uses browsers, websites, and web pages. Typical applications include electronic telephone directories, e-mail addresses, employee benefit information, internal job openings, and much more.
- **Extranet**—like intranet except connects *more than one* organization; typically allows suppliers and others limited access to their networks.

Network Security

Three technologies commonly used to ensure network security are firewalls, intrusion detection systems, and virtual private networks.

- **Firewall**—controls access; all communications pass through **proxy server.**
- **Intrusion detection systems (IDS)**—work with firewalls; use sophisticated statistical techniques to recognize and disable network attacks.
- **Virtual private network (VPN)**—creates secure private connection between remote user and organization's internal network.

CAREERS IN IT

Network administrators manage a company's LAN and WAN networks. Bachelor's or associate's degree in computer science, computer technology, or information systems and practical networking experience required. Salary range is $46,000 to $84,000.

KEY TERMS

1G (first-generation mobile telecommunications) (202)
2G (second-generation mobile telecommunications) (202)
3G (third-generation mobile telecommunications) (202)
4G (fourth-generation mobile telecommunications) (202)
analog signal (200)
asymmetric digital subscriber line (ADSL) (201)
backbone (209)
bandwidth (202)
base station (207)
baseband (202)
Bluetooth (199)
broadband (202)
bus (209)
bus network (209)
cable modem (201)
cable service (201)
cellular service provider (202)
client (205)
client/server network (210)
coaxial cable (198)
communication channel (198)
communication system (197)
computer network (205)
connectivity (196)
demodulation (200)
dial-up service (201)
digital signal (200)
digital subscriber line (DSL) (200)
digital subscriber line (DSL) service (201)
directory server (206)
domain name server (DNS) (204)
downlink (199)

DS3 (201)
Ethernet (207)
Ethernet cable (198)
extranet (211)
fiber-optic cable (198)
fiber-optic service (FiOS) (201)
firewall (212)
global positioning system (GPS) (199)
hierarchical network (210)
home network (207)
host (206)
hotspot (208)
http (hypertext transfer protocol) (204)
https (hypertext transfer protocol secure) (204)
hub (204)
infrared (206)
intranet (211)
intrusion detection system (IDS) (212)
IP address (Internet protocol address) (204)
local area network (LAN) (206)
low bandwidth (202)
LTE (Long Term Evolution) (199)
medium band (202)
megabits per second (Mbps) (200)
mesh network (210)
metropolitan area network (MAN) (208)
microwave (199)
modem (200)
modulation (200)
network administrator (206, 213)
network architecture (209)
network gateway (207)
network interface card (NIC) (206)
network operating system (NOS) (206)

node (205)
optical carrier (OC) (201)
packet (204)
peer-to-peer (P2P) network (211)
personal area network (PAN) (208)
protocol (204)
proxy server (212)
ring network (209)
router (206)
satellite (199)
satellite connection service (202)
server (205)
star network (209)
strategy (210)
switch (206)
T1 (201)
T3 (201)
telephone line (198)
telephone modem (200)
topology (209)
transfer rate (200)
transmission control protocol/Internet protocol (TCP/IP) (204)
tree network (210)
twisted-pair cable (198)
uplink (199)
virtual private network (VPN) (213)
voiceband (202)
wide area network (WAN) (208)
Wi-Fi (wireless fidelity) (199)
WiMax (Worldwide Interoperability for Microwave Access) (199)
wireless access point (207)
wireless LAN (WLAN) (207)
wireless modem (201)
wireless wide area network (WWAN) modem (201)

To test your knowledge of these key terms with animated flash cards, visit our website at www.mhhe.com/ce2015, select Student Edition, and choose Chapter 8 and then Flashcards.

MULTIPLE CHOICE

Circle the letter of the correct answer.

1. The concept related to using computer networks to link people and resources.
   - a. connectivity
   - b. GPS
   - c. TCP/IP
   - d. Wi-Fi

2. A high-frequency transmission cable that delivers television signals as well as connects computers in a network.
   - a. coaxial
   - b. hi def
   - c. 3-D
   - d. twisted pair

3. A short-range radio communication standard that transmits data over short distances of up to approximately 33 feet.
   - a. Bluetooth
   - b. broadband
   - c. DSL
   - d. TCP/IP

4. The speed with which a modem transmits data is called its:
   - a. digital velocity
   - b. dynamic rate
   - c. modular rating
   - d. transfer rate

5. The bandwidth typically used for DSL, cable, and satellite connections to the Internet.
   - a. baseband
   - b. broadband
   - c. medium band
   - d. voiceband

6. Every computer on the Internet has a unique numeric address called a(n):
   - a. IP address
   - b. DNS
   - c. broadcast
   - d. packet

7. Sometimes referred to as a LAN adapter, these expansion cards connect a computer to a network.
   - a. PCMCIA
   - b. NIC
   - c. server
   - d. VPN

8. A device that allows one LAN to be linked to other LANs or to larger networks.
   - a. IDS
   - b. network gateway
   - c. PAN
   - d. switch

9. Typically using Wi-Fi technology, these wireless access points are available from public places such as coffee shops, libraries, bookstores, colleges, and universities.
   - a. hotspots
   - b. extranets
   - c. PANs
   - d. LANs

10. Bus, ring, star, tree, and mesh are five types of network:
    - a. topologies
    - b. protocols
    - c. strategies
    - d. devices

For an interactive multiple-choice practice test, visit our website at www.mhhe.com/ce2015, select Student Edition, and choose Chapter 8 and then Multiple Choice.

MATCHING

Match each numbered item with the most closely related lettered item. Write your answers in the spaces provided.

a. analog
b. bus
c. intrusion detection systems
d. microwave
e. network administrator
f. node
g. peer-to-peer
h. protocols
i. TCP/IP
j. tree

_____ 1. Type of network topology in which each device is connected to a common cable called a backbone.

_____ 2. A widely used Internet protocol.

_____ 3. Uses high-frequency radio waves.

_____ 4. Signals that are continuous electronic waves.

_____ 5. Rules for exchanging data between computers.

_____ 6. Any device that is connected to a network.

_____ 7. A computer specialist responsible for efficient network operations and implementation of new networks.

_____ 8. This network, also known as a hierarchical network, is often used to share corporatewide data.

_____ 9. In this network, nodes have equal authority and can act as both clients and servers.

_____ 10. Work with firewalls to protect an organization's network.

For an interactive matching practice test, visit our website at www.mhhe.com/ce2015, select Student Edition, and choose Chapter 8 and then Matching.

OPEN-ENDED

On a separate sheet of paper, respond to each question or statement.

1. Define communications including connectivity, the wireless revolution, and communication systems.

2. Discuss communication channels including physical connections and wireless connections.

3. Discuss connection devices including modems (telephone, DSL, cable, and wireless modems) and connection services (DSL, ADSL, cable, satellite, and cellular connection services).

4. Discuss data transmission including bandwidths (voiceband, medium band, broadband, and baseband) as well as protocols (IP addresses, domain name servers, and packetization).

5. Discuss networks by identifying and defining specialized terms that describe computer networks.

6. Discuss network types including local area, home, wireless, personal, metropolitan, and wide area networks.

7. Define network architecture including topologies (bus, ring, star, tree, and mesh) and strategies (client/server and peer-to-peer).

8. Discuss organization networks including Internet technologies (intranets and extranets) and network security (firewalls, proxy servers, intrusion detection systems, and virtual private networks).

DISCUSSION

Respond to each of the following questions.

1 Making IT Work for You: MOBILE INTERNET

Is your smartphone or tablet always connected to the Internet? Review the Making IT Work for You: Mobile Internet on page 203, and then respond to the following: (a) What mobile Internet devices do you currently use? If you do not own any, which device do you feel would be most beneficial to you? (b) Do you currently have a 3G or 4G data plan for your mobile device? If so, provide details on your plan and why you chose it. Otherwise, describe what your ideal data plan would include. (c) Have you, a friend, or a family member ever gone over the data limit and/or been throttled? What sorts of activities are typically responsible for excessive data usage? (d) Go to the websites of at least two wireless companies, and compare their data plans. How are they similar? How are they different?

2 Privacy: UNAUTHORIZED NETWORK INTRUSION

Unauthorized network access is common today. Review the Privacy box on page 212, and then respond to the following: (a) Some argue that some networks must be penetrated and that the loss in privacy is outweighed by other concerns. Others suggest that we have already sacrificed too much privacy. What do you think? Defend your position. (b) Are there any circumstances when unauthorized network access can be justified? Be specific. (c) Is it acceptable for the U.S. government to support unauthorized network access to obtain information about other countries including terrorist activities? (d) Is it acceptable for other countries to attempt to gain unauthorized access to U.S. government networks? Why or why not?

3 Ethics: ELECTRONIC MONITORING

Many companies, websites, and law enforcement and various government agencies engage in monitoring or tracking Internet activity. Review the Ethics box on page 198, and respond to the following: (a) Is it unethical for an organization or corporation to use programs to monitor communications on its network? Why or why not? (b) Is it unethical for a government agency (such as the FBI) to monitor communications on the Internet or gather your records from the websites you visit? Why or why not? (c) Do you feel that new laws are needed to handle these issues? How would you balance the needs of companies and the government with the needs of individuals? Explain your answers.

4 Environment: GPS

Did you know that GPS technology might help protect the environment? Review the Environment box on page 199, and then respond to the following: (a) Identify ways in which GPS could benefit the environment. You need not limit your response to applications in motor vehicles. (b) Have you used a GPS device or mobile navigation app? If so, describe what you used it for. If not, do you think that you will in the near future? (c) Do you think that GPS should be standard equipment for every new car? Why or why not? (d) Do you think that it should be required by law? Why or why not?

chapter 9

Privacy, Security, and Ethics

222

Learning Objectives

After you have read this chapter, you should be able to:

1. Identify the most significant concerns for effective implementation of computer technology.

2. Discuss the primary privacy issues of accuracy, property, and access.

3. Describe the impact of large databases, private networks, the Internet, and the web on privacy.

4. Discuss online identity and the major laws on privacy.

5. Discuss cybercrimes including creation of malicious programs such as viruses, worms, Trojan horses, and zombies as well as denial of service attacks, Internet scams, identity theft, cyberbullying, rogue Wi-Fi hotspots, and data manipulation.

6. Detail ways to protect computer security including restricting access, encrypting data, anticipating disasters, and preventing data loss.

7. Discuss computer ethics including copyright law, software piracy, digital rights management, the Digital Millennium Copyright Act, as well as plagiarism and ways to identify plagiarism.

Why should I read this chapter?

Right now, criminals are trying to break into your email, your online bank account, and even your cell phone. Organizations are recording and analyzing your every digital decision, leading many to believe that the future of the Internet will result in the end of privacy as we know it.

This chapter covers the things you need to know to be prepared for this ever changing digital world, including:

- Cyber crime—protect yourself from viruses, Internet scams, and identity theft.
- Privacy rights—learn what companies can legally record about your internet usage and how they use that information.
- Safe computing—avoid embarrassment and worse by knowing the way Facebook and social media shares your information.

Introduction

"Hi, I'm Anthony, and I'm an IT security analyst. I'd like to talk with you about privacy, security, and ethics, three critical topics for anyone who uses computers today. I would also like to talk about how you can protect your privacy, ensure your security, and act ethically. "

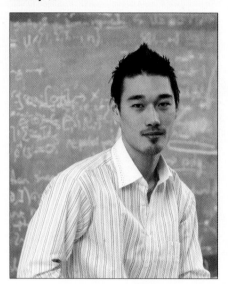

The tools and products of the information age do not exist in a world by themselves. As we said in Chapter 1, an information system consists not only of procedures, software, hardware, data, and the Internet but also of people. Because of people, computer systems may be used for both good and bad purposes.

There are more than one billion personal computers in use today. What are the consequences of the widespread presence of this technology? Does technology make it easy for others to invade our personal privacy? When we apply for a loan or for a driver's license, or when we check out at the supermarket, is that information about us being distributed and used without our permission? When we use the web, is information about us being collected and shared with others?

This technology prompts lots of questions—very important questions. Perhaps these are some of the most important questions for the 21st century. To efficiently and effectively use computers, you need to be aware of the potential impact of technology on people and how to protect yourself on the web. You need to be sensitive to and knowledgeable about personal privacy and organizational security.

People

As we have discussed, information systems consist of people, procedures, software, hardware, data, and the Internet. This chapter focuses on people. While most everyone agrees that technology has had a very positive impact on people, it is important to recognize the negative, or potentially negative, impacts as well.

Effective implementation of computer technology involves maximizing its positive effects while minimizing its negative effects. The most significant concerns are

- **Privacy:** What are the threats to personal privacy, and how can we protect ourselves?
- **Security:** How can access to sensitive information be controlled, and how can we secure hardware and software?
- **Ethics:** How do the actions of individual users and companies affect society?

Let us begin by examining privacy.

Privacy

Technology makes it possible to collect and use data of all kinds, including information about people. The websites you visit, the stores where you shop, and the telephone calls you make are all examples of information about you. How would you feel if you learned such information was being collected or shared? Would it matter who was collecting it, or how it was being used, or whether it was even correct?

Privacy concerns the collection and use of data about individuals. There are three primary privacy issues:

- **Accuracy** relates to the responsibility of those who collect data to ensure that the data is correct.
- **Property** relates to who owns data.
- **Access** relates to the responsibility of those who have data to control who is able to use that data.

Large Databases

Large organizations are constantly compiling information about us. The federal government alone has over 2,000 databases. Every day, data is gathered about us and stored in large databases. For example, telephone companies compile lists of the calls we make, the numbers called, locations from GPS-enabled smartphones, and so on. Credit card companies maintain user databases that track cardholder purchases, payments, and credit records. Supermarket scanners in grocery checkout counters record what we buy, when we buy it, how much we buy, and the price. Financial institutions, including banks and credit unions, record how much money we have, what we use it for, and how much we owe. Search engines record the search histories of their users including search topics and sites visited. Social networking sites collect every entry.

Effectively, every digital event—whether using a telephone or smartphone, buying a product or service, or sending or receiving any electronic communication—is collected and recorded. As a result, the size and the number of databases are exploding. In fact, it is widely reported that 90 percent of all of today's digitally stored data was collected in just the last two years. This ever-growing volume of data is often referred to as **big data.**

A vast industry of data gatherers known as **information resellers** or **information brokers** now exists that collects, analyzes, and sells such personal data. (See Figure 9-1.) Using publicly available databases and in many cases nonpublic

Figure 9-1 **Information reseller's website**

Figure 9-2 Google Street View

databases, information resellers create **electronic profiles** or highly detailed and personalized descriptions of individuals.

Almost certainly, you have an electronic profile that includes your name, address, telephone number, Social Security number, driver's license number, bank account numbers, credit card numbers, telephone records, shopping and purchasing patterns, and more. Information resellers sell these electronic profiles to direct marketers, fund-raisers, and others. Many provide these services on the web for free or for a nominal cost.

These profiles can reveal more than you might wish to make public and have an impact beyond what you might imagine. This raises many important issues, including

- **Collecting public, but personally identifying, information:** What if people anywhere in the world could view detailed images of you, your home, or your vehicle? Using detailed images captured with a specially equipped van, Google's Street View project allows just that. Street View makes it possible to take a virtual tour of many cities and neighborhoods from any computer with a connection to the Internet. (See Figure 9-2.) Although the images available on Street View are all taken in public locations, some have objected to the project as being an intrusion on their privacy.

  As digital cameras and webcams become cheaper and software becomes more sophisticated, it is likely that many more issues involving personal privacy in public spaces will need to be addressed. Such a combination of computing technologies could, for example, make real-time tracking of individuals in public places possible.

- **Spreading information without personal consent:** How would you feel if an employer were using your Facebook, Google+, or other social networking profiles to make decisions about hiring, placement, promotion, and firing? It is a common practice today for many organizations.

  As we have discussed in Chapter 2, social networking is designed for open sharing of information among individuals that share a common interest. Unfortunately, this openness can put individuals using social network sites at risk. In fact, some have lost their jobs after posting unflattering remarks about their supervisor or after discussing their dislike of their current job. Deeper analysis of your social networking profile may reveal even more about yourself than you intend.

The potential to inadvertently share personal information extends past what you might post to your social networking site. As an example, without your knowledge or permission, a social networking friend might tag or identify you in a photo on his or her site. Once tagged, that photo can become part of your electronic profile and available to others without your consent.

- **Spreading inaccurate information:** How would you like to be turned down for a home loan because of an error in your credit history? This is much more common than you might expect. What if you could not find a job or were fired from a job because of an error giving you a serious criminal history? This can and has happened due to simple clerical errors. In one case, an arresting officer while completing an arrest warrant incorrectly recorded the Social Security number of a criminal. From that time forward, this arrest and the subsequent conviction became part of another person's electronic profile. This is an example of **mistaken identity** in which the electronic profile of one person is switched with another.

It's important to know that you have some recourse. The law allows you to gain access to those records about you that are held by credit bureaus. Under the **Freedom of Information Act,** you are also entitled to look at your records held by government agencies. (Portions may be deleted for national security reasons.)

Private Networks

Suppose you use your company's electronic mail system to send a co-worker an unflattering message about your supervisor or to send a highly personal message to a friend. Later you find the boss has been reading these e-mails. In fact, many businesses search employees' electronic mail and computer files using **employee-monitoring software.** These programs record virtually everything you do on your computer. One proposed law would not prohibit this type of electronic monitoring but would require employers to provide prior written notice. Employers also would have to alert employees during the monitoring with some sort of audible or visual signal. If you are employed and would like to know your company's current policy on monitoring electronic communication, contact your human relations department.

Sharing personal information on a social network site like Facebook is a voluntary activity. However, many individuals do not fully understand the complex sharing and privacy policies of these networks. This often causes unintentional sharing with people outside their intended social circle. The social networks themselves have come under fire from privacy groups, saying that these companies use complex settings and policies to get users to share more information than intended. This information is in turn shared with advertisers. Do you think social network companies are a threat to privacy?
To see more privacy facts, visit our website at www.mhhe. com/ce2015 and select Student Edition **and then** Privacy.

concept check

Describe how large databases can effect our privacy.

What is big data? Information resellers? Electronic profiles?

List three important issues related to electronic profiles. What is mistaken identity? What is the Freedom of Information Act?

What are private networks? What is employee-monitoring software? Is it legal?

The Internet and the Web

When you send e-mail on the Internet or browse the web, do you have any concerns about privacy? Most people do not. They think that as long as they are using their own computer and are selective about disclosing their names or other personal

1 Select the *Favorites* button.

2 Select *History*.

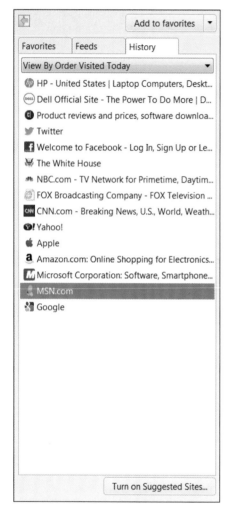

Figure 9-3 **Viewing history files**

information, then little can be done to invade their personal privacy. Experts call this the **illusion of anonymity** that the Internet brings.

As we discussed in Chapter 8, every computer on the Internet is identified by a unique number known as an IP address. IP addresses can be used to trace Internet activities to their origin, allowing computer security experts and law enforcement officers to investigate computer crimes such as unauthorized access to networks or sharing copyright files without permission.

When you browse the web, your browser stores critical information onto your hard disk, typically without you being aware of it. This information, which contains records about your Internet activities, includes history and temporary Internet files.

- **History files** include the locations, or addresses, of sites that you have recently visited. This history file can be displayed by your browser in various locations, including the address bar (as you type) and the *History* tab. To view your browsing history using Internet Explorer 9, follow the steps in Figure 9-3.
- **Temporary Internet files,** also known as the **browser cache,** contain web page content and instructions for displaying this content. Whenever you visit a website, these files are saved by your browser. If you leave a site and then return later, these files are used to quickly redisplay web content.

Another way your web activity can be monitored is with **cookies.** Cookies are small data files that are deposited on your hard disk from websites you have visited. Based on your browser's settings, these cookies can be accepted or blocked. To see how to block cookies using Internet Explorer 9, see Figure 9-4. Although you will generally not be aware when a website generates a cookie, the personalized experiences you enjoy on the web are often a result of those cookies. While cookies are harmless in and of themselves, what makes them a potential privacy risk is that they can store information about you, your preferences, and your browsing habits. The information stored generally depends on whether the cookie is a first-party or a third-party cookie.

- A **first-party cookie** is one that is generated (and then read) only by the website you are currently visiting. Many websites use first-party cookies to store information about the current session, your general preferences, and your activity on the site. The intention of these cookies is to provide a personalized experience on a particular site. For example, when you revisit a particular electronic commerce site, a previously deposited cookie can provide information so that you can be greeted by name and presented with sales and promotions that interest you.
- A **third-party cookie** is usually generated by an advertising company that is affiliated with the website you are currently visiting. They are used by the advertising company to keep track of your web activity as you move from one site to the next. For this reason, they are often referred to as **tracking cookies.** Critics of this practice claim that your privacy is being violated because your activity is being recorded across multiple websites. Defenders of this practice argue that these cookies are beneficial because it helps websites deliver ads that interest you. For example, suppose you visit four different websites that employ the same advertising agency. The first three sites are about cars, but the fourth is a search engine. When you visit the fourth site, you will likely see a car advertisement because your cookie showed that you had been visiting car-related websites.

1 • Select the *Tools* button.
   • Choose *Internet Options*.

2 • Select the *Privacy* tab.
   • Move the slide to the desired level of protection.
   • Click *OK*.

1 • Select the *Tools* button.
   • Choose *Safety*.
   • Choose *Delete browsing* history.

2 • Select check boxes for items to be deleted.
   • Choose *Delete*.

Figure 9-4 Blocking cookies

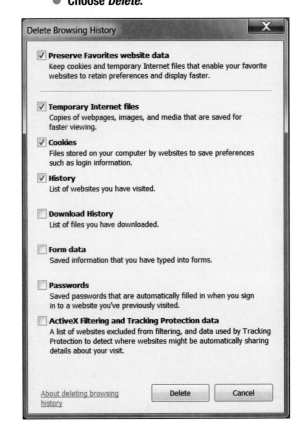

Figure 9-5 Deleting browsing history

Some users are not comfortable with idea of web browsers storing so much information in the form of temporary Internet files, cookies, and history. For this reason, browsers now offer users an easy way to delete their browsing history. To see how to delete browsing histories using Internet Explorer 9, see Figure 9-5. In addition, most browsers also offer a **privacy mode,** which ensures that your browsing activity is not recorded on your hard disk. For example, Internet Explorer 9 provides **InPrivate Browsing** accessible from the *Tools* button, and Safari provides **Private Browsing** accessible from the *Safari* option on the main menu.

Although these web browser files can concern many individuals, several other threats could potentially violate your privacy. **Web bugs,** which are invisible images or HTML code hidden within a web page or e-mail message, can be used to transmit information without your knowledge. When a user opens an e-mail containing a web bug, information is sent back to the source of the bug. The receiving server will now know that this e-mail address is active. One of the most common web bugs is used by companies that sell active mailing lists to spammers. Because of this deception, many e-mail programs now block images and HTML code from unknown senders. It is up to the user to decide whether or not to allow such content to be displayed for current and future messages. To see how

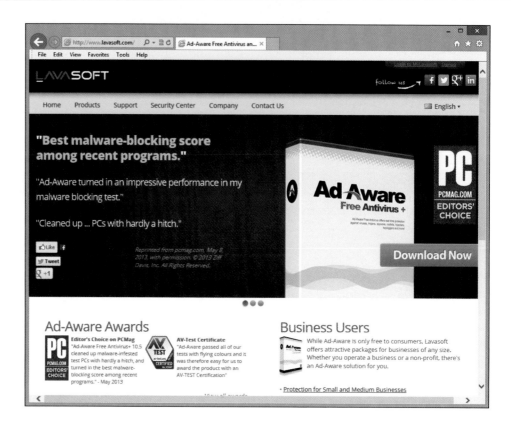

Figure 9-6 Antispyware

web bugs work, visit our website at www.mhhe.com/ce2015 and select Student Edition, then Explore, and then Bugs.

The most dangerous type of privacy threat comes in the form of spyware. The term **spyware** is used to describe a wide range of programs that are designed to secretly record and report an individual's activities on the Internet. Some of these programs can even make changes to your browser in order to deceive you and manipulate what you see online. **Computer monitoring software** is perhaps the most invasive and dangerous type of spyware. One type of computer monitoring software, known as a **keystroke logger,** records every activity and keystroke made on your computer system, including credit card numbers, passwords, and e-mail messages. Computer monitoring software can be deposited onto your hard drive without your knowledge by a malicious website or by someone installing the program directly onto your computer. While such software is deadly in the hands of criminals, it can be legally used by companies monitoring employees or law enforcement officials who are collecting evidence.

Unfortunately, many spyware programs go undetected, largely because users have no idea they are infected. Spyware will run in the background, invisible to the average user. Other times, it disguises itself as useful software, such as a security program. Various studies have demonstrated that an alarming number of computers are infected with spyware. The financial impact to individuals, companies, and financial institutions is estimated at billions of dollars.

One of the best defenses against spyware is to exercise caution when visiting new websites and downloading software from an unknown source. Another defense involves using a category of software known as **antispyware** or **spy removal programs,** which are designed to detect and remove various types of privacy threats. (See Figure 9-6.) For a list of some of these programs, see Figure 9-7.

Program	Website
Ad-Aware	www.lavasoft.com
SUPERAntiSpyware	www.superantispyware.com
Windows Defender	www.microsoft.com

Figure 9-7 Antispyware programs

Online Identity

Another aspect of Internet privacy comes from **online identity,** the information that people voluntarily post about themselves online. With the popularity of social networking, blogging, and photo- and video-sharing sites, many people post intimate details of their lives without considering the consequences. Although it is easy to think of online identity as something shared between friends, the archiving and search features of the web make it available indefinitely to anyone who cares to look.

There are any number of cases of people who have lost their jobs on the basis of posts on social media websites. These job losses range from a teacher (using off-color language and photos showing drinking) to a chief financial officer of a major corporation (discussing corporate dealings and financial data). The cases include college graduates being refused a job because of Facebook posts. How would you feel if information you posted about yourself on the web kept you from getting a job?

Major Laws on Privacy

Some federal laws governing privacy matters have been created. For example, the **Gramm-Leach-Bliley Act** protects personal financial information, the **Health Insurance Portability and Accountability Act (HIPAA)** protects medical records, and the **Family Educational Rights and Privacy Act (FERPA)** restricts disclosure of educational records. To learn more about existing privacy laws, visit our website at www.mhhe.com/ce2015 and select Student Edition, then Explore, and then Law.

Most of the information collected by private organizations is not covered by existing laws. However, as more and more individuals become concerned about controlling who has the right to personal information and how that information is used, companies and lawmakers will respond.

concept check

 What is the illusion of anonymity? Define and compare history files and temporary Internet file? What is Privacy mode?

 What is cookie? A first-party cookie? A third-party cookie?

 What is a web bug? Spyware? Keystroke logger? Antispyware? Online identity

Describe three federal laws to protect privacy.

Security

We are all concerned with having a safe and secure environment to live in. We are careful to lock our car doors and our homes. We are careful about where we walk at night and whom we talk to. This is personal security. What about computer security? What if someone gains unauthorized access to our computer or other computers that contain information about us? These people are commonly known as computer **hackers.** It should be noted that not all hackers are intent on malicious actions and that not all are criminals. **Security** involves protecting individuals and organizations from theft and danger. Computer security specifically focuses on protecting information, hardware, and software from unauthorized use, as well as preventing or limiting the damage from intrusions, sabotage, and natural disasters.

Cybercrime

Cybercrime or **computer crime** is any criminal offense that involves a computer and a network. It was recently estimated that cybercrime affects over 400 million people and costs over $400 billion each year. Cybercrimes can take various forms including the creation of malicious programs, denial of service attacks, Internet scams, identity theft, cyberbulling, rogue Wi-Fi hotspots, and data manipulation.

Malicious Programs A **cracker** is a computer criminal who creates and distributes malicious programs. These programs are called **malware,** which is short for **malicious software.** They are specifically designed to damage or disrupt a computer system. The three most common types of malware are viruses, worms, and Trojan horses.

- **Viruses** are programs that migrate through networks and operating systems, and most attach themselves to different programs and databases. While some viruses are relatively harmless, many can be quite destructive. Once activated, these destructive viruses can alter and/or delete files. Creating and knowingly spreading a virus is a very serious crime and a federal offense punishable under the **Computer Fraud and Abuse Act.**

  Unfortunately, new computer viruses are appearing all the time. The best way to stay current is through services that keep track of viruses on a daily basis. For example, Symantec, McAfee, and Microsoft all track the most serious virus threats. (See Figure 9-8.)

- **Worms** are programs that simply replicate themselves over and over again. Once active in a network, the self-replicating activity clogs computers and networks until their operations are slowed or stopped. A recent worm traveled across the world within hours, stopping tens of thousands of computers along its way. Unlike a virus, a worm typically does not attach itself to

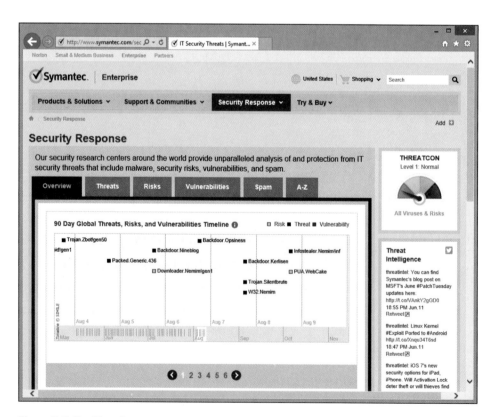

Figure 9-8 Tracking viruses

a program or alter and/or delete files. Worms, however, can carry a virus. Once a virus has been deposited by a worm onto an unsuspecting computer system, the virus will either activate immediately or lie dormant until some future time. For example in 2010, the Stuxnet worm infected several networks in Iran. One of these networks was used by Iran's nuclear program. Soon after the infection, several key pieces of nuclear equipment became permanently disabled.

Viruses and worms typically find their way into personal computers through e-mail attachments and programs downloaded from the Internet. Because viruses can be so damaging, computer users are advised to never open an e-mail attachment from an unknown source and to exercise great care in accepting new programs and data from any source.

As we discussed in Chapter 4, antivirus programs alert users when certain kinds of viruses and worms enter their system. Two of the most widely used are Avast! Free Antivirus and Microsoft Security Essentials. Unfortunately, new viruses are being developed all the time, and not all viruses can be detected.

- **Trojan horses** are programs that appear to be harmless; however, they contain malicious programs. Trojan horses are not viruses. Like worms, however, they can be carriers of viruses. The most common types of Trojan horses appear as free computer games and free screen saver programs that can be downloaded from the Internet. When a user installs one of these programs, the Trojan horse also secretly installs a virus on the computer system. The virus then begins its mischief. One of the most dangerous types of Trojan horse claims to provide free antivirus programs. When a user downloads one of these programs, the Trojan horse first installs a virus that locates and disables any existing virus protection programs before depositing other viruses.

Zombies are computers infected by a virus, worm, or Trojan horse that allows them to be remotely controlled for malicious purposes. A collection of zombie computers is known as a **botnet,** or **robot network.** Botnets harness the combined power of many zombies for malicious activities like password cracking or sending junk e-mail. Because they are formed by many computers distributed across the Internet, botnets are hard to shut down even after they are detected. Unfortunately for individual computer owners, it also can be difficult to detect when a personal computer has been compromised.

Denial of Service A **denial of service (DoS) attack** attempts to slow down or stop a computer system or network by flooding a computer or network with requests for information and data. The targets of these attacks are usually Internet service providers (ISPs) and specific websites. Once under attack, the servers at the ISP or the website become overwhelmed with these requests for service and are unable to respond to legitimate users. As a result, the ISP or website is effectively shut down.

Rogue Wi-Fi Hotspots Free Wi-Fi networks are available almost everywhere from libraries to fast-food restaurants and coffee shops. **Rogue Wi-Fi hotspots** imitate these free networks. These rogue networks operate close to the legitimate free hotspots and typically provide stronger signals that many users unsuspectingly connect to. Once connected, the rogue networks capture any and all information sent by the users to legitimate sites including user names and passwords.

Data Manipulation Finding entry into someone's computer network and leaving a prankster's message may seem like fun, which is why hackers do it. It is still against the law. Moreover, even if the manipulation seems harmless, it may cause a great deal of anxiety and wasted time among network users.

The **Computer Fraud and Abuse Act** makes it a crime for unauthorized persons even to view—let alone copy or damage—data using any computer across state lines. It also prohibits unauthorized use of any government computer or a computer used by any federally insured financial institution. Offenders can be sentenced to up to 20 years in prison and fined up to $100,000.

Identity Theft **Identity theft** is the illegal assumption of someone's identity for the purposes of economic gain. It is one of the fastest-growing crimes in the country and can financially devastate its victim. Once an identity is stolen, the criminal applies for and obtains new credit cards in the victim's name and then uses the cards to purchase clothes, cards, and even a house.

To commit this crime, identity thieves look for anything that can help them steal your identity, from your Social Security number and date of birth, to account information and passwords. Sometimes they gain this information from social networking sites, where users often post detailed personal information such as their birth dates, family member names, home addresses, and photos of their children. As mentioned previously, always exercise caution when providing information on Facebook, Twitter, and other social networking sites, and use the privacy settings and controls that are provided at the social networking sites you use.

Internet Scams A **scam** is a fraudulent or deceptive act or operation designed to trick individuals into providing personal information or spending their time and money for little or no return. An **Internet scam** is simply a scam using the Internet. Internet scams are becoming a serious problem and have created financial and legal problems for many thousands of people. Almost all the scams are initiated by a mass mailing to unsuspecting individuals.

A technique often employed by scammers is **phishing** (pronounced "fishing"). Phishing attempts to trick Internet users into thinking a fake but official-looking website or e-mail is legitimate. Phishing has grown in sophistication, replicating entire websites like PayPal to try to lure users into divulging their financial information.

See Figure 9-9 for a list of common types of Internet scams.

Type	Description
Chain letter	Classic chain letter instructing recipient to send a nominal amount of money to each of five people on a list. The recipient removes the first name on the list, adds his or her name at the bottom, and mails the chain letter to five friends. This is also known as a pyramid scheme. Almost all chain letters are fraudulent and illegal.
Auction fraud	Merchandise is selected and payment is sent. Merchandise is never delivered.
Vacation prize	"Free" vacation has been awarded. Upon arrival at vacation destination, the accommodations are dreadful but can be upgraded for a fee.
Advance fee loans	Guaranteed low-rate loans available to almost anyone. After applicant provides personal loan-related information, the loan is granted subject to payment of an "insurance fee."

Figure 9-9 Common Internet Scams

Computer Crime	Description
Malicious programs	Include viruses, worms, and Trojan horses
DoS	Causes computer systems to slow down or stop
Rogue Wi-Fi hotspots	Imitate legitimate Wi-Fi hotspot in order to capture personal information
Data manipulation	Involves changing data or leaving prank messages
Identity theft	Is illegal assumption of a person's identity for economic gain
Cyberbullying	Is using the Internet, cell phones, or other devices to send/post content intended to hurt or embarrass another person
Internet scams	Are scams over the Internet usually initiated by e-mail and involving phishing

Figure 9-10 **Computer crimes**

Cyberbullying A fairly recent and all-too-common phenomenon, **cyberbullying** is the use of the Internet, cell phones, or other devices to send or post content intended to hurt or embarrass another person. Although not always a crime, it can lead to criminal prosecution. Cyberbullying includes sending repeated unwanted e-mails to an individual who has stated that he or she wants no further contact with the sender, ganging up on victims in electronic forums, posting false statements designed to injure the reputation of another, maliciously disclosing personal data about a person that could lead to harm to that person, and sending any type of communication that is threatening or harassing. Never participate in cyberbullying, and discourage others from participating in this dangerous and hateful activity.

For a summary of computer crimes, see Figure 9-10. For a brief history of computer crimes, visit our website at www.mhhe.com/ce2015 and select Student Edition, then Explore, and then Crime.

concept check

What are hackers? What is cybercrime? What are malicious programs?

Compare viruses, worms, and Trojan horses. What are zombies? What is a botnet?

What are denial of service attacks? Rogue Wi-Fi hotspots? Data theft and manipulation?

What is identity theft? What is cyberbullying? Describe some common Internet scams.

Measures to Protect Computer Security

There are numerous ways in which computer systems and data can be compromised and many ways to ensure computer security. Some of the principal measures to ensure computer security are restricting access, encrypting messages, anticipating disasters, and preventing data loss.

Restricting Access Security experts are constantly devising ways to protect computer systems from access by unauthorized persons. Sometimes security is a matter of putting guards on company computer rooms and checking the identification of everyone admitted. Other times it is using **biometric scanning** devices such as fingerprint and iris (eye) scanners. (See Figure 9-11.) There are numerous applications that use face recognition to allow access to a computer system. For example,

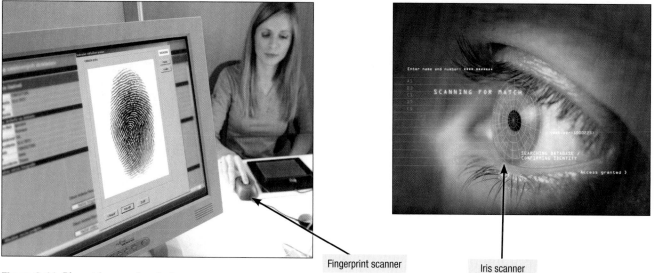

Fingerprint scanner

Iris scanner

Figure 9-11 **Biometric scanning devices**

many personal computer systems use Dell's FastAccess face recognition application to prevent unauthorized access. There are also several face recognition apps for mobile devices including Face Recognition by iNFINITE Studios LLC.

Oftentimes it is a matter of being careful about assigning passwords to people and of changing the passwords when people leave a company. **Passwords** are secret words or phrases (including numbers, letters, and special characters) that must be keyed into a computer system to gain access. For many applications on the web, users assign their own passwords. Windows 8 includes an application, Picture Password, that accepts a series of gestures over a picture of the user's choice to gain access.

The strength of a password depends on how easily it can be guessed. A **dictionary attack** uses software to try thousands of common words sequentially in an attempt to gain unauthorized access to a user's account. For this reason, words, names, and simple numeric patterns make weak or poor passwords. Strong passwords have at least eight characters and use a combination of letters, numbers, and symbols. It is also important not to reuse passwords for different accounts. If one account is compromised, that password might be tried for access to other systems as well. For example, if a low-security account such as an online web forum is compromised, that password could also be tried on higher-security accounts such as banking websites.

As mentioned in previous chapters, individuals and organizations use security suites and firewalls to protect and control access to their computers and the flow of information.

- **Security suites** provide a collection of utility programs designed to protect your privacy and security while you are on the web.

- **Firewalls** act as a security buffer between a corporation's private network and all external networks, including the Internet. All electronic communications coming into and leaving the corporation must pass through the company's firewall where it is evaluated. Security is maintained by denying access to unauthorized communications.

Encrypting Data Whenever information is sent over a network or stored on a computer system, the possibility of unauthorized access exists. The solution is **encryption,** the process of coding information to make it unreadable except to

Figure 9-12 **Encrypted e-mail**

those who have a special piece of information known as an **encryption key,** or, simply, a **key.** Some common uses for encryption include

- **E-mail encryption:** Protects e-mail messages as they move across the Internet. One of the most widely used personal e-mail encryption programs is Pretty Good Privacy. (See Figure 9-12.)

- **File encryption:** Protects sensitive files by encrypting them before they are stored on a hard drive. Files can be encrypted individually, or specialized software can be used to encrypt all files automatically each time they are saved to a certain hard drive location. (See Figure 9-13.)

- **Website encryption:** Secures web transactions, especially financial transactions. Web pages that accept passwords or confidential information like a credit card number are often encrypted.

Figure 9-13 **File encryption**

The most common protocol for website encryption is **https (hypertext transfer protocol secure).** As we discussed in Chapter 2, **http (hypertext transfer protocol)** is the most widely used Internet protocol. The https protocol adds another protection level to http. Every URL that begins with *https* requires that the browser and the connecting site encrypt all messages, providing a safer and more secure transmission.

- **Virtual private networks: Virtual private networks (VPNs)** encrypt connections between company networks and remote users such as workers connecting from home. This connection creates a secure virtual connection to a company LAN across the Internet.
- **Wireless network encryption:** Restricts access to authorized users on wireless networks. **WPA2 (Wi-Fi Protected Access)** is the most widely used wireless network encryption for home wireless networks. WPA2 is typically established for a wireless network through the network's wireless router. While the specifics vary between routers, WPA2 is usually set through the router's settings options.

Anticipating Disasters Companies (and even individuals) should prepare themselves for disasters. **Physical security** is concerned with protecting hardware from possible human and natural disasters. **Data security** is concerned with protecting software and data from unauthorized tampering or damage. Most large organizations have **disaster recovery plans** describing ways to continue operating until normal computer operations can be restored.

Preventing Data Loss Equipment can always be replaced. A company's *data*, however, may be irreplaceable. Most companies have ways of trying to keep software and data from being tampered with in the first place. They include careful screening of job applicants, guarding of passwords, and auditing of data and programs from time to time. Some systems use redundant storage to prevent loss of data even when a hard drive fails. We discussed RAID in Chapter 7, which is a commonly used type of redundant storage. Backup batteries protect against data loss due to file corruption during unexpected power outages.

Making frequent backups of data is essential to prevent data loss. Backups are often stored at an off-site location to protect data in case of theft, fire, flood, or other disasters. Students and others often use flash drives and cloud storage as discussed in Chapter 7 to back up homework and important papers. Incremental backups store multiple versions of data at different points in time to prevent data loss due to unwanted changes or accidental deletion.

To see how you could use a cloud-based backup service, see Making IT Work for You: Cloud-Based Backup on pages 239 and 240.

See Figure 9-14 for a summary of the different measures to protect computer security.

Measure	Description
Restricting access	Limit access to authorized persons using such measures as passwords and firewalls.
Encrypting data	Code all messages sent over a network.
Anticipating disasters	Prepare for disasters by ensuring physical security and data security through a disaster recovery plan.
Preventing data loss	Routinely copy data and store it at a remote location.

Figure 9-14 **Measures to protect computer security**

CLOUD-BASED BACKUP

Do you remember to make frequent backups of your irreplaceable data files, such as photos and documents? Would you like a service that remembers to do the backups for you and places them in a very reliable location? If so, then a cloud-based backup service, such as Carbonite, is the solution for you.

Getting Started Carbonite offers a free trial to its backup service. Once the trial ends, you will have to pay an annual fee to continue using it. To get started with the trial:

1. Visit www.carbonite.com, and click the *Try It For Free* button for home users.

2. Create an account, and then click the *Install Now* button to download the software.

3. Start the installation process, and when prompted, select the *Automatic* backup settings for easy setup.

After installation, Carbonite InfoCenter will launch and begin scanning your system for files to back up.

Managing Files for Backup During the free trial, Carbonite will not automatically back up certain types of files (such as music and video). Regardless, you can still select these files manually and request that they be backed up.

1. Go to a folder that contains photos, such as *Sample Pictures* in Windows. If you see an orange or a green icon at the bottom left of the files, that means they have been backed up (green) or are waiting to be backed up (orange).

2. Now, go to a folder where you have music files. Notice that they do not have an icon in the corner.

3. Right-click a music file, select *Carbonite*, and click *Back this up*. This file is now marked with an orange icon (you may have to refresh your window) and will be backed up in due time.

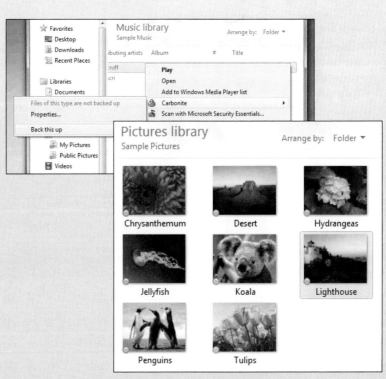

Restoring your Files   Both your files and folder structure are securely backed up on Carbonite's servers. Although the Carbonite InfoCenter window has a restore area, this guide will show you how to view your backups on Carbonite's website for easy downloading from wherever you are.

1 Go to Carbonite's website, and click the *Log In* button. Enter your log-in information. You will be taken to a screen where you can see both computer and account information.

2 Click the *Restore* button, and you will be given a choice to restore all your files or to select individual files to be downloaded.

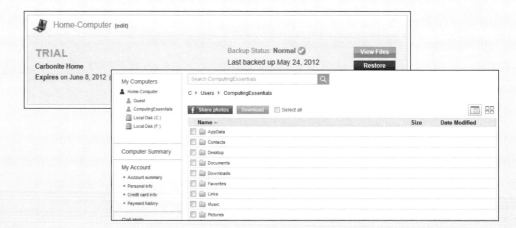

3 Click the *Remote Access* button.

4 Browse your backups by drives, folders, or users on your machine.

5 Select a particular file or folder, and then click the *Download* button.

To maintain access to your files, you will have to sign up for a yearly subscription once the free trial ends. The affordable "Home" option is sufficient for most users. However, if you need to back up files that are stored on an external hard drive, the "HomePlus" plan may be best.

The web is continually changing, and some of the specifics presented in this Making IT Work for You may have changed.

To learn about other ways to make information technology work for you, visit our website at www.mhhe.com/ce2015 and select Student Edition and then Making IT Work.

- Define each of the following: biometric scanning, password, dictionary attack, security suite, and firewalls.

- What is encryption and an encryption key? What is the difference between http and https? What is a VPN? WPA2?

- Define physical security, data security, and disaster recovery plans.

- Describe how to prevent data loss.

Ethics

What do you suppose controls how computers can be used? You probably think first of laws. Of course, that is right, but technology is moving so fast that it is very difficult for our legal system to keep up. The essential element that controls how computers are used today is *ethics.*

Ethics, as you may know, are standards of moral conduct. **Computer ethics** are guidelines for the morally acceptable use of computers in our society. Ethical treatment is critically important to us all, and we are all entitled to ethical treatment. This includes the right to keep personal information, such as credit ratings and medical histories, from getting into unauthorized hands. These issues, largely under the control of corporations and government agencies, were covered earlier in this chapter. These issues and many more have been addressed in the Ethics boxes throughout this book. Now we'll examine two important issues in computer ethics where average users have a role to play.

Copyright and Digital Rights Management

Copyright is a legal concept that gives content creators the right to control use and distribution of their work. Materials that can be copyrighted include paintings, books, music, films, and even video games. Some users choose to make unauthorized copies of digital media, which violates copyright. For example, making an unauthorized copy of a digital music file for a friend might be a copyright violation.

Software piracy is the unauthorized copying and/or distribution of software. According to a recent study, software piracy costs the software industry over $60 billion annually. To prevent copyright violations, corporations often use **digital rights management (DRM).** DRM encompasses various technologies that control access to electronic media and files. Typically, DRM is used to (1) control the number of devices that can access a given file and (2) limit the kinds of devices that can access a file. Although some companies see DRM as a necessity to protect their rights, some users feel they should have the right to use the media they buy—including movies, music, software, and video games—as they choose.

The **Digital Millennium Copyright Act** makes it illegal to deactivate or otherwise disable any antipiracy technologies including DRM technologies. The act also establishes that copies of commercial programs may not be legally resold or given away. It further makes it a crime to sell or to use programs or devices that are used to illegally copy software. This may come as a surprise to those who copy software, movies, or music from a friend or from the Internet. The law is clear: It is illegal to copy or download copyright-protected music and videos from the Internet without appropriate authorization.

Today, there are many legal sources for digital media. Television programs can be watched online, often for free, on television-network-sponsored sites. Sites like

Figure 9-15 **iTunes Music Store**

Pandora allow listeners to enjoy music at no cost. There are several online stores for purchasing music and video content. A pioneer in this area is Apple's iTunes Music Store. (See Figure 9-15.)

Plagiarism

Another ethical issue is **plagiarism,** which means representing some other person's work and ideas as your own without giving credit to the original source. Although plagiarism was a problem long before the invention of computers, computer technology has made plagiarism easier. For example, simply cutting and pasting content from a web page into a report or paper may seem tempting to an overworked student or employee.

Correspondingly, computer technology has made it easier than ever to recognize and catch **plagiarists.** For example, services such as Turnitin are dedicated to preventing Internet plagiarism. This service will examine the content of a paper and compare it to a wide range of known public electronic documents including web page content. In this way, Turnitin can identify an undocumented paper or even parts of an undocumented paper. (See Figure 9-16.)

 ## concept check

What is the distinction between ethics and computer ethics?

Define copyright, software privacy, digital rights management, and the Digital Millennium Copyright Act.

What is plagiarism? What is Turnitin and what does it do?

ethics

Do you know of anyone who has copied parts of a web page from a variety of sites and combined the parts to form a term paper? Of course, such a practice is unethical and most likely illegal. Many schools and universities now use a program that can compare the content of a student's paper to published material on the web and previously submitted papers. Do you think it is ethical for instructors to employ a program that checks for plagiarism? Is there a risk that the program may confuse proper citations from the web with obvious cases of plagiarism?

To see more ethical issues, visit our website at www.mhhe. com/ce2015 and select Student Edition **and then** Ethics.

Figure 9-16 **Turnitin website**

Careers in IT

IT security analysts are responsible for maintaining the security of a company's networks, systems, and data. Their goal is to ensure the confidentiality, integrity, and availability of information. These analysts must safeguard information systems against a variety of external threats, such as hackers and viruses, as well be vigilant of threats that may come from within the company.

Employers typically look for candidates with a bachelor's or associate's degree in information systems or computer science. Experience in this field or in network administration is usually required. IT security analysts should possess good communication and research skills, and be able to handle high-stress situations.

IT security analysts can expect to earn an annual salary of $62,000 to $101,000. Opportunities for advancement typically depend on experience. Demand for this position is expected to grow as malware, hackers, and other types of threats become more complex and prevalent. To learn about other careers in information technology, visit us at www.mhhe.com/ce2015 and select Student Edition and then Careers.

A LOOK TO THE FUTURE

The End of Anonymity

Do you enjoy the ability to interact with others on the web anonymously? Is there a sense of comfort knowing that you can express yourself freely without others knowing your identity? Anonymity has been a way of life on the Internet since the very beginning. However, various organizations, ranging from advertisers to governments, are questioning whether the Internet can continue like this. And based on the amount of information currently shared by people online, one wonders whether anonymity will be valued at all in the future.

There are many factors that are causing many to question the value of anonymity. First is the issue of harassment. Most forums and comment areas on websites allow users to post messages anonymously. Some individuals use this ability to write abusive or threatening comments. Many children and teenagers have been victims of online harassment, or cyberbullying, at some point in their lives. Others have been stalked online to the point where they have experienced psychological harm. Experts feel that if anonymous comments

were disallowed, those same individuals would not be willing to write those types of messages, as their anonymity would be stripped. The other area where anonymity has become a problem is the legal field. Some anonymous web users have posted lies about individuals or businesses that have damaged the target's reputation. In the real world, those types of false and damaging comments could lead to lawsuits. For these reasons, many legislators are proposing laws aimed at discouraging the sort of anonymity that allows various online crimes to occur. In the future, it may even be a requirement to provide a real-world ID in order to use the Internet.

Many online companies are also fighting to end anonymity. This is because they make most of their money off targeted advertising. For these companies to deliver the proper advertisement to you, they need to know quite a bit about you and your online activities. By having a profile with your real name and interests, they can follow your activity throughout the web to get to know you better. At present, many advertisements you see online are for a product or service that does not interest you. In the future, every advertisement you see will be selected just for you, as marketing companies develop a complete profile that lets them know everything about you. Now, many online businesses do aim to protect your privacy, but this is only with respect to what the public knows about you. When it comes to their advertising partners, they don't hide much because it is not in their interest to do so. Essentially, it is a trade-off for users, whether to give up some (or all) of your anonymity in return for targeted advertising.

Although many organizations are working toward ending or severely limiting anonymity, some would like to keep the Internet the way it is. Many civil rights groups and journalists support anonymity as a basic right. If you cannot be anonymous, then it would be difficult, for example, to post information that uncovers abuses in government or in a business. Some psychologists also support anonymity, stating that creating a separate online identity can be useful for personal development, allowing an individual to explore interests without leaving a record that is tied to his or her own life.

How do you feel about the possible end to anonymity? Do you agree that there will be less negativity on the web if everyone had to provide real names? Since advertisements pay for free services, will you at least tolerate future ads more if they contain something that interests you?

PRIVACY

Privacy concerns the collection and use of data about individuals. There are three primary privacy issues: **accuracy** (who is responsible to ensure data is correct), **property** (who owns data), **access** (who controls access to data).

Large Databases

Large organizations are constantly compiling information about us. This ever-growing volume of data is often referred to as **big data**. **Information resellers (information brokers)** collect and sell personal data. **Electronic profiles** are compiled from databases to provide highly detailed and personalized descriptions of individuals.

Mistaken identity occurs when an electronic profile of one person is switched with another. **The Freedom of Information Act** entitles individuals access to governmental records relating to them.

Private Networks

Many organizations monitor employee e-mail and computer files using special software called **employee-monitoring software**.

The Internet and the Web

Many people believe that, while using the web, little can be done to invade their privacy. This is called the **illusion of anonymity**.

PRIVACY

Information stored by browsers includes **history files** (record sites visited) and **temporary Internet files** or **browser cache** (contain website content and display instructions). **Cookies** store and track information. **Privacy mode (InPrivate Browsing; Private Browsing)** ensures that your browsing activity is not recorded.

Spyware secretly records and reports Internet activities. **Keystroke loggers** (one type of **computer monitoring software**) records every activity and keystroke. **Antispyware (spy removal programs)** detects and removes various privacy threats.

Online Identity

Many people post personal information and sometimes intimate details of their lives without considering the consequences. This creates an **online identity**. With the archiving and search features of the web, this identity is indefinitely available to anyone who cares to look for it.

Major Laws on Privacy

The **Gramm-Leach-Bliley Act** protects personal financial information; the **Health Insurance Portability and Accountability Act (HIPAA)** protects medical records; and the **Family Educational Rights and Privacy Act (FERPA)** restricts disclosure of educational records.

To efficiently and effectively use computers, you need to be aware of the potential impact of technology on people. You need to be sensitive to and knowledgeable about personal privacy, organizational security, and ethics.

SECURITY

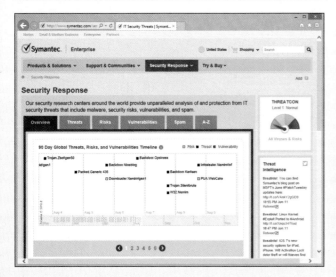

Computer **security** focuses on protecting information, hardware, and software from unauthorized use as well as preventing damage from intrusions, sabotage, and natural disasters. Someone who gains unauthorized access to computers that contain information about us is commonly known as a computer **hacker**. Not all hackers are intent on malicious actions and not all are criminals.

Cybercrime

Cybercrime (computer crime) is an illegal action involving special knowledge of computer technology.

- Malicious programs (**malware**) include **viruses** (the **Computer Fraud and Abuse Act** makes spreading a virus a federal offense), **worms**, and **Trojan horses**. **Zombies** are remotely controlled infected computers used for malicious purposes. A collection of zombie computers is known as a **botnet**, or **robot network**.
- **Denial of service (DoS) attack** is an attempt to shut down or stop a computer system or network.
- **Rogue Wi-Fi hotspots** imitate legitimate hotspots to capture personal information.
- Data manipulation involves changing data or leaving prank messages. **The Computer Fraud and Abuse Act** helps protect against data manipulation.
- **Identity theft** is the illegal assumption of someone's identity for the purposes of economic gain.

SECURITY

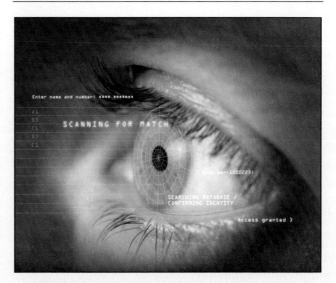

- **Scams** are designed to trick individuals into spending their time and money with little or no return. Common **Internet scams** are frequently coupled with **phishing** websites or e-mails.
- **Cyberbullying** is the use of the Internet, cell phones, or other devices to send or post content intended to hurt or embarrass another person.

Measures to Protect Computer Security

There are numerous ways in which computer systems and data can be compromised and many ways to protect computer security. These measures include

- Access can be restricted through **biometric scanning** devices and **passwords** (secret words or phrases; **dictionary attacks** use thousands of words to attempt to gain access).
- **Encrypting** is coding information to make it unreadable except to those who have the **encryption key**. **Virtual private networks (VPNs)** encrypt connections between company networks and remote users. **WPA2 (Wi-Fi Protected Access)** is the most widely used wireless network encryption for home wireless networks.
- Anticipating disasters involves physical security, data security, and disaster recovery plans.
- Preventing data loss involves protecting data by screening job applicants, guarding passwords, and auditing and backing up data.

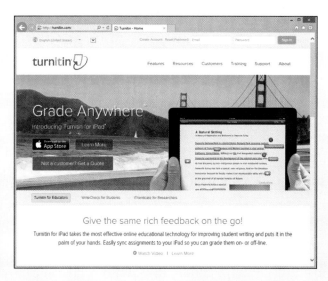

What do you suppose controls how computers can be used? You probably think first of laws. Of course, that is right, but technology is moving so fast that it is very difficult for our legal system to keep up. The essential element that controls how computers are used today is *ethics*.

Ethics are standards of moral conduct. **Computer ethics** are guidelines for the morally acceptable use of computers in our society. We are all entitled to ethical treatment. This includes the right to keep personal information, such as credit ratings and medical histories, from getting into unauthorized hands.

Copyright and Digital Rights Management

Copyright is a legal concept that gives content creators the right to control use and distribution of their work. Materials that can be copyrighted include paintings, books, music, films, and even video games.

Software piracy is the unauthorized copying and distribution of software. The software industry loses over $60 billion annually to software piracy. Two related topics are the Digital Millennium Copyright Act and digital rights management.

- **Digital Millennium Copyright Act** establishes the right of a program owner to make a backup copy of any program and disallows the creation of copies to be sold or given away. It is also illegal to download copyright-protected music and videos from the Internet.
- **Digital rights management (DRM)** is a collection of technologies designed to prevent copyright violations. Typically, DRM is used to (1) control the number of devices that can access a given file and (2) limit the kinds of devices that can access a file.

Today, many legal sources for digital media exist, including

- Television programs that can be watched online, often for free, on television-network-sponsored sites.
- Sites like Pandora that allow listeners to enjoy music at no cost.
- Online stores that legally sell music and video content. A pioneer in this area is Apple's iTunes Music Store.

Plagiarism

Plagiarism is the illegal and unethical representation of some other person's work and ideas as your own without giving credit to the original source. Examples of plagiarism include cutting and pasting web content into a report or paper.

Recognizing and catching **plagiarists** is relatively easy. For example, services such as **Turnitin** are dedicated to preventing Internet plagiarism. This service examines a paper's content and compares it to a wide range of known public electronic documents including web page content. Exact duplication or paraphrasing is readily identified.

CAREERS IN IT

IT security analysts are responsible for maintaining the security of a company's network, systems, and data. Employers look for candidates with a bachelor's or associate's degree in information systems or computer science and network experience. Salary range is $62,000 to $101,000.

KEY TERMS

access   (225)
accuracy   (225)
antispyware   (230)
big data   (225)
biometric scanning   (235)
botnet   (233)
browser cache   (228)
computer crime   (232)
computer ethics   (241)
Computer Fraud and
Abuse Act (232, 233)
computer monitoring software   (230)
cookies   (228)
copyright   (241)
cracker   (232)
cyberbullying   (235)
cybercrime   (232)
data security   (238)
denial of service (DoS) attack   (233)
dictionary attack   (236)
Digital Millennium Copyright Act   (241)
digital rights management (DRM)   (241)
disaster recovery plan   (238)
electronic profile   (226)
employee-monitoring software   (227)
encryption   (236)
encryption key   (237)
ethics   (241)
Family Educational Rights and Privacy
Act (FERPA)   (231)
firewall   (236)
first-party cookie   (228)
Freedom of Information Act   (227)
Gramm-Leach-Bliley Act   (231)
hacker   (231)
Health Insurance Portability and
Accountability Act (HIPAA)   (231)
history file   (228)
http (hypertext transfer protocol)   (238)
https (hypertext transfer protocol
secure)   (238)

identity theft   (234)
illusion of anonymity   (228)
information broker   (225)
information reseller   (225)
InPrivate Browsing   (229)
Internet scam   (234)
IT security analyst   (243)
key   (237)
keystroke logger   (230)
malware   (232)
mistaken identity   (227)
online identity   (231)
password   (236)
phishing   (234)
physical security   (238)
plagiarism   (242)
plagiarist   (242)
privacy   (225)
privacy mode   (229)
Private Browsing   (229)
property   (225)
robot network   (233)
rogue Wi-Fi hotspot   (233)
scam   (234)
security   (231)
security suites   (236)
software piracy   (241)
spy removal program   (230)
spyware   (230)
temporary Internet file   (228)
third-party cookie   (228)
tracking cookies   (228)
Trojan horse   (233)
virtual private network (VPN)   (238)
virus   (232)
web bugs   (229)
wireless network encryption   (238)
worm   (232)
WPA2 (Wi-Fi Protected Access 2)   (238)
zombie   (233)

To test your knowledge of these key terms with animated flash cards, visit us at www.
mhhe.com/ce2015, select Student Edition, and choose Chapter 9 and then Flashcards.

MULTIPLE CHOICE

Circle the letter of the correct answer.

1. The three primary privacy issues are accuracy, property, and:
   - a. access
   - b. ethics
   - c. ownership
   - d. security

2. Highly detailed and personalized descriptions of individuals are electronic:
   - a. cookies
   - b. histories
   - c. profiles
   - d. web bugs

3. Browsers store the locations of sites visited in a:
   - a. history file
   - b. menu
   - c. tool bar
   - d. firewall

4. The browser mode that ensures your browsing activity is not recorded.
   - a. detect
   - b. insert
   - c. privacy
   - d. sleep

5. The information that people voluntarily post in social networking sites, blogs, and photo- and video-sharing sites is used to create their:
   - a. access approval
   - b. firewall
   - c. online identity
   - d. phish

6. Computer criminals who create and distribute malicious programs.
   - a. antispies
   - b. crackers
   - c. cyber traders
   - d. identity thieves

7. Programs that come into a computer system disguised as something else are called:
   - a. Trojan horses
   - b. viruses
   - c. web bugs
   - d. zombies

8. The use of the Internet, cell phones, or other devices to send or post content intended to hurt or embarrass another person is known as:
   - a. cyberbullying
   - b. online harassment
   - c. social media discrimination
   - d. unethical communication

9. Special hardware and software used to control access to a corporation's private network is known as a(n):
   - a. antivirus program
   - b. communication gate
   - c. firewall
   - d. spyware removal program

10. To prevent copyright violations, corporations often use:
    - a. ACT
    - b. DRM
    - c. VPN
    - d. WPA2

For an interactive multiple-choice practice test, visit us at www.mhhe.com/ce2015, select Student Edition, and choose Chapter 9 and then Multiple Choice.

MATCHING

Match each numbered item with the most closely related lettered item. Write your answers in the spaces provided.

a. accuracy
b. biometric
c. cookies
d. encryption
e. information brokers
f. malware
g. phishing
h. plagiarism
i. spyware
j. zombies

_____ 1. Privacy concern that relates to the responsibility to ensure correct data collection.

_____ 2. Individuals who collect and sell personal data.

_____ 3. Small data files deposited on your hard disk from websites you have visited.

_____ 4. Wide range of programs that secretly record and report an individual's activities on the Internet.

_____ 5. Malicious programs that damage or disrupt a computer system.

_____ 6. Infected computers that can be remotely controlled.

_____ 7. Used by scammers to trick Internet users with official-looking websites.

_____ 8. A type of scanning device such as fingerprint and iris (eye) scanner.

_____ 9. Process of coding information to make it unreadable except to those who have a key.

_____ 10. An ethical issue relating to using another person's work and ideas as your own without giving credit to the original source.

For an interactive matching practice test, visit our website at www.mhhe.com/ce2015, select Student Edition, and choose Chapter 9 and then Matching.

OPEN-ENDED

On a separate sheet of paper, respond to each question or statement.

1. Define privacy, and discuss the impact of large databases, private networks, the Internet, and the web.
2. Define and discuss online identity and the major privacy laws.
3. Define security. Define computer crime and the impact of malicious programs, including viruses, worms, Trojan horses, and zombies, as well as denial of service attacks, rogue Wi-Fi hotspots, data manipulation, identity theft, Internet scams, and cyberbullying.
4. Discuss ways to protect computer security including restricting access, encrypting data, anticipating disasters, and preventing data loss.
5. Define ethics, and describe copyright law and plagiarism.

DISCUSSION

Respond to each of the following questions.

1 Making IT Work for You: CLOUD-BASED BACKUP

Review the Making IT Work for You: Cloud-Based Backup on pages 239 and 240, and then respond to the following: (a) How do you currently back up your important files? How often do you create these backups? (b) Have you ever used Carbonite or a similar cloud-based service? If so, which service have you used, and what do you typically use it for? If you have not used Carbonite or a similar service, describe how and why you might use one. (c) Do you see yourself signing up for a paid, yearly subscription to a service such as Carbonite? Why or why not?

2 Privacy: SOCIAL NETWORKING

Review the Privacy box on page 227, and then answer the following: (a) Do you use any social networking sites? If so, which ones and do you know their policy of sharing your posts and photos to others without your expressed consent? (b) Do you believe that social networks violate your privacy when they share information with advertisers? Why or why not? (c) Suppose that a high school teacher posts photos on her Facebook page showing her drinking at a party. When the school board becomes aware of these photos, the teacher is suspended. Is this a violation of her rights? Why or why not? (d) In late 2009, Facebook allowed user's names, pictures, and basic information to appear in Google search results. Do you think this is ethical? Why or why not.

3 Ethics: PLAGIARISM

Review the Ethics box on page 242, and then respond to the following: (a) Do you think it is ethical for instructors to employ a program that checks for plagiarism? Why or why not? (b) Do you think it is ethical for students or any individuals to copy all or part of a web page's content and then present the information without crediting the source? Why or why not? (c) How would you distinguish between using the web for research and plagiarizing web content? Be as specific as possible. (d) Does your school have a policy specifically regarding plagiarism of web content? If yes, what is the policy? If not, what would you suggest would be an appropriate policy?

4 Environment: ENVIRONMENTAL ETHICS AND IT

Review the Environment box on page 241, and then respond to the following: (a) Do you feel that IT professionals should receive training or education in environmental issues? Why or why not? (b) Can a person be considered unethical if he or she fails to consider the environment in any decisions? Discuss your response. (c) Do you feel that governments should create laws that govern the energy consumption of computers and other electronic devices? Why or why not? (d) Using a search engine, find the website of the Energy Star program. Which government agencies are responsible for this program? What environmental benefits has this program already given us?

The Evolution of the Computer Age

Many of you probably can't remember a world without computers, but for some of us, computers were virtually unknown when we were born and have rapidly come of age during our lifetime.

Although there are many predecessors to what we think of as the modern computer—reaching as far back as the 18th century, when Joseph Marie Jacquard created a loom programmed to weave cloth and Charles Babbage created the first fully modern computer design (which he could never get to work)—the computer age did not really begin until the first computer was made available to the public in 1951.

The modern age of computers thus spans slightly more than 60 years (so far), which is typically broken down into five generations. Each generation has been marked by a significant advance in technology.

- **First Generation (1951–57):** During the first generation, computers were built with vacuum tubes— electronic tubes that were made of glass and were about the size of lightbulbs.

- **Second Generation (1958–63):** This generation began with the first computers built with transistors—small devices that transfer electronic signals across a resistor. Because transistors are much smaller, use less power, and create less heat than vacuum tubes, the new computers were faster, smaller, and more reliable than the first-generation machines.

- **Third Generation (1964–69):** In 1964, computer manufacturers began replacing transistors with integrated circuits. An integrated circuit (IC) is a complete electronic circuit on a small chip made of silicon (one of the most abundant elements in the earth's crust). These computers were more reliable and compact than computers made with transistors, and they cost less to manufacture.

- **Fourth Generation (1970–90):** Many key advances were made during this generation, the most significant being the microprocessor—a specialized chip developed for computer memory and logic. Use of a single chip to create a smaller "personal" computer (as well as digital watches, pocket calculators, copy machines, and so on) revolutionized the computer industry.

- **Fifth Generation (1991–2015 and beyond):** Our current generation has been referred to as the "Connected Generation" because of the industry's massive effort to increase the connectivity of computers. The rapidly expanding Internet, World Wide Web, and intranets have created an information superhighway that has enabled both computer professionals and home computer users to communicate with others across the globe.

This appendix provides you with a timeline that describes in more detail some of the most significant events in each generation of the computer age.

First Generation: **The Vacuum Tube Age**

1951 Dr. John W. Mauchly and J. Presper Eckert Jr. introduce the first commercially available electronic digital computer—the UNIVAC—built with vacuum tubes. This computer was based on their earlier ENIAC (Electronic Numerical Integrator and Computer) design completed in 1946.

1951–53 IBM adds computers to its business equipment products and sells over 1,000 IBM 650 systems.

IBM 650 DATA PROCESSING SYSTEM

1951 1952 1953 1954 1955 1956 1957

1957 Introduction of first high-level programming language—FORTRAN (FORmula TRANslator).

1952 Development team led by Dr. Grace Hopper, former U.S. Navy programmer, introduces the A6 Compiler—the first example of software that converts high-level language symbols into instructions that a computer can execute.

Second Generation: **The Transistor Age**

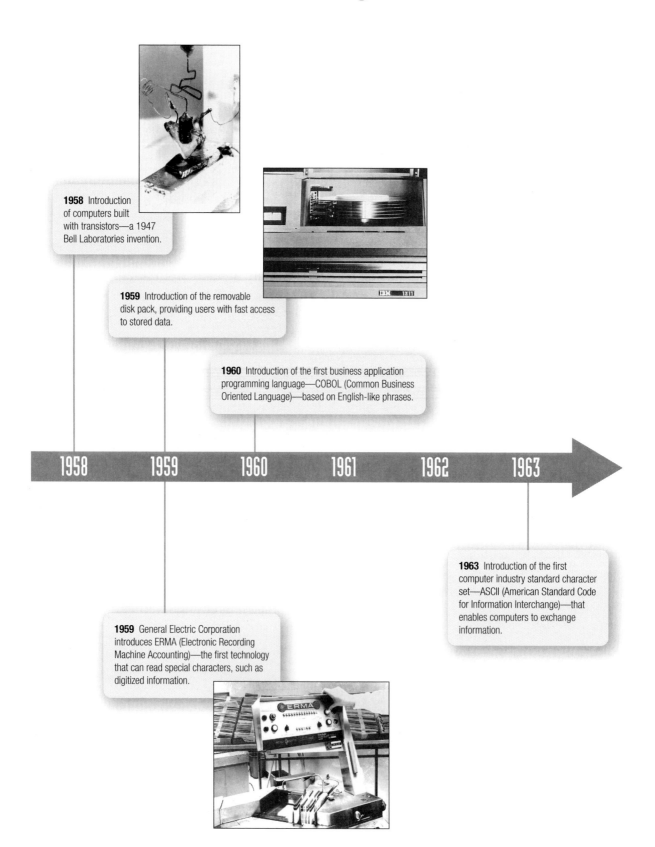

1958 Introduction of computers built with transistors—a 1947 Bell Laboratories invention.

1959 Introduction of the removable disk pack, providing users with fast access to stored data.

1960 Introduction of the first business application programming language—COBOL (Common Business Oriented Language)—based on English-like phrases.

1958 1959 1960 1961 1962 1963

1963 Introduction of the first computer industry standard character set—ASCII (American Standard Code for Information Interchange)—that enables computers to exchange information.

1959 General Electric Corporation introduces ERMA (Electronic Recording Machine Accounting)—the first technology that can read special characters, such as digitized information.

Third Generation: **The Integrated Circuit Age**

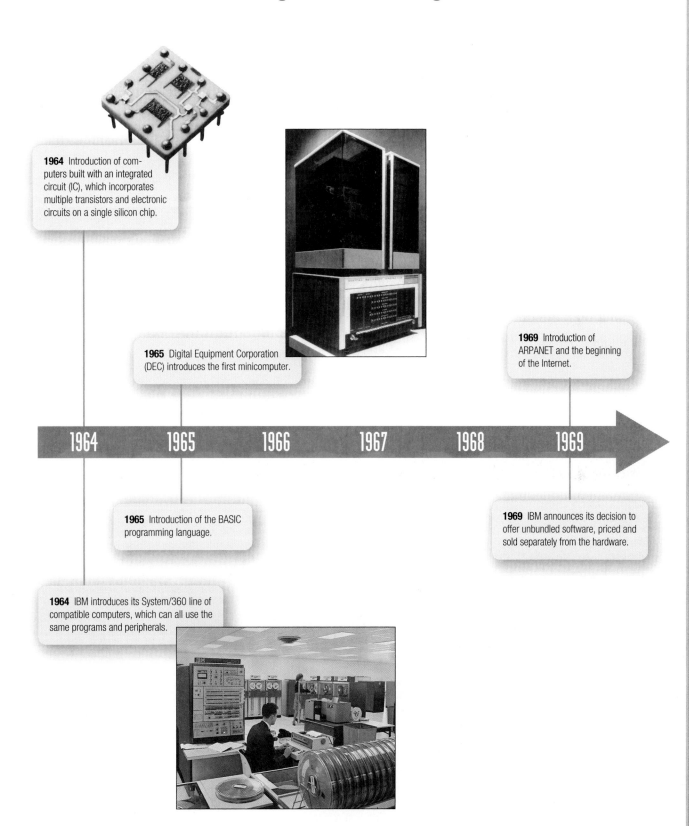

1964 Introduction of computers built with an integrated circuit (IC), which incorporates multiple transistors and electronic circuits on a single silicon chip.

1965 Digital Equipment Corporation (DEC) introduces the first minicomputer.

1969 Introduction of ARPANET and the beginning of the Internet.

1964　1965　1966　1967　1968　1969

1965 Introduction of the BASIC programming language.

1969 IBM announces its decision to offer unbundled software, priced and sold separately from the hardware.

1964 IBM introduces its System/360 line of compatible computers, which can all use the same programs and peripherals.

Fourth Generation: **The Microprocessor Age**

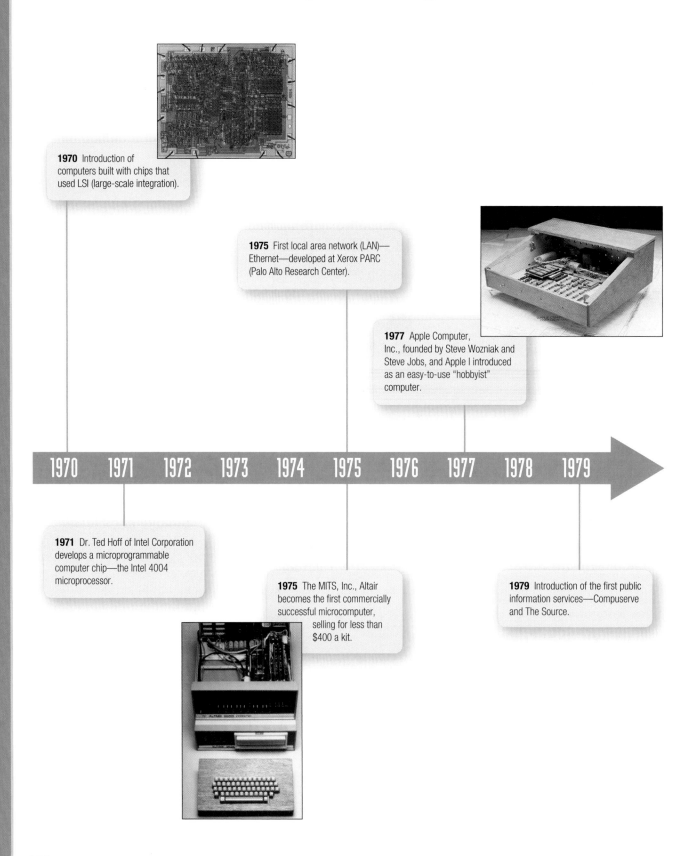

1970 Introduction of computers built with chips that used LSI (large-scale integration).

1975 First local area network (LAN)—Ethernet—developed at Xerox PARC (Palo Alto Research Center).

1977 Apple Computer, Inc., founded by Steve Wozniak and Steve Jobs, and Apple I introduced as an easy-to-use "hobbyist" computer.

1970 1971 1972 1973 1974 1975 1976 1977 1978 1979

1971 Dr. Ted Hoff of Intel Corporation develops a microprogrammable computer chip—the Intel 4004 microprocessor.

1975 The MITS, Inc., Altair becomes the first commercially successful microcomputer, selling for less than $400 a kit.

1979 Introduction of the first public information services—Compuserve and The Source.

1980 IBM asks Microsoft founder, Bill Gates, to develop an operating system—MS-DOS—for the soon-to-be-released IBM personal computer.

1981 Introduction of the IBM PC, which contains an Intel microprocessor chip and Microsoft's MS-DOS operating system.

1989 Introduction of Intel 486—the first 1,000,000-transistor microprocessor.

1980 1981 1982 1983 1984 1985 1986 1987 1988 1989 1990

1984 Apple introduces the Macintosh Computer, with a unique, easy-to-use graphical user interface.

1985 Microsoft introduces its Windows graphical user interface.

1990 Microsoft releases Windows 3.0, with an enhanced graphical user interface and the ability to run multiple applications.

THE EVOLUTION OF THE COMPUTER AGE **257**

Fifth Generation: **The Age of Connectivity**

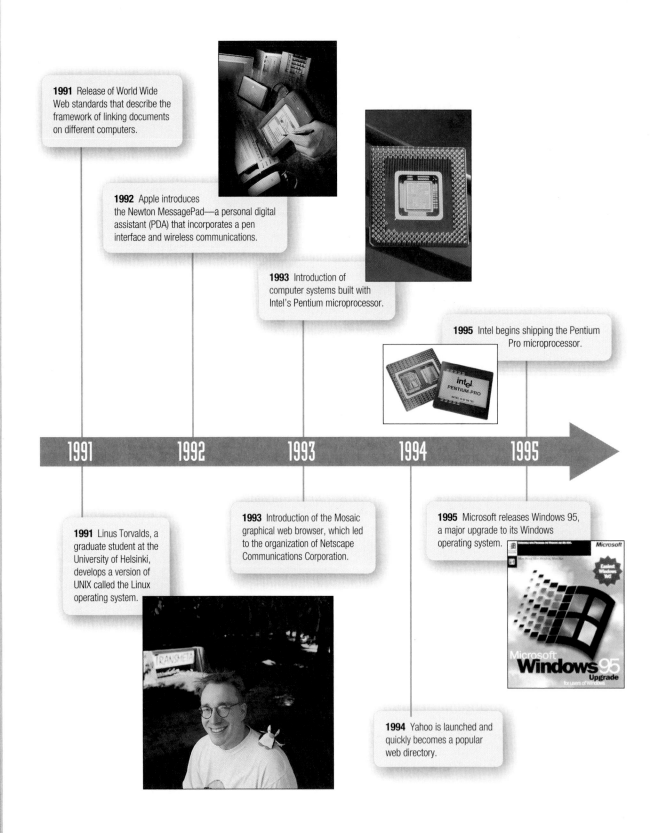

1991 Release of World Wide Web standards that describe the framework of linking documents on different computers.

1992 Apple introduces the Newton MessagePad—a personal digital assistant (PDA) that incorporates a pen interface and wireless communications.

1993 Introduction of computer systems built with Intel's Pentium microprocessor.

1995 Intel begins shipping the Pentium Pro microprocessor.

1991   1992   1993   1994   1995

1991 Linus Torvalds, a graduate student at the University of Helsinki, develops a version of UNIX called the Linux operating system.

1993 Introduction of the Mosaic graphical web browser, which led to the organization of Netscape Communications Corporation.

1995 Microsoft releases Windows 95, a major upgrade to its Windows operating system.

1994 Yahoo is launched and quickly becomes a popular web directory.

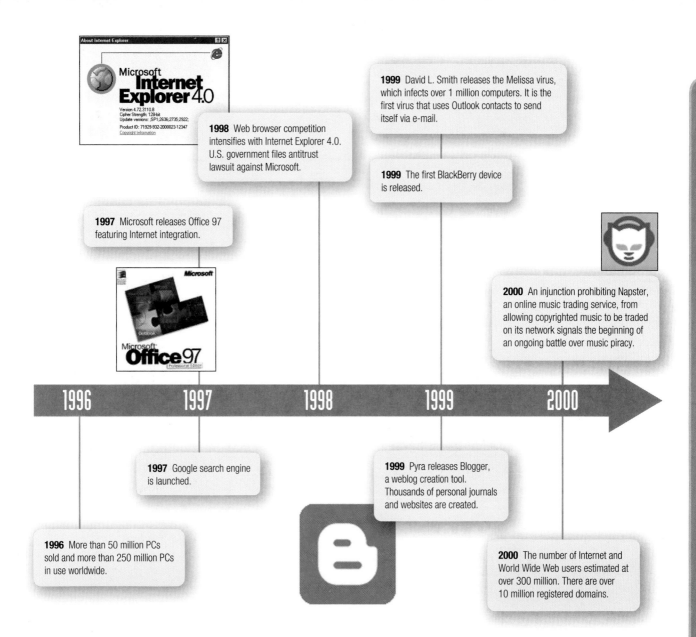

1999 David L. Smith releases the Melissa virus, which infects over 1 million computers. It is the first virus that uses Outlook contacts to send itself via e-mail.

1998 Web browser competition intensifies with Internet Explorer 4.0. U.S. government files antitrust lawsuit against Microsoft.

1999 The first BlackBerry device is released.

1997 Microsoft releases Office 97 featuring Internet integration.

2000 An injunction prohibiting Napster, an online music trading service, from allowing copyrighted music to be traded on its network signals the beginning of an ongoing battle over music piracy.

1996   1997   1998   1999   2000

1997 Google search engine is launched.

1999 Pyra releases Blogger, a weblog creation tool. Thousands of personal journals and websites are created.

1996 More than 50 million PCs sold and more than 250 million PCs in use worldwide.

2000 The number of Internet and World Wide Web users estimated at over 300 million. There are over 10 million registered domains.

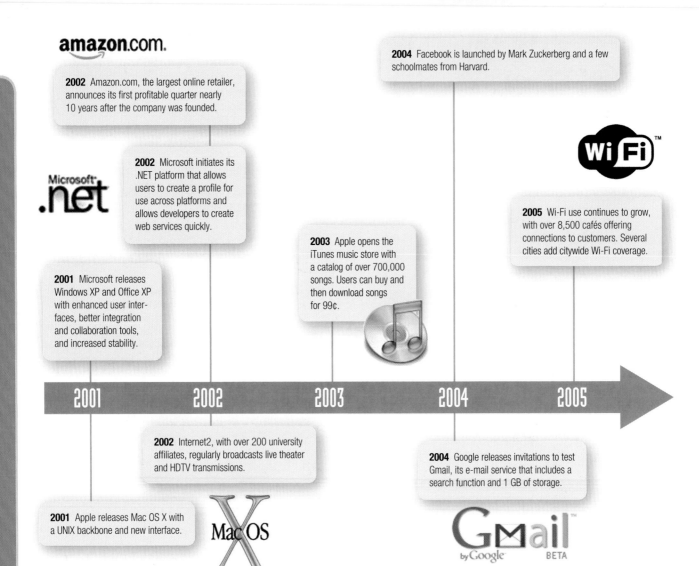

amazon.com.

2002 Amazon.com, the largest online retailer, announces its first profitable quarter nearly 10 years after the company was founded.

2004 Facebook is launched by Mark Zuckerberg and a few schoolmates from Harvard.

Wi Fi™

Microsoft®
.net

2002 Microsoft initiates its .NET platform that allows users to create a profile for use across platforms and allows developers to create web services quickly.

2003 Apple opens the iTunes music store with a catalog of over 700,000 songs. Users can buy and then download songs for 99¢.

2005 Wi-Fi use continues to grow, with over 8,500 cafés offering connections to customers. Several cities add citywide Wi-Fi coverage.

2001 Microsoft releases Windows XP and Office XP with enhanced user inter-faces, better integration and collaboration tools, and increased stability.

| 2001 | 2002 | 2003 | 2004 | 2005 |

2002 Internet2, with over 200 university affiliates, regularly broadcasts live theater and HDTV transmissions.

2004 Google releases invitations to test Gmail, its e-mail service that includes a search function and 1 GB of storage.

2001 Apple releases Mac OS X with a UNIX backbone and new interface.

Mac OS X

Gmail™
by Google   BETA

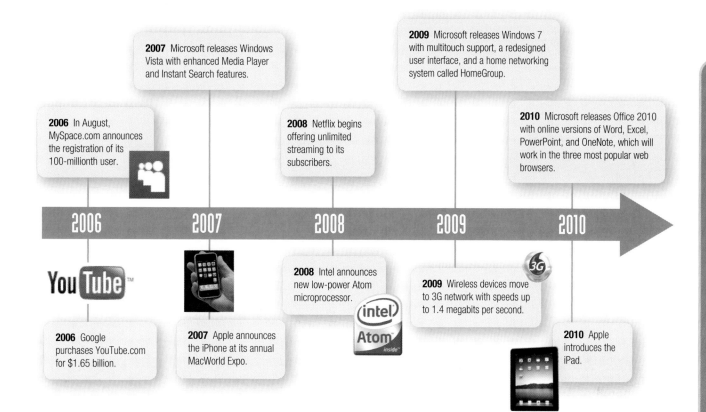

2006 In August, MySpace.com announces the registration of its 100-millionth user.

2007 Microsoft releases Windows Vista with enhanced Media Player and Instant Search features.

2009 Microsoft releases Windows 7 with multitouch support, a redesigned user interface, and a home networking system called HomeGroup.

2008 Netflix begins offering unlimited streaming to its subscribers.

2010 Microsoft releases Office 2010 with online versions of Word, Excel, PowerPoint, and OneNote, which will work in the three most popular web browsers.

2006   2007   2008   2009   2010

2006 Google purchases YouTube.com for $1.65 billion.

2007 Apple announces the iPhone at its annual MacWorld Expo.

2008 Intel announces new low-power Atom microprocessor.

2009 Wireless devices move to 3G network with speeds up to 1.4 megabits per second.

2010 Apple introduces the iPad.

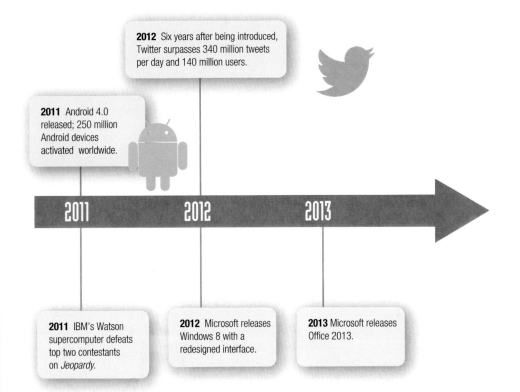

2012 Six years after being introduced, Twitter surpasses 340 million tweets per day and 140 million users.

2011 Android 4.0 released; 250 million Android devices activated worldwide.

2011   2012   2013

2011 IBM's Watson supercomputer defeats top two contestants on *Jeopardy*.

2012 Microsoft releases Windows 8 with a redesigned interface.

2013 Microsoft releases Office 2013.

The Computer Buyer's Guide

PART 1: WHICH TYPES OF COMPUTERS SHOULD YOU PURCHASE?

Many individuals feel confused and overwhelmed when it comes to buying a new computer. In today's market, there are various categories of computers ranging from desktops and laptops to ultraportable tablets and smartphones. And within each category, there are countless choices and a wide range of prices. This buying guide will help you choose the best combination of computers for your needs, as well as point out some key specifications that they should have.

LAPTOPS COMPUTERS: TODAY'S STANDARD

Typical Recommendation: Buy a $500 to $700 laptop with a 15-inch screen.

The laptop computer has become the must-have device that can do everything you need, wherever you need it. They are powerful enough to be your primary home computer (replacing desktops) while portable enough to take to school, work, the local coffee shop, and even on your next trip. Many students are bringing them to classes to take notes and perform research. If you can only own one computer, make it a laptop. Affordable ones start at under $500.

If you have decided that you want to buy a laptop computer, be sure to read Part 2 for additional tips and recommendations.

SMARTPHONES: COMPUTERS IN YOUR POCKET

Typical Recommendation: Obtain a free or low-cost smartphone by signing a two-year wireless contract with a data plan.

For many individuals, the smartphone has become much like a wallet, purse, or keys—you don't leave home without it. This single, pocket-sized device fills many roles. It is a mobile phone, digital camera, video recorder, gaming device, and personal digital assistant. Most individuals purchase a smartphone because they need to access information quickly and easily, regardless of where they are.

With many smartphones now available for free with two-year contracts, it is easier than ever to replace your older cell phone. The biggest drawback to owning a smartphone is that its "use anywhere" benefit is limited if it is not paired with a wireless data plan, which can often cost around $30 per month.

Although Apple's iPhone was once the clear leader in the smartphone market, various Android devices include competitive features and are enjoying favorable reviews. If you have decided that you want to buy a smartphone, be sure to read Part 2 for additional tips and recommendations.

TABLETS: THE RISING STARS

Typical Recommendation: Buy a 10-inch tablet with 16 GB of storage.

The release of the iPad has revived this category of computers. With an attractive, 10-inch touch-screen surface, it has quickly become a popular device for watching videos, playing games, reading e-books, and browsing the web. Tablets are light enough to hold comfortably for many hours, yet powerful enough to use a variety of apps. They generally have a much longer battery life than laptop computers.

If you are a typical computer user, then you may not benefit much from purchasing a tablet computer. Most of your computing time will be spent on your laptop computer (at home and at school, for example) or on your smartphone. Although tablets are very popular right now, you must remember that they cost several hundred dollars. You should have a very clear need for this sort of device before you decide to spend the money on it.

Many students consider buying tablets because the low weight makes a tablet easy to carry around. Although this is true, there are lightweight laptop computers that weigh only one or two pounds more and are much more versatile than tablets. Such versatility is crucial for various types of software that are not available as apps and require installation on a Windows or Mac computer. Before you decide between a tablet and lightweight laptop, consider the type of software you will need for your schoolwork, business, or personal use. If everything you need is available as a mobile app, then a tablet (paired with a wireless keyboard) will be more affordable than a lightweight laptop computer.

In conclusion, purchase a tablet computer only if you see yourself using it often. The touch-screen interface, low weight, and long battery life do indeed make it easy to carry around and use almost anywhere you go. However, the price tag does not make the decision an obvious one if you already own a laptop computer and smartphone. If you have decided that you want to buy a tablet, be sure to read Part 2 for additional tips and recommendations.

DESKTOPS

Typical Recommendation: Buy a tower system with a 20- to 24-inch monitor for approximately $600.

Desktop (or tower) computers have been around for a long time. You will still find them in many offices and homes. However, they are steadily losing popularity because laptop computers have become very powerful and affordable. Why have a computer that remains stuck in your home or office when you can have a laptop that can be taken almost anywhere?

Although laptop computers seem to be the better choice, there are several reasons why you might want to purchase a desktop computer. First, the use of a laptop computer as your primary computer can be uncomfortable. After prolonged use, it can place stress on your neck, back, and wrists. Desktops typically come with large monitors, and various types of ergonomic keyboards are available. However, desktop critics will point out that laptop computers can be connected to external monitors and keyboards as well. The only downside is that a laptop requires the purchase of extra equipment.

The other reason to get a desktop is if you have a specific need that cannot be addressed by a laptop computer. For example, some families have a media center computer that holds all the videos, photos, and music for the entire home network. Another example involves gamers, who often seek to build or customize extremely powerful computers. They often choose desktops for this endeavor.

Most users will not need to purchase a desktop computer. In fact, they are currently the least popular of the four categories in this buying guide. However, if you have decided that you want to buy a desktop, be sure to read Part 2 for additional tips and recommendations.

PART 2: PERSONALIZED BUYING GUIDE

Now that you have decided which types of computers you need, it is time to explore computer specifications. The areas below explore the decision-making process from the perspective of various buyers.

LAPTOPS

There are two basic categories of laptop: the traditional laptop and the ultrabook. Although these two categories of laptop computers have the same general appearance, they vary greatly in power, storage capacity, weight, and battery life. The following section helps you find the device that best meets your needs.

User #1: I am a power user. I need a portable computer that can handle the latest video games or process-intensive operations such as video editing, engineering, and design.

Response #1: Purchase a traditional laptop computer that includes the following minimum specs:

- **The fastest categories of processors with large number of cores and high GHz count**
- **A graphics processor (GPU) outside of the main CPU**
- **8-GB RAM**
- **750-GB hard drive**
- **17-inch screen**

Expect to pay approximately $1000, perhaps more. For games, many individuals choose Windows-based PCs. The video and design industries usually use Macs.

User #2: I am a regular user. I need a desktop replacement and portable computer. I typically run office software, use the Internet, and listen to music.

Response #2: Purchase an affordable traditional laptop computer that includes the following specs:

- **Middle-tier processors—not the fastest but not the slowest either**
- **4- to 8-GB RAM**
- **500-GB hard drive**
- **15-inch screen**

Expect to pay approximately $500 to $700. For maximum savings, as well as compatibility with most software, many buyers choose Windows-based PCs. Be sure to purchase an external monitor, keyboard, and mouse if you plan on heavy use while at home.

User #3: I want a small, lightweight computer that I can carry anywhere. I would like long battery life for extended use.

Response #3: Purchase an ultrabook with

- 11- to 13-inch screen
- Solid-state hard drive
- 4-GB RAM
- Weight under 4 pounds

Expect to pay $700 to $1000. Many ultrabooks will not include a DVD drive. Windows-based ultrabooks tend to be more affordable. The MacBook Air is slightly more expensive, but it has always been considered a leader in the lightweight laptop field.

SMARTPHONES

Shopping for a smartphone involves three separate processes: (1) choosing an operating system, such iOS, Android, or Windows; (2) choosing a device; and (3) choosing a wireless carrier. Although the following section does not review different wireless companies or data plans, it presents a list of smartphone features that you should always consider before making your choice. In addition, it presents each smartphone operating system from the perspective of typical users.

Features to Consider

- *Screen and device size:* **Consider a size (and weight) that is comfortable for you to use and carry around. Four-inch screens are now typical.**
- *Screen resolution:* **Some devices deliver HD quality for sharp photos and videos.**
- *Integrated keyboard:* **consider one if you type often on these devices.**
- *Storage:* **Having 8 GB is enough for most users. Choose 16 GB or more if you plan to store large quantities of music, photos, and videos. Some devices allow you to increase storage by using memory cards.**
- *Battery life:* **About 7 to 8 hours is typical. Some devices have removable batteries.**
- *Cameras:* **Many include front- and rear-facing cameras. Compare megapixels and photo quality.**
- *App market:* **Consider the number of apps, and ensure that any apps you need are available for this operating system.**

Operating Systems

- *iOS:* **The iPhone is considered by many to be the standard against which all smartphones are measured. Buyers typically choose the iPhone if they are Mac owners or prefer a tightly controlled "eco-system" from Apple where stability and ease of use are favored over heavy customization.**

- *Android:* **There are many Android devices available from various manufacturers, some free with a wireless contract. Buyers who enjoy customizing their interface typically choose Android. In addition, this operating system is tightly integrated with many of Google's products and services.**
- *BlackBerry:* **Many of these devices contain integrated keyboards for faster and more comfortable typing. Many business users choose BlackBerry for typing e-mail and notes on the go.**
- *Windows Phone:* **The newcomer to the smartphone market features an interface that will seem familiar to those using Windows 8 laptop and tablets. Users enjoy the "live tiles," which constantly update information, such as social network activity.**

Remember that smartphones can cost very little when you sign a two-year contract with a wireless company. Consider whether you want to make that sort of commitment.

TABLET COMPUTERS

Because of their increased popularity, tablets are available in several sizes from many different companies. The following section helps you find the device that best meets your needs.

User #1: *I want to watch videos, play games, create notes, and browse websites.*

Response #1: Purchase a 10-inch tablet. Expect to pay $400 to $500. Most weigh about 1.5 pounds. Apple's iPad was very popular when first released, and it continues to be a popular choice among buyers today. Other things to consider:

- For greater customization, consider an Android-based tablet. There are several models that are comparable to the iPad, which is considered by many reviewers to be the standard bearer.
- The Microsoft Surface tablet includes a keyboard that is integrated into the cover. However, any tablet can be paired with a Bluetooth keyboard, which is crucial if you plan to type often.
- Make sure the apps you plan on using are available for the tablet's operating system.
- Having 16 GB of storage is typical. Some tablets let you expand this by using flash memory cards.

User #2: *I want to read e-books, browse websites, and have a lightweight device that I can hold with one hand.*

Response #2: Purchase a 7-inch tablet. Expect to pay around $200. Most weigh less than 1 pound. Google's

Nexus 7 and Amazon's Kindle Fire are popular Android-based tablets.

DESKTOP COMPUTERS

Desktops remain popular for offices, both at home and in many companies. In addition, many power users require them for graphics-intensive tasks. The following section helps you find the device that best meets your needs.

User #1: *I need a powerful computer that can handle the latest video games or process-intensive operations such as video editing, engineering, and design.*

Response #1: Purchase a tower-based computer with the following minimum specs:

- **The fastest categories of processors with large number of cores and high GHz count**
- **High-performance video card**
- **16-GB RAM**
- **2-TB hard drive**
- **24-inch monitor**
- **Specialty peripherals (such as game controllers) when needed**

Expect to pay at least $1,500 for these powerful computers. For games, many individuals choose Windows-based PCs. The video and design industries usually use Macs.

User #2: *I would like a computer that can be used by the entire family for many years.*

Response #2: Purchase a tower or all-in-one computer with the following minimum specs:

- **Middle-tier processor**
- **4-GB RAM**
- **500-GB hard drive (increase to 2 TB if you plan to store a large number of videos)**
- **20- to 24-inch monitor**
- **Ergonomic keyboard**

Tower-based systems are usually offered in a package that includes the monitor and several peripherals. All-in-one systems will, of course, include the monitor, some of which are touch screens. Spending approximately $600 to $800 will help ensure that the components remain relevant for several years. For a stylish and powerful all-in-one computer, consider the slightly more expensive iMac from Apple.

1G (first-generation mobile telecommunications): Started in 1980s using analog signals to provide voice transmission service.

2G (second-generation mobile telecommunications): Started in the 1990s using digital radio signals.

3-D printer: A printer that creates objects by adding layers of material onto one another. Also known as additive manufacturing.

3G (third-generation mobile telecommunications): Started in the 2000s and provided services capable of effective connectivity to the Internet, marking the beginning of smartphones.

4G (fourth-generation mobile telecommunications): Replacing 3G networks in some areas with providers using WiMax and LTE connections to provide faster transmission speeds.

3GLs (third-generation languages): High-level procedural language. *See* Procedural language.

4G (fourth-generation mobile telecommunications): Provides faster transmission speeds than 3G. 3G started in the 2000s providing services capable of effective connectivity to the Internet and marked the beginning of smartphones.

4GLs (fourth-generation languages): Very high level or problem-oriented languages. *See* Task-oriented language.

5GLs (fifth-generation languages): *See* Fifth-generation language.

802.11: *See* Wi-Fi (wireless fidelity).

a

AC adapter: Notebook computers use AC adapters that are typically outside the system unit. They plug into a standard wall outlet, convert AC to DC, provide power to drive the system components, and can recharge batteries.

Access: Refers to the responsibility of those who have data to control who is able to use that data.

Access speed: Measures the amount of time required by the storage device to retrieve data and programs.

Accounting: The organizational department that records all financial activity from billing customers to paying employees.

Accounts payable: The activity that shows the money a company owes to its suppliers for the materials and services it has received.

Accounts receivable: The activity that shows what money has been received or is owed by customers.

Accuracy: Relates to the responsibility of those who collect data to ensure that the data is correct.

Active display area: The diagonal length of a monitor's viewing area.

Add a Device Wizard: A Windows wizard that provides step-by-step guidance for selecting and installing an appropriate printer driver for a new printer.

Additive manufacturing: *See* 3-D printer.

Address: Located in the header of an e-mail message; the e-mail address of the persons sending, receiving, and, optionally, anyone else who is to receive copies.

Advanced Research Project Agency Network (ARPANET): A national computer network from which the Internet developed.

Agile development: A development methodology that starts by getting core functionality of a program working, then expands on it until the customer is satisfied with the results.

AJAX: An advanced use of JavaScript found on many interactive sites. This technology is used to create interactive websites that respond quickly like traditional desktop application software.

All-in-one: A desktop computer that has the monitor and system unit housed together in the same case (e.g., Apple's iMac).

Analog: Continuous signals that vary to represent different tones, pitches, and volume.

Analog signals: Signals that represent a range of frequencies, such as the human voice. They are a continuous electronic wave signal as opposed to a digital signal that is either on or off.

Android: Mobile operating system originally developed by Android Inc. and later purchased by Google.

Animation: Feature involving special visual and sound effects like moving pictures, audio, and video clips that play automatically when selected.

Antispyware: *See* Spy removal programs.

Antivirus program: A utility program that guards a computer system from viruses or other damaging programs.

App: *See* Application software.

App store: A website that provides access to specific mobile apps that can be downloaded either for a nominal fee or free of charge.

Applets: Web pages contain links to programs called applets, which are written in a programming language called Java. These programs are used to add interest to a website by presenting animation, displaying graphics, providing interactive games, and so forth.

Application generation subsystem: Provides tools to create data entry forms and specialized programming languages that interface or work with common languages, such as C or Visual Basic.

Application generator: Also called program coder; provides modules of prewritten code to accomplish various tasks, such as calculation of overtime pay.

Application software: Also referred to as apps. Software that can perform useful work, such as word processing, cost estimating, or accounting tasks. The user primarily interacts with application software.

Arithmetic-logic unit (ALU): The part of the CPU that performs arithmetic and logical operations.

Arithmetic operation: Fundamental math operations: addition, subtraction, multiplication, and division.

Artificial intelligence (AI): A field of computer science that attempts to develop computer systems that can mimic or simulate human thought processes and actions.

Artificial reality: *See* Virtual reality.

ASCII (American Standard Code for Information Interchange): Binary coding scheme widely used on all computers, including personal computers. Eight bits form each byte, and each byte represents one character.

Aspect ratio: The width of a monitor divided by its height. Common aspect ratios for monitors are 4:3 (standard) and 16:9 (wide screen).

Assembly language: A step up from machine language, using names instead of numbers. These languages use abbreviations or mnemonics, such as ADD, that are automatically converted to the appropriate sequence of 1s and 0s.

Asymmetric digital subscriber line (ADSL): One of the most widely used types of telephone high-speed connections (DSL).

Attachment: A file, such as a document or worksheet, that is attached to an e-mail message.

Attribute: A data field represents an attribute (description or characteristic) of some entity (person, place, thing, or object). For example, an employee is an entity with many attributes, including his or her last name, address, phone, etc.

Automated design tool: Software package that evaluates hardware and software alternatives according to requirements given by the systems analyst. Also called computer-aided software engineering (CASE) tools.

b

Backbone: *See* Bus.

Background: Other programs running simultaneously with the program being used in an operating system. *See* Foreground.

Backup: A Windows utility program. *See* Backup program.

Backup program: A utility program that helps protect you from the effects of a disk failure by making a copy of selected or all files that have been saved onto a disk.

Balance sheet: Lists the overall financial condition of an organization.

Bandwidth: Bandwidth determines how much information can be transmitted at one time. It is a measurement of the communication channel's capacity. There are three bandwidths: voice band, medium band, and broadband.

Bar code: Code consisting of vertical zebra-striped marks printed on product containers, read with a bar code reader.

Bar code reader: Photoelectric scanner that reads bar codes for processing.

Bar code scanner: *See* Bar code reader.

Base station: *See* Wireless access point.

Baseband: Bandwidth used to connect individual computers that are located close to one another. Though it supports high-speed transmission, it can only carry a single signal at a time.

Batch processing: Processing performed all at once on data that has been collected over time.

BD (Blu-ray disc): A type of high-definition disc with a capacity of 25 to 50 gigabytes.

Beta testing: Testing by a select group of potential users in the final stage of testing a program.

Big data: Term given to describe the ever-growing volume of data currently being collected.

Binary system: Numbering system in which all numbers consist of only two digits: 0 and 1.

Biometric scanning: Devices that check fingerprints or retinal scans.

BIOS (basic input/output system): Information including the specifics concerning the amount of RAM and the type of keyboard, mouse, and secondary storage devices connected to the system unit.

Bit (binary digit): Each 1 or 0 is a bit; short for binary digit.

Bitmap image: Graphic file in which an image is made up of thousands of dots (pixels).

BitTorrent: A peer-to-peer file-sharing protocol used for distributing large amounts of data over the Internet.

Blog: *See* Web log.

Bluetooth: A wireless technology that allows nearby devices to communicate without the connection of cables or telephone systems.

Booting: Starting or restarting your computer.

Botnet: A collection of zombie computers.

Broadband: Bandwidth that includes microwave, satellite, coaxial cable, and fiber-optic channels. It is used for very-high-speed computers.

Browser: Special Internet software connecting you to remote computers; opens and transfers files, displays text and images, and provides an uncomplicated interface to the Internet and web documents. Examples of browsers are Internet Explorer, Mozilla Firefox, and Google Chrome.

Browser cache: A collection of temporary Internet files that contain web page content and instructions for displaying this content.

Bus: All communication travels along a common connecting cable called a bus or a backbone. As information passes along the bus, it is examined by each device on the system board to see if the information is intended for that device. *See* Bus line and Ethernet.

Bus line: Electronic data roadway, along which bits travel; connects the parts of the CPU to each other and links the CPU with other important hardware. The common connecting cable in a bus network.

Bus network: Each device is connected to a common cable called a bus or backbone, and all communications travel along this bus.

Bus width: The number of bits traveling simultaneously down a bus is the bus width.

Business suite: *See* Productivity suites.

Business-to-business (B2B): A type of electronic commerce that involves the sale of a product or service from one business to another. This is typically a manufacturer-supplier relationship.

Business-to-consumer (B2C): A type of electronic commerce that involves the sale of a product or service to the general public or end users.

Button: A special area you can click to make links that "navigate" through a presentation.

Byte: Unit consisting of eight bits. There are 256 possible bit combinations in a byte, and each byte represents one character.

C

Cable: Cords used to connect input and output devices to the system unit.

Cable modem: Type of modem that uses coaxial cable to create high-speed computer connections.

Cable service: Service provided by cable television companies using existing television cables.

Cache memory: Area of random-access memory (RAM) set aside to store the most frequently accessed information. Cache memory improves processing by acting as a temporary high-speed holding area between memory and the CPU, allowing the computer to detect which information in RAM is most frequently used.

Capacity: Capacity is how much data a particular storage medium can hold and is another characteristic of secondary storage.

Card reader: A device that interprets the encoded information contained on credit, debit, access, and identification cards.

Carpal tunnel syndrome: A repetitive strain injury consisting of damage to the nerves and tendons in the hands.

Cascading style sheets (CSS): Files inserted into an HTML document that control the appearance of web pages including layout, colors, and fonts.

Cathode-ray tube (CRT) monitor: Older type of monitor that is similar in size and technology to older television sets.

CD: *See* Compact disc.

CD-R: Stands for CD-recordable. This optical disc can be written to only once. After that it can be read many times without deterioration but cannot be written on or erased. Used to create custom music CDs and to archive data.

CD-ROM (compact disc–read-only memory): CD format that allows data to be read but not recorded. Used to distribute large databases, references, and software application packages.

CD-RW (compact disc rewriteable): A reusable, optical disc that is not permanently altered when data is recorded. Used to create and edit large multimedia presentations.

Cell: The space created by the intersection of a vertical column and a horizontal row within a worksheet in a program like Microsoft Excel. A cell can contain text or numeric entries.

Cellular service provider: Supports voice and data transmission to wireless devices.

Center for European Nuclear Research (CERN): In Switzerland, where the web was introduced in 1992.

Central processing unit (CPU): The part of the computer that holds data and program instructions for processing the data. The CPU consists of the control unit and the arithmetic-logic unit. In a personal computer, the CPU is on a single electronic component called a microprocessor chip.

Character: A single letter, number, or special character, such as a punctuation mark or $.

Character encoding standards: Assign unique sequence of bits to each character.

Child node: A node one level below the node being considered in a hierarchical database or network. *See* Parent node.

Chip: A tiny circuit board etched on a small square of sandlike material called silicon. A chip is also called a silicon chip, semiconductor, or integrated circuit.

Chip carrier: The device onto which chips are mounted and plugged into the system board.

Chrome OS: An operating system designed by Google for netbook computers and Internet connectivity through cloud computing.

Circles: A service offered through Google Plus, for grouping individuals according to common interests or other criteria.

Clarity: Indicated by the resolution, or number of pixels, on a monitor. The greater the resolution, the better the clarity.

Class: In an object-oriented database, classes are similar objects grouped together.

Client: A node that requests and uses resources available from other nodes. Typically, a client is a user's personal computer.

Client-based e-mail system: A system that requires a special program known as an e-mail client to be installed on your computer.

Client/server network: Network in which one powerful computer coordinates and supplies services to all other nodes on the network. Server nodes coordinate and supply specialized services, and client nodes request the services.

Clip art: Graphic illustrations representing a wide variety of topics.

Clock speed: Also called clock rate. It is measured in gigahertz, or billions of beats per second. The faster the clock speed, the faster the computer can process information and execute instructions.

Cloud computing: Data stored at a server on the Internet and available anywhere the Internet can be accessed.

Cloud printer: A printer connected to the Internet that provides printing services to others on the Internet.

Cloud storage: Also known as online storage. An Internet-based space for storing data and files.

Cloud suite: Suite stored at a server on the Internet and available anywhere from the Internet.

Coaxial cable: High-frequency transmission cable that replaces the multiple wires of telephone lines with a single solid-copper core. It is used to deliver television signals as well as to connect computers in a network.

Code: Writing a program using the appropriate computer language.

Code review: *See* Desk checking.

Coding: Actual writing of a computer program, using a programming language.

Cold boot: Starting the computer after it has been turned off.

Combination key: Keys such as the Ctrl key that perform an action when held down in combination with another key.

Commercial database: Enormous database an organization develops to cover certain particular subjects. Access to this type of database is usually offered for a fee or subscription. Also known as data bank and informational utility.

Common data item: In a relational database, all related tables must have a common data item or key field.

Communication channel: The actual connecting medium that carries the message between sending and receiving devices. This medium can be a physical wire, cable, or wireless connection.

Communication device: Computer systems that communicate with other computer systems using modems. For example, it modifies computer output into a form that can be transmitted across standard telephone lines.

Communication system: Electronic system that transmits data over communication lines from one location to another.

Compact disc (CD): Widely used optical disc format. It holds 650 MB (megabytes) to 1 GB (gigabyte) of data on one side of the CD.

Compact disc–read-only memory: *See* CD-ROM.

Compact disc rewriteable: *See* CD-RW.

Company database: Also called shared database. Stored on a mainframe, users throughout the company have access to the database through their personal computers linked by a network.

Compiler: Software that converts the programmer's procedural language program (source code) into machine language (object code). This object code can then be saved and run later.

Computer-aided design/computer-aided manufacturing (CAD/CAM) system: Knowledge work systems that run programs to integrate the design and manufacturing activities. CAD/CAM is widely used in manufacturing automobiles.

Computer-aided software engineering (CASE) tool: A type of software development tool that helps provide some automation and assistance in program design, coding, and testing. *See* Automated design tool.

Computer crime: *See* Cybercrime.

Computer ethics: Guidelines for the morally acceptable use of computers in our society.

Computer Fraud and Abuse Act: Law allowing prosecution of unauthorized access to computers and databases.

Computer monitoring software: The most invasive and dangerous type of spyware. These programs record every activity made on your computer, including credit card numbers, bank account numbers, and e-mail messages.

Computer network: Communications system connecting two or more computers and their peripheral devices to exchange information and share resources.

Computer support specialist: Specialists include technical writers, computer trainers, computer technicians, and help-desk specialists who provide technical support to customers and other users.

Computer technician: Specialist who installs hardware and software and troubleshoots problems for users.

Connectivity: Capability of the personal computer to use information from the world beyond one's desk. Data and information can be sent over telephone or cable lines and through the air so that computers can talk to each other and share information.

Consumer-to-consumer (C2C): A type of electronic commerce that involves individuals selling to individuals.

Contextual tab: A type of tab found in Microsoft Word that only appears when needed and anticipates the next operations to be performed by the user.

Contrast ratio: Indicates a monitor's ability to display colors. It compares the light intensity of the brightest white to the darkest black.

Control unit: Section of the CPU that tells the rest of the computer how to carry out program instructions.

Conversion: Also known as systems implementation; four approaches to conversion: direct, parallel, pilot, and phased. *See* Systems implementation.

Cookies: Small data files that are deposited on your hard disk from websites you have visited.

Coprocessor: Specialized processing chip designed to improve specific computer operations, such as the graphics coprocessor.

Copyright: A legal concept that gives content creators the right to control use and distribution of their work.

Cordless mouse: A battery-powered mouse that typically uses radio waves or infrared light waves to communicate with the system unit. Also known as wireless mouse.

Cracker: One who gains unauthorized access to a computer system for malicious purposes.

Cyberbullying: The use of the Internet, a cell phone, or other device to deliver content intended to hurt or embarrass another person.

Cybercash: *See* Digital cash.

Cybercrime: Any criminal offense that involves a computer and a network. Criminals may be employees, outside users, hackers and crackers, or organized crime members.

Cylinder: Hard disks store and organize files using tracks, sectors, and cylinders. A cylinder runs through each track of a stack of platters. Cylinders differentiate files stored on the same track and sector of different platters.

d

Dance pad: An input device for dance games where signals are sent via a pressure-sensitive mat.

Data: Raw, unprocessed facts that are input to a computer system that will give compiled information when the computer processes those facts. Data is also defined as facts or observations about people, places, things, and events.

Data administration subsystem: Helps manage the overall database, including maintaining security, providing disaster recovery support, and monitoring the overall performance of database operations.

Data bank: *See* Commercial database.

Data cube: A multidimensional data model. *Also see* Multidimensional database.

Data definition subsystem: This system defines the logical structure of the database by using a data dictionary.

Data dictionary: Dictionary containing a description of the structure of data in a database.

Data flow diagram: Diagram showing data or information flow within an information system.

Data integrity: Database characteristics relating to the consistency and accuracy of data.

Data maintenance: Maintaining data includes adding new data, deleting old data, and editing existing data.

Data manipulation subsystem: Provides tools to maintain and analyze data.

Data mining: Technique of searching data warehouses for related information and patterns.

Data processing system (DPS): Transaction processing system that keeps track of routine operations and records these events in a database. Also called transaction processing system (TPS).

Data redundancy: A common database problem in which data is duplicated and stored in different files.

Data security: Protection of software and data from unauthorized tampering or damage.

Data warehouse: Data collected from a variety of internal and external databases and stored in a database called a data warehouse. Data mining is then used to search these databases.

Data worker: Person involved with the distribution and communication of information, such as administrative assistants and clerks.

Database: A collection of related information, like employee names, addresses, and phone numbers. It is organized so that a computer program can quickly select the desired pieces of information and display them for you.

Database administrator (DBA): Uses database management software to determine the most efficient way to organize and access data.

Database file: File containing highly structured and organized data created by database management programs.

Database management system (DBMS): To organize, manage, and retrieve data. DBMS programs have five subsystems: DBMS engine, data definition, data manipulation, applications generation, and data administration. An example of a database management system is Microsoft Access. *See* Database manager.

Database manager: Software package used to set up, or structure, a database such as an inventory list of supplies. It also provides tools to edit, enter, and retrieve data from the database.

Database model: Defines rules and standards for all data in a database. There are five database models: hierarchical, network, relational, multidimensional, and object-oriented. For example, Access uses the relational data model.

DBMS engine: Provides a bridge between the logical view of data and the physical view of data.

Debugging: Programmer's word for testing and then eliminating errors in a program. Programming errors are of two types: syntax and logic errors.

Decision model: The decision model gives the decision support system its analytical capabilities. There are three types of models included in the decision model: tactical, operational, and strategic.

Decision support system (DSS): Flexible analysis tool that helps managers make decisions about unstructured problems, such as effects of events and trends outside the organization.

Demand report: A demand report is produced on request. An example is a report on the numbers and types of jobs held by women and minorities done at the request of the government.

Demodulation: Process performed by a modem in converting analog signals to digital signals.

Denial of service (DoS) attack: A variant virus in which websites are overwhelmed with data and users are unable to access the website. Unlike a worm that self-replicates, a DoS attack floods a computer or network with requests for information and data.

Density: Refers to how tightly the bits (electromagnetic charges) can be packed next to one another on a disk.

Desk checking: Process of checking out a computer program by studying a printout of the program line by line, looking for syntax and logic errors.

Desktop: (1) The screen that is displayed on the monitor when the computer starts up. All items and icons on the screen are considered to be on your desktop and are used to interact with the computer. (2) A system unit that typically contains the system's electronic components and selected secondary storage devices. Input and output devices, such as the mouse, keyboard, and monitor, are located outside the system unit.

Desktop computer: Computer small enough to fit on top of or along the side of a desk and yet too big to carry around.

Desktop operating system: *See* Stand-alone operating system.

Desktop publisher: One who creates and formats publication-ready material.

Desktop publishing program: Program that allows you to mix text and graphics to create publications of professional quality.

Device driver: Every device that is connected to the computer has a special program associated with it called a device driver that allows communication between the operating system and the device.

Diagnostic program: *See* Troubleshooting program.

Dial-up service: Antiquated method of connecting to the Internet using telephones and telephone modems, which has been replaced with higher-speed connection services.

Dialog box: Provides additional information and requests user input.

Dictionary attack: Uses software to try thousands of common words sequentially in an attempt to gain unauthorized access to a user's account.

Digital: Computers are digital machines because they can only understand 1s and 0s. It is either on or off. For example, a digital watch states the exact time on the face, whereas an analog watch has the second hand moving in constant motion as it tells the time.

Digital camera: Similar to a traditional camera except that images are recorded digitally in the camera's memory rather than on film.

Digital cash: Currency for Internet purchases. Buyers purchase digital cash from a third party (a bank that specializes in electronic currency) by transferring funds from their banks.

Digital Millennium Copyright Act: Law that makes it legal for a program owner to make only his or her own backup copies of a software program. However, it is illegal for those copies to be resold or given away.

Digital rights management (DRM): Encompasses various technologies that control access to electronic media and files.

Digital signal: Computers can only understand digital signals. Before processing can occur within the system unit, a conversion must occur from what we understand (analog) to what the system unit can electronically process (digital). *See* Analog signals.

Digital subscriber line (DSL): Provides high-speed connection using existing telephone lines.

Digital subscriber line (DSL) service: Service provided by telephone companies using existing telephone lines to provide high-speed connections.

Digital versatile disc (DVD): A type of optical disc similar to CD-ROMs except that more data can be packed into the same amount of space. *Also see* DVD (digital versatile disc).

Digital video disc: *See* DVD (digital versatile disc).

Digital wallet: Information to make online shopping more convenient. A digital wallet typically resides on a user's smartphone and contains an individual's mailing address, credit card, and other information typically required to make an online purchase.

Digital whiteboard: A specialized device with a large display connected to a computer or projector.

DIMM (dual in-line memory module): An expansion module used to add memory to the system board.

Direct approach: Approach for systems implementation whereby the old system is simply abandoned for the new system.

Directory server: A specialized server that manages resources such as user accounts for an entire network.

Disaster recovery plan: Plan used by large organizations describing ways to continue operations following a disaster until normal computer operations can be restored.

Disaster recovery specialist: Worker responsible for recovering systems and data after a disaster strikes an organization.

Disk caching: Method of improving hard-disk performance by anticipating data needs. Frequently used data is read from the hard disk into memory (cache). When needed, data is then accessed directly from memory, which has a much faster transfer rate than from the hard disk. Increases performance by as much as 30 percent.

Disk Cleanup: A Windows troubleshooting utility that eliminates nonessential files.

Display: Output device like a television screen that displays data processed by the computer.

Display screen: *See* Display.

Distributed database: Database that can be made accessible through a variety of communications networks, which allow portions of the database to be located in different places.

Document: Any kind of text material.

Document file: File created by a word processor to save documents such as letters, research papers, and memos.

Document scanner: Similar to a flatbed scanner except that it can quickly scan multipage documents. It automatically feeds one page of a document at a time through a scanning surface.

Documentation: Written descriptions and procedures about a program and how to use it. *See* Program documentation.

Domain name: The second part of the URL; it is the name of the server where the resource is located. For example, www.mtv.com.

Domain name server (DNS): Internet addressing method that assigns names and numbers to people and computers. Because the numeric IP addresses are difficult to remember, the DNS server was developed to automatically convert text-based addresses to numeric IP addresses.

Dot pitch: Distance between each pixel. The lower the dot pitch, the shorter the distance between pixels, and the higher the clarity of images produced.

Dots per inch (dpi): Printer resolution is measured in dpi. The higher the dpi, the better the quality of images produced.

Downlink: To receive data from a satellite.

Downloading: Process of transferring information from a remote computer to the computer one is using.

Drawing program: Program used to help create artwork for publications. *See* Illustration program.

Driver: *See* Device driver.

DS3: Provides support for very high speed, all-digital transmission for large corporations.

DSL: *See* Digital subscriber line.

Duplex printing: Allows automatic printing on both sides of a sheet of paper.

DVD (digital versatile disc or digital video disc): Similar to CD-ROMs except that more data can be packed into the same amount of space. DVD drives can store a typical capacity of 4.7 GB on one side.

DVD player: Also known as DVD-ROM drives. *See* DVD.

DVD-R (DVD recordable): A DVD with a write-once format that differs slightly from the format of DVD+R. Typically used to create permanent archives for large amounts of data and to record videos.

DVD+R (DVD recordable): A DVD with a write-once format that differs slightly from the format of DVD-R. Typically used to create permanent archives for large amounts of data and to record videos.

DVD-RAM (DVD random-access memory): A high-capacity, maximum-performance disc that allows the user to read the information, write over it, and erase the data if necessary. Used like a floppy disk to copy, delete files, and run programs. It has up to 8 times the storage capacity of a CD and also can be used to read CD and DVD formats.

DVD-ROM (DVD–read-only memory): Used to distribute full-length feature films with theater-quality video and sound. Also known as DVD players. Are read-only.

DVD-RW (DVD rewriteable): A type of reusable DVD disc that is more flexible than the DVD-RAM. DVD-RW is able to create and read CD discs along with creating and editing large-scale multimedia presentations.

DVD+RW (DVD rewriteable): Another DVD format to record and erase repeatedly. Able to create and read CD discs along with creating and editing large-scale multimedia presentations.

DVI (Digital Video Interface) port: A type of port that provides a connection to a digital monitor.

e

E-book: *See* E-book reader.

E-book reader: Handheld, book-sized device that displays text and graphics. Using content downloaded from the web or special cartridges, these devices are used to read newspapers, magazines, and books.

E-commerce: Buying and selling goods over the Internet.

E-ink: A black and white output from some e-book readers producing images that reflect light like ordinary paper.

E-learning: A web application that allows one to take educational courses online.

E-mail: Communicate with anyone in the world who has an Internet address or e-mail account with a system connected to the Internet. You can include a text message, graphics, photos, and file attachments.

E-mail client: A special program that communicates with the e-mail service provider and must be installed on the computer first.

E-reader: Dedicated mobile devices for storing and displaying e-books and other electronic media including electronic newspapers and magazines.

EBCDIC (Extended Binary Coded Decimal Interchange Code): Binary coding scheme that is a standard for minicomputers and mainframe computers.

Economic feasibility: Comparing the costs of a new system to the benefits it promises.

Electronic books: Traditional printed books in electronic format.

Electronic commerce (e-commerce): Buying and selling goods over the Internet.

Electronic mail: Transmission of electronic messages over the Internet. Also known as e-mail.

Electronic profile: Using publicly and privately available databases, information resellers create electronic profiles, which are highly detailed and personalized descriptions of individuals.

Embedded operating system: An operating system that is completely stored within the ROM (read-only memory) of the device that it is in; used for handheld computers and smaller devices like PDAs.

Employee-monitoring software: Programs that record virtually every activity on a computer system.

Encryption: Coding information so that only the user can read or otherwise use it.

Encryption key: A number used to gain access to encrypted information.

End user: Person who uses personal computers or has access to larger computers.

Enterprise storage system: Using mass storage devices, a strategy designed for organizations to promote efficient and safe use of data across the networks within their organizations.

Entity: In an object-oriented database, a person, place, thing, or event that is to be described.

Erasable optical disc: Optical disc on which the disk drive can write information and also erase and rewrite information. Also known as CD-RW or compact disc rewriteable.

Ergonomics: The study of human factors related to things people use.

Ethernet: Otherwise known as Ethernet bus or Ethernet LAN. The Ethernet bus is the pathway or arterial to which all nodes (PCs, file servers, print servers, web servers, etc.) are connected. All of this is connected to a local area network (LAN) or a wide area network (WAN). *See* Bus network.

Ethernet cable: Twisted-pair cable commonly used in networks and to connect a variety of components to the system unit.

Ethernet port: A high-speed networking port that allows multiple computers to be connected for sharing files or for high-speed Internet access.

Ethics: Standards of moral conduct.

Exception report: Report that calls attention to unusual events.

Executive information system (EIS): Sophisticated software that can draw together data from an organization's databases in meaningful patterns and highly summarized forms.

Executive support system (ESS): *See* Executive information system.

Expansion bus: Connects the CPU to slots on the system board. There are different types of expansion buses such as industry standard architecture (ISA), peripheral component interconnect (PCI), accelerated graphics port (AGP), universal serial bus (USB), and FireWire buses. *See* System bus.

Expansion card: Optional device that plugs into a slot inside the system unit to expand the computer's abilities. Ports on the system board allow cables to be connected from the expansion board to devices outside the system unit.

Expansion slots: Openings on a system board. Users can insert optional devices, known as expansion cards, into these slots, allowing users to expand their systems. *See* Expansion card.

Expert system: Computer program that provides advice to decision makers who would otherwise rely on human experts. It's a type of artificial intelligence that uses a database to provide assistance to users.

ExpressCard: Technology replacing the PC card to provide a direct connection to the system bus. *Also see* PC card slots.

External data: Data gathered from outside an organization. Examples are data provided by market research firms.

External hard drive: Uses the same technology as an internal hard disk but is used primarily to complement an internal hard disk by providing additional storage. They are typically connected to a USB or FireWire port on the system unit and are easily removed.

External Serial Advanced Technology Attachment (eSATA): A port that provides very high speed connections for external hard-disk drives, optical discs, and other large secondary storage devices.

Extranet: Private network that connects more than one organization.

f

Facebook: One of the best known social networking sites.

Facebook groups: Communities of individuals who share common interest on Facebook.

Facebook Pages: Often used by businesses and public figures to promote ideas, products, and services.

Facebook Profile: An individual's Facebook page, which may include photos, lists of personal interests, contact information, and other personal information.

Family Educational Rights and Privacy Act (FERPA): A federal law that restricts disclosure of educational records.

Fiber-optic cable: Special transmission cable made of glass tubes that are immune to electronic interference. Data is transmitted through fiber-optic cables in the form of pulses of light.

Fiber-optic service (FiOS): An Internet connection service that is not yet widely available. Current providers of FiOS include Google and Verizon with speeds faster than cable or DSL connections.

Field: Each column of information within a record is called a field. A field contains related information on a specific item like employee names within a company department.

Fifth-generation language (5GL): Computer language that incorporates the concept of artificial intelligence to allow direct human communication.

File: A collection of related records that can store data and programs. For example, the payroll file would include payroll information (records) for all of the employees (entities).

File compression: Process of reducing the storage requirements for a file.

File compression program: Utility program that reduces the size of files so they require less storage on the computer and can be sent more efficiently over the Internet. Examples of such programs are WinZip and Wizard.

File decompression: Process of expanding a compressed file.

File History: A utility program included with many versions of Windows that makes a copy of all files or selected files that have been saved onto a disk.

File server: Dedicated computer with large storage capacity providing users access to shared folders or fast storage and retrieval of information used in that business.

File transfer protocol (FTP): Internet service for uploading and downloading files.

Filter: (1) A filter blocks access to selected websites. (2) A filter will locate or display records from a table that fit a set of conditions or criteria when using programs like Excel.

Firewall: Security hardware and software. All communications into and out of an organization pass through a special security computer, called a proxy server, to protect all systems against external threats.

FireWire bus: Operates much like USB buses on the system board but at higher speeds.

FireWire port: Used to connect high-speed printers, and even video cameras, to system unit.

First-party cookie: A cookie that is generated and then read only by the website you are currently visiting.

Flash: An interactive animation program from Adobe that is usually full screen and highly dynamic, displaying moving text or complicated interactive features.

Flash drive: *See* USB drive.

Flash memory: RAM chips that retain data even when power is disrupted. Flash memory is an example of solid-state storage and is typically used to store digitized images and record MP3 files.

Flash memory card: A solid-state storage device widely used in notebook computers. Flash memory also is used in a variety of specialized input devices to capture and transfer data to desktop computers.

Flat-panel monitor: Or liquid crystal display (LCD) monitor. These monitors are much thinner than CRTs and can be used for desktop systems as well.

Flatbed scanner: An input device similar to a copying machine.

Folder: A named area on a disk that is used to store related subfolders and files.

Foreground: The current program when multitasking or running multiple programs at once.

Fourth-generation language (4GL): Task-oriented language designed to solve a specific problem and requiring little special training on the part of the end user.

Fragmented: Storage technique that breaks up large files and stores the parts wherever space is available.

Freedom of Information Act of 1970: Law giving citizens the right to examine data about them in federal government files, except for information restricted for national security reasons.

Friend: An individual on a list of contacts for an instant messaging server.

g

Galleries: Feature of Microsoft Office 2007, 2010, and 2013 that simplifies the process of making selections from a list of alternatives by replacing dialog boxes with visual presentations of results.

Game controller: A device that provides input to computer games.

Gamepad: An input device designed to be held by two hands and provide a wide array of inputs including motion, turning, stopping, and firing.

General ledger: Activity that produces income statements and balance sheets based on all transactions of a company.

General-purpose application: Application used for doing common tasks, such as browsers and word processors, spreadsheets, databases, management systems, and presentation graphics. Also known as productivity applications.

Generations (of programming languages): The five generations are machine languages, assembly languages, procedural languages, problem-oriented languages, and natural languages. *See* Levels.

Gesture control: The ability to control operations with finger movements, such as swiping, sliding, and pinching.

Gestures: A feature of Mac OS 10.7 that allows the use of fingers to run programs and to control the content of a display screen.

Global positioning system (GPS): Devices that use location information to determine the geographic location of your car, for example.

Gloves: Interactive sensory equipment that collects data from your hand movements.

Google+: *See* Google Plus.

Google Cloud Print: A Google service that supports cloud printing.

Google Plus: A combination of some of Google's previously existing services with some new services, many of which are similar to Facebook's services.

GPU (graphics processing unit): *See* Graphics coprocessor.

Gramm-Leach-Bliley Act: A law that protects personal financial information.

Graphical site map: Diagram of a website's overall design.

Graphical user interface (GUI): Special screen that allows software commands to be issued through the use of graphic symbols (icons) or pull-down menus.

Graphics card: Device that provides high-quality 3-D graphics and animation for games and simulations.

Graphics coprocessor: Designed to handle requirements related to displaying and manipulating 2-D and 3-D graphic images.

Grayscale: The most common black ink selection in which images are displayed using many shades of gray.

Grid chart: Chart that shows the relationship between input and output documents.

Group decision support system (GDSS): System used to support the collective work of a team addressing large problems.

Groups: In Microsoft Word, each tab is organized into groups that contain related items.

Guest operating system: Operating system that operates on virtual machines.

h

Hacker: Person who gains unauthorized access to a computer system for the fun and challenge of it.

Handwriting recognition software: Translates handwritten notes into a form that the system unit can process.

Hangouts: A service offered through Google Plus, for communicating with up to 10 people at a time.

Hard copy: Information presented on paper; also referred to as printer output.

Hard disk: Enclosed disk drive containing one or more metallic disks. Hard disks use magnetic charges to record data and have large storage capacities and fast retrieval times.

Hardware: Equipment that includes a keyboard, monitor, printer, the computer itself, and other devices that are controlled by software programming.

Head crash: When a read-write head makes contact with the hard disk's surface or particles on its surface, the disk surface becomes scratched and some or all data is destroyed.

Header: A typical e-mail has three elements: header, message, and signature. The header appears first and includes addresses, subject, and attachments.

Headgear: Interactive sensory equipment that collects data from embedded earphones and three-dimensional stereoscopic screens.

Headsets: Audio-output devices connected to a sound card in the system unit. The sound card is used to capture as well as play back recorded sound.

Health Insurance Portability and Accountability Act (HIPAA): A federal law that protects medical records.

Help: A feature in most application software providing options that typically include an index, a glossary, and a search feature to locate reference information about specific commands.

Hexadecimal system (hex): Uses 16 digits to represent binary numbers.

Hi def (high definition): The next generation of optical disc, with increased storage capacity. *See* BD (Blu-ray disc).

Hierarchical database: Database in which fields or records are structured in nodes. Organized in the shape of a pyramid, and each node is linked directly to the nodes beneath it. Also called one-to-many relationship.

Hierarchical network: *See* Tree network.

High Definition Multimedia Interface (HDMI): Port that provides high-definition video and audio, making it possible to use a computer as a video jukebox or an HD video recorder.

High-definition television (HDTV): All-digital television that delivers a much clearer and more detailed wide-screen picture.

Higher level: Programming languages that are closer to the language humans use.

History file: Created by the browser to store information on websites visited by your computer system.

Hits: The sites that a search engine returns after running a keyword search, ordered from most likely to least likely to contain the information requested.

Home network: LAN network for homes allowing different computers to share resources, including a common Internet connection.

Host: Also called a server or provider, is a large centralized computer.

Host operating system: Operating system that runs on the physical machine.

Hotspot: Wireless access points that provide Internet access and are often available in public places such as coffee shops, libraries, bookstores, colleges, and universities.

HTML: *See* Hypertext Markup Language.

HTML editor: *See* Web authoring program.

Hub: The center or central node for other nodes. This device can be a server or a connection point for cables from other nodes.

Human resources: The organizational department that focuses on the hiring, training, and promoting of people, as well as any number of human-centered activities within the organization.

Hyper-V: A program created by Microsoft used to create and run a virtual machine.

Hyperlink: Connection or link to other documents or web pages that contain related information.

Hypertext Markup Language (HTML): Programming language that creates document files used to display web pages.

Hypertext transfer protocol (http): A widely used protocol for web traffic.

Hypertext transfer protocol secure (https): A widely used protocol for web traffic and to protect the transfer of sensitive information.

i

Icons: Graphic objects on the desktop used to represent programs and other files.

Identity theft: The illegal assumption of someone's identity for the purpose of economic gain.

IF-THEN-ELSE structure: Logical selection structure whereby one of two paths is followed according to IF, THEN, and ELSE statements in a program. *See* Selection structure.

IFPS (interactive financial planning system): A 4GL language used for developing financial models.

Illusion of anonymity: The misconception that being selective about disclosing personal information on the Internet can prevent an invasion of personal privacy.

Illustration program: Also known as drawing programs; used to create digital illustrations and modify vector images and thus create line art, 3-D models, and virtual reality.

Image editor: An application for modifying bitmap images.

Image gallery: Libraries of electronic images.

Immersive experience: Allows the user to walk into a virtual reality room or view simulations on a virtual reality wall.

Income statement: A statement that shows a company's financial performance, income, expenses, and the difference between them for a specific time period.

Individual database: Collection of integrated records used mainly by just one person. Also called personal computer database.

Information: Data that has been processed by a computer system.

Information broker: *See* Information reseller.

Information reseller: Also known as information broker. It gathers personal data on people and sells it to direct marketers, fund-raisers, and others, usually for a fee.

Information system: Collection of hardware, software, people, data, and procedures that work together to provide information essential to running an organization.

Information systems manager: Oversees the work of programmers, computer specialists, systems analysts, and other computer professionals.

Information technology (IT): Computer and communication technologies, such as communication links to the Internet, that provide help and understanding to the end user.

Information utility: *See* Commercial database.

Information worker: Employee who creates, distributes, and communicates information.

Infrared: Uses infrared light waves to communicate over short distances. Sometimes referred to as line-of-sight communication because light waves can only travel in a straight line.

Inkjet printer: Printer that sprays small droplets of ink at high speed onto the surface of the paper, producing letter-quality images, and can print in color.

InPrivate Browsing: A privacy mode provided by Internet Explorer that eliminates history files as well as blocks most cookies.

Input: Any data or instructions used by a computer.

Input device: Piece of equipment that translates data into a form a computer can process. The most common input devices are the keyboard and the mouse.

Instant messaging (IM): A program allowing communication and collaboration for direct, "live" connections over the Internet between two or more people.

Integrated circuit: *See* Silicon chip.

Interactive whiteboard: *See* Digital whiteboard.

Internal data: Data from within an organization consisting principally of transactions from the transaction processing system.

Internal hard disk: Storage device consisting of one or more metallic platters sealed inside a container. Internal hard disks are installed inside the system cabinet of a personal computer. It stores the operating system and major applications like Word.

Internet: A huge computer network available to everyone with a personal computer and a means to connect to it. It is the actual physical network made up of wires, cables, and satellites as opposed to the web, which is the multimedia interface to resources available on the Internet.

Internet scam: Using the Internet, a fraudulent act or operation designed to trick individuals into spending their time and money for little or no return.

Internet security suite: Collection of utility programs designed to make using the Internet easier and safer.

Internet service provider (ISP): Provides access to the Internet.

Internet telephone: Low-cost alternative to long-distance telephone calls using electronic voice delivery.

Internet telephony: *See* Telephony.

Interpreter: Software that converts a procedural language one statement at a time into machine language just before the statement is executed. No object code is saved.

Intranet: Like the Internet, it typically provides e-mail, mailing lists, newsgroups, and FTP services, but it is accessible only to those within the organization. Organizations use intranets to provide information to their employees.

Intrusion detection system (IDS): Using sophisticated statistical techniques to analyze all incoming and outgoing network traffic, this system works with firewalls to protect an organization's network.

Inventory: Material or products that a company has in stock.

Inventory control system: A system that keeps records of the number of each kind of part or finished good in the warehouse.

iOS: Previously known as iPhone OS, mobile operating system developed for Apple's iPhone, iPod Touch, and iPad.

IP address (Internet Protocol address): The unique numeric address of a computer on the Internet that facilitates the delivery of e-mail.

IP telephony: *See* Telephony.

iPhone OS: *See* iOS.

IT security analyst: Person responsible for maintaining the security of a company's network, systems, and data. Employers look for candidates with a bachelor's or associate's degree in information systems or computer science and network experience.

j

JavaScript: A scripting language that adds basic interactivity to web pages.

Joystick: Popular input device for computer games. You control game actions by varying the pressure, speed, and direction of the joystick.

k

Key: Another term for encryption key.

Key field: The common field by which tables in a database are related to each other. This field uniquely identifies the record. For example, in university databases, a key field is the Social Security number. Also known as primary key.

Keyboard: Input device that looks like a typewriter keyboard but has additional keys.

Keystroke logger: Also known as computer monitoring software and sniffer programs. They can be loaded onto your computer without your knowledge.

Knowledge base: A system that uses a database containing specific facts, rules to relate these facts, and user input to formulate recommendations and decisions.

Knowledge-based systems: Programs duplicating human knowledge. A type of artificial intelligence that uses a database to provide assistance to users.

Knowledge work system (KWS): Specialized information system used to create information in a specific area of expertise.

Knowledge worker: Person involved in the creation of information, such as an engineer or a scientist.

l

Land: *See* Lands and pits.

Lands and pits: Flat and bumpy areas, respectively, that represent 1s and 0s on the optical disc surface to be read by a laser.

Language translator: Converts programming instructions into a machine language that can be processed by a computer.

Laptop: A small, portable system unit that contains electronic components, selected secondary storage devices, and input devices.

Laptop computer: Portable computer, also known as a notebook computer, weighing between 4 and 10 pounds.

Laptop keyboard: Almost all laptops have attached keyboards and screens.

Laser printer: Printer that creates dotlike images on a drum, using a laser beam light source.

Levels: Generations or levels of programming languages ranging from "low" to "high." *See* Generations (of programming languages).

Light-emitting diode (LED): A technology for flat-panel monitors that have a more advanced backlighting technology. They produce better-quality images, are slimmer, and are more environmentally friendly as they require less power and use fewer toxic chemicals to manufacture. Most new monitors are LED.

Link: A connection to related information.

LinkedIn: The premier business-oriented social networking site.

Linux: Type of UNIX operating system initially developed by Linus Torvalds, it is one of the most popular and powerful alternatives to the Windows operating system.

Liquid crystal display (LCD): A technology used for flat-panel monitors.

Local area network (LAN): Network consisting of computers and other devices that are physically near each other, such as within the same building.

Location: For browsers to connect to resources, locations or addresses must be specified. Also known as uniform resource locators or URLs.

Logic error: Error that occurs when a programmer has used an incorrect calculation or left out a programming procedure.

Logic structure: Programming statements or structures called sequence, selection, or loop that control the logical sequence in which computer program instructions are executed.

Logical operation: Comparing two pieces of data to see whether one is equal to (=), less than (<), or greater than (>) the other.

Logical view: Focuses on the meaning and content of the data. End users and computer professionals are concerned with this view as opposed to the physical view, with which only specialized computer professionals are concerned.

Loop structure: Logic structure in which a process may be repeated as long as a certain condition remains true. This structure is called a "loop" because the program loops around or repeats again and again.

Low bandwidth: *See* Voiceband.

Lower level: Programming language closer to the language the computer itself uses. The computer understands the 0s and 1s that make up bits and bytes.

LTE (Long Term Evolution): A wireless standard, comparable to WiMax.

m

Mac OS: Operating system designed for Macintosh computers.

Mac OS X: Macintosh operating system featuring a user interface called Aqua.

Machine language: Language in which data is represented in 1s and 0s. Most languages have to be translated into machine language for the computer to process the data. Either a compiler or an interpreter performs this translation.

Magnetic card reader: A card reader that reads encoded information from a magnetic strip on the back of a card.

Magnetic-ink character recognition (MICR): Direct-entry scanning devices used in banks. This technology is used to automatically read the numbers on the bottom of checks.

Mainboard: *See* Motherboard or System board.

Mainframe computer: This computer can process several million program instructions per second. Sizable organizations rely on these room-size systems to handle large programs and a great deal of data.

Maintenance programmer: Programmer who maintains software by updating programs to protect them from errors, improve usability, standardize, and adjust to organizational changes.

Malware: Short for malicious software.

MAN: *See* Metropolitan area network.

Management information system (MIS): Computer-based information system that produces standardized reports in a summarized and structured form. Generally used to support middle managers.

Many-to-many relationship: In a network database, each child node may have more than one parent node and vice versa.

Marketing: The organizational department that plans, prices, promotes, sells, and distributes an organization's goods and services.

Mass storage: Refers to the tremendous amount of secondary storage required by large organizations.

Mass storage devices: Devices such as file servers, RAID systems, tape libraries, optical jukeboxes, and more.

MaxiCode: A code widely used by the United Parcel Service (UPS) and others to automate the process of routing packages, tracking in-transit packages, and locating lost packages.

Media: Media are the actual physical material that holds the data, such as a hard disk, which is one of the important characteristics of secondary storage. Singular of media is medium.

Medium: *See* Media.

Medium band: Bandwidth of special leased lines, used mainly with minicomputers and mainframe computers.

Megabits per second (Mbps): The transfer rate of millions of bits per second.

Memory: Memory is contained on chips connected to the system board and is a holding area for data instructions and information (processed data waiting to be output to secondary storage). RAM, ROM, and CMOS are three types of memory chips.

Menu: List of commands.

Menu bar: Menus are displayed in a menu bar at the top of the screen.

Mesh network: A topology requiring each node to have more than one connection to the other nodes so that if a path between two nodes is disrupted, data can be automatically rerouted around the failure using another path.

Message: The content portion of e-mail correspondence.

Metropolitan area network (MAN): These networks are used as links between office buildings in a city.

Microblog: Publishes short sentences that only take a few seconds to write, rather than long stories or posts like a traditional blog.

Microprocessor: The central processing unit (CPU) of a personal computer controls and manipulates data to produce information. The microprocessor is contained on a single integrated circuit chip and is the brains of the system. Also known as a processor.

Microwave: Communication using high-frequency radio waves that travel in straight lines through the air.

Middle management: Middle-level managers deal with control and planning. They implement the long-term goals of the organization.

MIDI: *See* Musical instrument digital interface.

Midrange computer: Refrigerator-sized machines falling in between personal computers and mainframes in processing speed and data-storing capacity. Medium-sized companies or departments of large companies use midrange computers.

Mini DisplayPort (MiniDP or mDP): A port that an audiovisual device typically uses to connect large monitors. These ports are used with many Apple Macintosh computers.

Mini notebook: A type of very portable laptop. They are lighter and thinner and have a longer battery life than other laptops. Also known as ultrabooks or ultraportables.

Mini tablets: A type of tablet with a smaller screen.

Mistaken identity: When the electronic profile of one person is switched with another.

Mobile apps (applications): Add-on features for a variety of mobile devices, including smartphones, netbooks, and tablets.

Mobile browser: Special browsers designed to run on portable devices.

Mobile device: The smallest type of system unit, designed to fit into the palm of one's hand.

Mobile operating system: Embedded operating system that controls a smartphone.

Mobile OS: *See* Mobile operating system.

Modem: Short for modulator-demodulator. It is a communication device that translates the electronic signals from a computer into electronic signals that can travel over telephone lines.

Modulation: Process of converting digital signals to analog signals.

Module: *See* Program module.

Monitor: *See* Display.

Motherboard: Also called a system board; the communications medium for the entire system.

Motion-sensing device: An input device that controls games with user movements.

Mouse: Device that typically is moved across the desktop and directs the cursor on the display screen.

Mouse pointer: Typically in the shape of an arrow.

Multicore processor: A new type of chip that provides two or more separate and independent CPUs.

Multidimensional database: Data can be viewed as a cube having three or more sides consisting of cells. Each side of the cube is considered a dimension of the data; thus, complex relationships between data can be represented and efficiently analyzed. Sometimes called a data cube and designed for analyzing large groups of records.

Multifunctional devices (MFD): Devices that typically combine the capabilities of a scanner, printer, fax, and copying machine.

Multitasking: Operating system that allows a single user to run several application programs at the same time.

Multitouch screen: Can be touched with more than one finger, which allows for interactions such as rotating graphical objects on the screen with your hand or zooming in and out by pinching and stretching your fingers.

Musical instrument digital interface (MIDI): A standard that allows musical instruments to connect to the system using MIDI ports.

n

Network: The arrangement in which various communications channels are connected through two or more computers. The largest network in the world is the Internet.

Network adapter card: Connects the system unit to a cable that connects to other devices on the network.

Network administrator: Also known as network manager. Computer professional who ensures that existing information and communication systems are operating effectively and that new ones are implemented as needed. Also responsible for meeting security and privacy requirements.

Network architecture: Describes how networks are configured and how the resources are shared.

Network attached storage (NAS): Similar to a file server except simpler and less expensive. Widely used for home and small business storage needs.

Network database: Database with a hierarchical arrangement of nodes, except that each child node may have more than one parent node. Also called many-to-many relationship.

Network gateway: Connection by which a local area network may be linked to other local area networks or to larger networks.

Network interface card (NIC): Also known as a network adapter card. Used to connect a computer to one or more computers forming a communication network whereby users can share data, programs, and hardware.

Network operating system (NOS): Interactive software between applications and computers coordinating and directing activities between computers on a network. This operating system is located on one of the connected computers' hard disks, making that system the network server.

Network server: *See also* Network operating system. This computer coordinates all communication between the other computers. Popular network operating systems include NetWare and Windows NT Server.

Node: Any device connected to a network. For example, a node is a computer, printer, or data storage device and each device has its own address on the network. Also, within hierarchical databases, fields or records are structured in nodes.

Notebook: *See* Laptop and Laptop computer.

o

Object: An element, such as a text box, that can be added to a workbook and can be selected, sized, and moved. For example, if a chart (object) in an Excel workbook file (source file) is linked to a Word document (destination file), the chart appears in the Word document. In this manner, the object contains both data and instructions to manipulate the data.

Object code: Machine language code converted by a compiler from source code. Object code can be saved and run later.

Object-oriented database: A more flexible type of database that stores data as well as instructions to manipulate data and is able to handle unstructured data such as photographs, audio, and video. Object-oriented databases organize data using objects, classes, entities, attributes, and methods.

Object-oriented programming (OOP): Methodology in which a program is organized into self-contained, reusable modules called objects. Each object contains both the data and processing operations necessary to perform a task.

Object-oriented software development: Software development approach that focuses less on the tasks and more on defining the relationships between previously defined procedures or objects.

Objectives: In programming, it is necessary to make clear the problems you are trying to solve to create a functional program.

Office automation system (OAS): System designed primarily to support data workers. It focuses on managing documents, communicating, and scheduling.

Office software suites: *See* Productivity suites.

Office suites: *See* Productivity suites.

One-to-many relationship: In a hierarchical database, each entry has one parent node, and a parent may have several child nodes.

Online: Being connected to the Internet is described as being online.

Online identity: The information that people voluntarily post about themselves online.

Online office suite: Office suite stored online and available anywhere the Internet can be accessed.

Online processing: *See* Real-time processing.

Online storage: Provides users with storage space that can be accessed from a website.

Open source: A free and openly distributed software program intended to allow users to improve upon and further develop the program.

Operating system (OS): Software that interacts between application software and the computer, handling such details as running programs, storing and processing data, and coordinating all computer resources, including attached peripheral devices. It is the most important program on the computer. Windows 7, Windows 8, and Mac OS X are examples of operating systems.

Operational feasibility: Making sure the design of a new system will be able to function within the existing framework of an organization.

Operational model: A decision model that helps lower-level managers accomplish the organization's day-to-day activities, such as evaluating and maintaining quality control.

Operators: Operators handle correcting operational errors in any programs. To do that, they need documentation, which lets them understand the program, thus enabling them to fix any errors.

Optical carrier (OC): Provides support for very high speed, all-digital transmission for large corporations.

Optical-character recognition (OCR): Scanning device that uses special preprinted characters, such as those printed on utility bills, that can be read by a light source and changed into machine-readable code.

Optical disc: Storage device that can hold over 17 gigabytes of data, which is the equivalent of several million typewritten pages. Lasers are used to record and read data on the disc. The three basic types of optical discs are compact discs (CDs), digital versatile or video discs (DVDs), and Blu-ray discs (BDs).

Optical disc drive: A disc is read by an optical disc drive using a laser that projects a tiny beam of light. The amount of reflected light determines whether the area represents a 1 or a 0.

Optical-mark recognition (OMR): Device that senses the presence or absence of a mark, such as a pencil mark. As an example, an OMR device is used to score multiple-choice tests.

Optical mouse: A type of mouse that emits and senses light to detect mouse movement.

Optical scanner: Device that identifies images or text on a page and automatically converts it to electronic signals that can be stored in a computer to copy or reproduce.

Optimize Drives: A Windows utility that optimizes disk performance by eliminating unnecessary fragments and rearranging files.

Organization chart: Chart showing the levels of management and formal lines of authority in an organization.

Organizational cloud storage: High-speed Internet connection to a dedicated remote organizational Internet drive site.

OS X Mavericks: Mac operating system announced in 2013 that provided better power management and enhanced workflow options for multiple monitor setups.

OS X Mountain Lion: An OS for Mac that was released in 2012 and designed for desktops and laptops.

Output: Processed data or information.

Output device: Equipment that translates processed information from the central processing unit into a form that can be understood by humans. The most common output devices are monitors and printers.

p

Packet: Before a message is sent on the Internet, it is broken down into small parts called packets. Each packet is then sent separately over the Internet. At the receiving end, the packets are reassembled into the correct order.

Page layout program: *See* Desktop publishing program.

Parallel approach: Systems implementation in which old and new systems are operated side by side until the new one has shown it is reliable.

Parallel processing: Used by supercomputers to run large and complex programs.

Parent node: Node one level above the node being considered in a hierarchical database or network. Each entry has one parent node, although a parent may have several child nodes. Also called one-to-many relationship.

Password: Special sequence of numbers or letters that limits access to information, such as electronic mail.

Patches: Programming modifications or corrections.

Payroll: Activity concerned with calculating employee paychecks.

PC: *See* Personal computer.

PC card: A small, credit card–sized expansion card developed to meet the size constraints of notebook, tablet, and handheld computers.

PC card slot: Also known as Personal Computer Memory Card International Association (PCMCIA) card slot. Credit card–sized expansion cards developed for portable computers.

PCI Express (PCIe): New type of bus that is 30 times faster than PCI bus.

PCMCIA slot: *See* PC card slot.

Peer-to-peer (P2P) network: Network in which nodes can act as both servers and clients. For example, one personal computer can obtain files located on another personal computer and also can provide files to other personal computers.

People: End users who use computers to make themselves more productive.

Periodic report: Reports for a specific time period as to the health of the company or a particular department of the company.

Personal area network (PAN): A type of wireless network that works within a very small area—your immediate surroundings.

Personal computer: Small, low-cost computer designed for individual users. These include desktop computers, laptops, and mobile devices.

Personal computer database: *See* Individual database.

Personal laser printer: Inexpensive laser printer widely used by single users to produce black-and-white documents.

Phased approach: Systems implementation whereby a new system is implemented gradually over a period of time.

Phishing: An attempt to trick Internet users into thinking a fake but official-looking website or e-mail is legitimate.

Photo editor: *See* Image editor.

Physical security: Activity concerned with protecting hardware from possible human and natural disasters.

Physical view: This focuses on the actual format and location of the data. *See* Logical view.

Picture element: *See* Pixel.

Pilot approach: Systems implementation in which a new system is tried out in only one part of the organization. Later it is implemented throughout the rest of the organization.

Pit: *See* Lands and pits.

Pixel (picture element): Smallest unit on the screen that can be turned on and off or made different shades. Pixels are individual dots that form images on a monitor. The greater the resolution, the more pixels and the better the clarity.

Pixel pitch: The distance between each pixel on a monitor.

Plagiarism: Representation of some other person's work and ideas as your own without giving credit to the original source.

Plagiarist: Someone who engages in plagiarism.

Platform: The operating system. Application programs are designed to run with a specific platform. *See* Operating system.

Platform scanner: Handheld direct-entry device used to read special characters on price tags. Also known as wand reader.

Platter: Rigid metallic disk; multiple platters are stacked one on top of another within a hard disk drive.

Plotter: Special-purpose output device for producing bar charts, maps, architectural drawings, and three-dimensional illustrations.

Plug and Play: Set of hardware and software standards developed to create operating systems, processing units, expansion cards, and other devices that are able to configure themselves. When the computer starts up, it will search for the Plug and Play device and automatically configure it to the system.

Plug-in: Program that is automatically loaded and operates as part of a browser.

Podcast: An Internet-based medium for delivering music and movie files from the Internet to a computer.

Pointer: For a monitor, a pointer is typically displayed as an arrow and controlled by a mouse. For a database, a pointer is a connection between a parent node and a child node in a hierarchical database.

Pointers: Within a network database, pointers are additional connections between parent nodes and child nodes. Thus, a node may be reached through more than one path and can be traced down through different branches.

Pointing device: A device that provides an intuitive interface with the system unit by accepting pointing gestures and converting them into machine-readable input.

Port: Connecting socket on the outside of the system unit. Used to connect input and output devices to the system unit.

Portable language: Language that can be run on more than one type of computer.

Portable scanner: A handheld device that slides across an image to be scanned, making direct contact.

Power supply unit: Desktop computers have a power supply unit located within the system unit that plugs into a standard wall outlet, converting AC to DC, which becomes the power to drive all of the system unit components.

Preliminary investigation: First phase of the systems life cycle. It involves defining the problem, suggesting alternative systems, and preparing a short report.

Presentation file: A file created by presentation graphics programs to save presentation materials. For example, a file might contain audience handouts, speaker notes, and electronic slides.

Presentation graphics: Graphics used to combine a variety of visual objects to create attractive and interesting presentations.

Primary key: *See* Key field.

Primary storage: Holds data and program instructions for processing data. It also holds processed information before it is output. *See* Memory.

Printer: Device that produces printed paper output.

Privacy: Computer ethics issue concerning the collection and use of data about individuals.

Privacy mode: A browser feature that eliminates history files and blocks most cookies.

Private Browsing: A privacy mode provided by Safari. *See* Privacy mode.

Procedural language: Programming language designed to focus on procedures and how a program will accomplish a specific task. Also known as 3GL or third-generation language.

Procedures: Rules or guidelines to follow when using hardware, software, and data.

Processing rights: Refers to which people have access to what kind of data.

Processor: *See* Central processing unit.

Production: The organizational department that actually creates finished goods and services using raw materials and personnel.

Productivity suites: Also known as office suites; contain professional-grade application programs, including word processing, spreadsheets, and more. A good example is Microsoft Office.

Program: Instructions for the computer to follow to process data. *See* Software.

Program analysis: *See* Program specification.

Program coder: *See* Application generator.

Program definition: *See* Program specification.

Program design: Creating a solution using programming techniques, such as top-down program design, pseudocode, flowcharts, logic structures, object-oriented programming, and CASE tools.

Program documentation: Written description of the purpose and process of a program. Documentation is written within the program itself and in printed documents. Programmers will find themselves frustrated without adequate documentation, especially when it comes time to update or modify the program.

Program flowchart: Flowchart graphically presents a detailed sequence of steps needed to solve a programming problem.

Program maintenance: Activity of updating software to correct errors, improve usability, standardize, and adjust to organizational changes.

Program module: Each module is made up of logically related program statements. The program must pass in sequence from one module to the next until the computer has processed all modules.

Program specification: Programming step in which objectives, output, input, and processing requirements are determined.

Programmer: Computer professional who creates new software or revises existing software.

Programming: A program is a list of instructions a computer will follow to process data. Programming, also known as software development, is a six-step procedure for creating that list of instructions. The six steps are program specification, program design, program code (or coding), program test, program documentation, and program maintenance.

Programming language: A collection of symbols, words, and phrases that instruct a computer to perform a specific task.

Project manager: Software that enables users to plan, schedule, and control the people, resources, and costs needed to complete a project on time.

Property: Computer ethics issue relating to who owns data and rights to software.

Protocol: Rules for exchanging data between computers. The protocol http:// is the most common.

Prototyping: Building a model or prototype that can be modified before the actual system is installed.

Proxy server: Computer that acts as a gateway or checkpoint in an organization's firewall. *See* Firewall.

Pseudocode: An outline of the logic of the program to be written. It is the steps or the summary of the program before you actually write the program for the computer. Consequently, you can see beforehand what the program is to accomplish.

Purchase order: A form that shows the name of the company supplying the material or service and what is being purchased.

Purchasing: Buying of raw materials and services.

q

QR code: Graphics that typically appear as black and white boxes that automatically link mobile devices to a variety of different content including games, text, videos, and websites.

Query-by-example: A specific tool in database management that shows a blank record and lets you specify the information needed, like the fields and values of the topic you are looking to obtain.

Query language: Easy-to-use language and understandable to most users. It is used to search and generate reports from a database. An example is the language used on an airline reservation system.

Quick response code: *See* QR code.

r

RAID system: Several inexpensive hard-disk drives connected to improve performance and provide reliable storage.

RAM: *See* Random-access memory.

Random-access memory (RAM): Volatile, temporary storage that holds the program and data the CPU is presently processing. It is called temporary storage because its contents will be lost if electrical power to the computer is disrupted or the computer is turned off.

Rapid applications development (RAD): Involves the use of powerful development software and specialized teams as an alternative to the systems development life cycle approach. Time for development is shorter and quality of the completed systems development is better, although cost is greater.

Raster: *See* Bitmap image.

Read-only memory (ROM): Refers to chips that have programs built into them at the factory. The user cannot change the contents of such chips. The CPU can read or retrieve the programs on the chips but cannot write or change information. ROM stores programs that boot the computer, for example. Also called firmware.

Real-time processing: Or online processing. Occurs when data is processed at the same time a transaction occurs.

Record: Each row of information in a database is a record. Each record contains fields of data about some specific item, like employee name, address, phone, and so forth. A record represents a collection of attributes describing an entity.

Redundant arrays of inexpensive disks (RAID): Groups of inexpensive hard-disk drives related or grouped together using networks and special software. They improve performance by expanding external storage.

Relation: A table in a relational database in which data elements are stored in rows and columns.

Relational database: A widely used database structure in which data is organized into related tables. Each table is made up of rows called records and columns called fields. Each record contains fields of data about a specific item.

Repetition structure: *See* Loop structure.

Repetitive strain injury (RSI): Any injury that is caused by fast, repetitive work that can generate neck, wrist, hand, and arm pain.

Research: The organizational department that identifies, investigates, and develops new products and services.

Resolution: A measurement in pixels of a monitor's clarity. For a given monitor, the greater the resolution, the more pixels and the clearer the image.

RFID (radio-frequency identification) reader: A device used to read radio-frequency identification information.

RFID tags: Microchips that contain electronically stored information and can be embedded in items such as consumer products, driver's licenses, passports, etc.

Ribbon GUI: An interface that uses a system of ribbons, tabs, and galleries to make it easier to find and use all the features of an application.

Ribbons: Feature of Microsoft Office 2007, 2010, and 2013 that replaces menus and toolbars by organizing commonly used commands into a set of tabs.

Ring network: Network in which each device is connected to two other devices, forming a ring. There is no host computer, and messages are passed around the ring until they reach the correct destination.

Robot network: *See* Botnet.

Rogue Wi-Fi hotspot: Imitation hotspot intended to capture personal information.

ROM: *See* Read-only memory.

Router: A node that forwards or routes data packets from one network to their destination in another network.

S

Sales order processing: Activity that records the demands of customers for a company's products or services.

Satellite: This type of communication uses satellites orbiting about 22,000 miles above the earth as microwave relay stations.

Satellite connection services: Connection services that use satellites and the air to download or send data to users at a rate seven times faster than dial-up connections.

Scam: A fraudulent or deceptive act or operation designed to trick individuals into spending their time and money for little or no return.

Scanner: *See* Optical scanner.

Scanning devices: Convert scanned text and images into a form that the system unit can process.

Schema: *See* Data dictionary.

Search engine: Specialized programs assisting in locating information on the web and the Internet.

Search services: Organizations that maintain databases relating to information provided on the Internet and also provide search engines to locate information.

Secondary storage: Permanent storage used to preserve programs and data that can be retained after the computer is turned off. These devices include hard disks, magnetic tape, CDs, DVDs, and more.

Secondary storage device: These devices are used to save, backup, and transport files from one location or computer to another. *See* Secondary storage.

Sector: Section shaped like a pie wedge that divides the tracks on a disk.

Secure file transfer protocol (SFTP): *See* File transfer protocol.

Security: The protection of information, hardware, and software.

Security suites: A collection of utility programs designed to protect your privacy and security while you are on the web.

Selection structure: Logic structure that determines which of two paths will be followed when a program must make a decision. Also called IF-THEN-ELSE structures. IF something is true, THEN do option one, or ELSE do option two.

Semiconductor: Silicon chip through which electricity flows with some resistance.

Sequential structure: Logic structure in which one program statement follows another.

Server: A host computer with a connection to the Internet that stores document files used to display web pages. Depending on the resources shared, it may be called a file server, printer server, communication server, web server, or database server.

Shared laser printer: More expensive laser printer used by a group of users to produce black-and-white documents. These printers can produce over 30 pages a minute.

Signature: Provides additional information about a sender of an e-mail message, such as name, address, and telephone number.

Silicon chip: Tiny circuit board etched on a small square of sandlike material called silicon. Chips are mounted on carrier packages, which then plug into sockets on the system board.

Skype: An audio and video communication service that does not require any dedicated hardware.

Slot: Area on a system board that accepts expansion cards to expand a computer system's capabilities.

Smartphone: A type of cell phone that offers a variety of advanced functionality, including Internet and e-mail.

SMS (short messaging service): Texting or process of sending a short electronic message using a wireless network to another person.

Social networking: Using the Internet to connect individuals.

Socket: Sockets provide connection points on the system board for holding electronic parts.

Soft copy: Output from a monitor.

Software: Computer program consisting of step-by-step instructions, directing the computer on each task it will perform.

Software development: *See* Programming.

Software development life cycle (SDLC): A six-step procedure for software development.

Software engineer: Programming professional or programmer who analyzes users' needs and creates application software.

Software environment: Operating system, also known as software platform, consisting of a collection of programs to handle technical details depending on the type of operating system. For example, software designed to run on an Apple computer is compatible with the Mac OS environment.

Software piracy: Unauthorized copying of programs for personal gain.

Software platform: *See* Software environment.

Software suite: Individual application programs that are sold together as a group.

Software updates: Patches in which modifications to the software are typically more extensive and significant.

Solid-state drive (SSD): Designed to be connected inside a microcomputer system the same way an internal hard disk would be but contains solid-state memory instead of magnetic disks to store data.

Solid-state storage: A secondary storage device that has no moving parts. Data is stored and retrieved electronically directly from these devices, much as they would be from conventional computer memory.

Sort: Tool that rearranges a table's records numerically or alphabetically according to a selected field.

Sound card: Device that accepts audio input from a microphone and converts it into a form that can be processed by the computer. Also converts internal electronic signals to audio signals so they can be heard from external speakers.

Source code: When a programmer originally writes the code for a program in a particular language. This is called source code until it is translated by a compiler for the computer to execute the program. It then becomes object code.

Spam: Unwelcome and unsolicited e-mail that can carry attached viruses.

Spam blocker: Also referred to as spam filter. Software that uses a variety of different approaches to identify and eliminate spam or junk mail.

Spam filter: *See* Spam blocker.

Sparks: A Google Plus service that automatically provides news on selected topics of interest and facilitates sharing this information with others to spark further discussion.

Speakers: Audio-output devices connected to a sound card in the system unit. The sound card is used to capture as well as play back recorded sound.

Specialized applications: Programs that are narrowly focused on specific disciplines and occupations. Some of the best known are multimedia, web authoring, graphics, virtual reality, and artificial intelligence.

Specialized search engine: Search engine that focuses on subject-specific websites.

Specialized suite: Programs that focus on specialized applications such as graphics or financial planning.

Spider: Special program that continually looks for new information and updates a search server's databases.

Spreadsheet: Computer-produced spreadsheet based on the traditional accounting worksheet that has rows and columns used to present and analyze data.

Spy removal programs: Programs such as Spybot and Spysweeper, designed to detect web bugs and monitor software.

Spyware: Wide range of programs designed to secretly record and report an individual's activities on the Internet.

Stand-alone operating system: Also called desktop operating system; a type of operating system that controls a single desktop or notebook computer.

Star network: Network of computers or peripheral devices linked to a central computer through which all communications pass. Control is maintained by polling. The configuration of the computers looks like a star surrounding and connected to the central computer in the middle.

Start screen: Offered in Windows 8 consisting of tiles to link to applications.

Stock photograph: Photographs of a variety of subject material from professional models to natural landscapes.

Storage area network (SAN): An architecture that links remote computer storage devices such as enterprise storage systems to computers so that the devices are available as locally attached drives.

Storage device: Hardware that reads data and programs from storage media. Most also write to storage media.

Strategic model: A decision model that assists top managers in long-range planning, such as stating company objectives or planning plant locations.

Strategy: A way of coordinating the sharing of information and resources. The most common network strategies are terminal, peer-to-peer, and client/server networks.

Streaming: *See* Webcast.

Structured program: Program that uses logic structures according to the program design and the language in which you have chosen to write the program. Each language follows techniques like pseudocode, flowcharts, and logic structures.

Structured programming techniques: Techniques consisting of top-down program design, pseudocode, flowcharts, and logic structures.

Structured query language (SQL): A program control language used to create sophisticated database applications for requesting information from a database.

Stylus: Penlike device used with tablets and PDAs that uses pressure to draw images on a screen. A stylus interacts with the computer through handwriting recognition software.

Subject: Located in the header of an e-mail message; a one-line description used to present the topic of the message.

Supercomputer: Fastest calculating device ever invented, processing billions of program instructions per second. Used by very large organizations like NASA.

Supervisor: Manager responsible for managing and monitoring workers. Supervisors have responsibility for operational matters.

Switch: The center or central node for other nodes. This device coordinates the flow of data by sending messages directly between sender and receiver nodes.

Syntax error: Violation of the rules of a language in which the computer program is written. For example, leaving out a semicolon would stop the entire program from working because it is not the exact form the computer expects for that language.

System: Collection of activities and elements designed to accomplish a goal.

System board: Flat board that usually contains the CPU and memory chips connecting all system components to one another.

System bus: There are two categories of buses. One is the system bus that connects the CPU to the system board. The other is the expansion bus that connects the CPU to slots on the system board.

System chassis: *See* System unit.

System flowchart: A flowchart that shows the flow of input data to processing and finally to output, or distribution of information.

System software: "Background" software that enables the application software to interact with the computer. System software consists of the operating system, utilities, device drivers, and language translators. It works with application software to handle the majority of technical details.

System unit: Part of a personal computer that contains the CPU. Also known as the system cabinet or chassis, it is the container that houses most of the electronic components that make up the computer system.

Systems analysis: This second phase of the systems life cycle determines the requirements for a new system. Data is collected about the present system and analyzed, and new requirements are determined.

Systems analysis and design: Six phases of problem-solving procedures for examining information systems and improving them.

Systems analysis report: Report prepared for higher management describing the current information system, the requirements for a new system, and a possible development schedule.

Systems analyst: Plans and designs information systems.

Systems audit: A systems audit compares the performance of a new system to the original design specifications to determine if the new procedures are actually improving productivity.

Systems design: Phase three of the systems life cycle, consisting of designing alternative systems, selecting the best system, and writing a systems design report.

Systems design report: Report prepared for higher management describing alternative designs, presenting costs versus benefits, and outlining the effects of alternative designs on the organization.

Systems development: Phase four of the systems life cycle, consisting of developing software, acquiring hardware, and testing the new system.

Systems implementation: Phase five of the systems life cycle is converting the old system to the new one and training people to use the new system. Also known as conversion.

Systems life cycle: The six phases of systems analysis and design are called the systems life cycle. The phases are preliminary investigation, systems analysis, systems design, systems development, systems implementation, and systems maintenance.

Systems maintenance: Phase six of the systems life cycle consisting of a systems audit and periodic evaluation.

t

T1: High-speed lines that support all digital communications, provide very high capacity, and are very expensive.

T3: Copper lines combined to form higher-capacity options.

Tab: Used to divide the ribbon into major activity areas, with each tab being organized into groups that contain related items.

Table (in database): The list of records in a database. Tables make up the basic structure of a database. Their columns display field data and their rows display records. *See* Field and Record.

Tablet: A type of personal computer that contains a thin system unit, most of which is the monitor. The best-known tablets are Apple's iPad, Motorola's Xoom, and HP's Slate.

Tablet computer: *See* Tablet.

Tactical model: A decision model that assists middle-level managers to control the work of the organization, such as financial planning and sales promotion planning.

Task-oriented language: Programming language that is nonprocedural and focuses on specifying what the program is to accomplish. Also known as 4GL or very high level language.

Technical feasibility: Making sure hardware, software, and training will be available to facilitate the design of a new system.

Technical writer: Prepares instruction manuals, technical reports, and other scientific or technical documents.

Telephone line: A transmission medium for both voice and data.

Telephone modem: Used to connect a computer directly to a telephone line.

Telephony: Communication that uses the Internet rather than traditional communication lines to connect two or more people via telephone.

Temporary Internet file: File that has web page content and instructions for displaying this content.

Text messaging (texting): The process of sending a short electronic message typically less than 160 characters using a wireless network to another person who views the message on a mobile device, such as a smartphone.

Thermal printer: Printer that uses heat elements to produce images on heat-sensitive paper.

Third-generation language (3GL): *See* Procedural language.

Third-party cookie: A cookie generated by an advertising company that is affiliated with the website you are currently visiting. Often also referred to as a tracking cookie.

Thumb keyboard: Small thumb-operated keyboard for smartphones and other portable devices. Designed primarily for texting and connecting to the web.

Thunderbolt: A specialty port for high-speed connections to up to seven separate devices connected one to another.

Tile: Part of the Windows 8 start screen that displays active content.

Toggle key: These keys turn a feature on or off, like the Caps Lock key.

Toolbar: Bar located typically below the menu bar containing icons or graphical representations for commonly used commands.

Top-down analysis method: Method used to identify top-level components of a system, then break these components down into smaller parts for analysis.

Top-down program design: Used to identify the program's processing steps, called program modules. The program must pass in sequence from one module to the next until the computer has processed all modules.

Top-level domain (TLD): Last part of an Internet address; identifies the geographic description or organizational identification. For example, using www.aol.com, the .com is the top-level domain code and indicates it is a commercial site. *Also see* Domain name.

Top management: Top-level managers are concerned with long-range (strategic) planning. They supervise middle management.

Topology: The configuration of a network. The five principal network topologies are *ring, bus, star, tree,* and *mesh.*

Touch pad: Used to control the pointer by moving and tapping your finger on the surface of a pad.

Touch screen: Monitor screen allowing actions or commands to be entered by the touch of a finger.

Tower computer: A desktop system unit placed vertically.

Tower unit: *See* Tower computer.

Track: Closed, concentric ring on a disk on which data is recorded. Each track is divided into sections called sectors.

Tracking cookies: *See* Third-party cookie.

Traditional keyboard: Full-sized, rigid, rectangular keyboard that includes function, navigational, and numeric keys.

Transaction processing system (TPS): System that records day-to-day transactions, such as customer orders, bills, inventory levels, and production output. The TPS tracks operations and creates databases.

Transfer rate: Or transfer speed, is the speed at which modems transmit data, typically measured in bits per second (bps).

Transmission control protocol/Internet protocol (TCP/IP): TCP/IP is the standard protocol for the Internet. The essential features of this protocol involve (1) identifying sending and receiving devices and (2) reformatting information for transmission across the Internet.

Tree network: Also known as a hierarchical network. A topology in which each device is connected to a central node, either directly or through one or more other devices. The central node is then connected to two or more subordinate nodes that in turn are connected to other subordinate nodes, and so forth, forming a treelike structure.

Trojan horse: Program that is not a virus but is a carrier of virus(es). The most common Trojan horses appear as free computer games, screen savers, or antivirus programs. Once downloaded they locate and disable existing virus protection and then deposit the virus.

Troubleshooting program: A utility program that recognizes and corrects computer-related problems before they become serious. Also called diagnostic program.

Twisted-pair cable: Cable consisting of pairs of copper wire that are twisted together.

Twitter: The most popular microblogging site that enables you to add new content from your browser, instant messaging application, or even a mobile phone.

U

Ultrabook: Very portable laptops that are lighter and thinner with a longer battery life than other laptops.

Ultraportable: See ultrabooks.

Unicode: A 16-bit code designed to support international languages, like Chinese and Japanese.

Uniform resource locator (URL): For browsers to connect you to resources on the web, the location or address of the resources must be specified. These addresses are called URLs.

Universal Product Code (UPC): A bar code system that identifies the product to the computer, which has a description and the latest price for the product.

Universal serial bus (USB): Combines with a PCI bus on the system board to support several external devices without inserting cards for each device. USB buses are used to support high-speed scanners, printers, and video-capturing devices.

Universal serial bus (USB) port: They have replaced serial and parallel ports. They are faster, and one USB port can be used to connect several devices to the system unit.

UNIX: An operating system originally developed for mid-range computers. It is now important because it can run on many of the more powerful personal computers.

Uplink: To send data to a satellite.

Uploading: Process of transferring information from the computer the user is operating to a remote computer.

USB drive: The size of a key chain, these hard drives connect to a computer's USB port enabling a transfer of files.

User: Any individual who uses a computer. *See* End user.

User interface: Means by which users interact with application programs and hardware. A window is displayed with information for the user to enter or choose, and that is how users communicate with the program.

Utility: Performs specific tasks related to managing computer resources or files. Norton Utility for virus control and system maintenance is a good example of a utility. Also known as service programs.

Utility suite: A program that combines several utilities in one package to improve system performance.

V

Vector illustration: *See* Vector image.

Vector image: Graphics file made up of a collection of objects such as lines, rectangles, and ovals. Vector images are more flexible than bitmaps because they are defined by mathematical equations so they can be stretched and resized. Illustration programs create and manipulate vector graphics. Also known as vector illustrations.

Very high level languages: Task-oriented languages that require little special training on the part of the user.

VGA (Video Graphic Adapter) port: A type of port that provides a connection to an analog monitor.

Videoconferencing system: Computer system that allows people located at various geographic locations to have in-person meetings.

Virtual keyboard: Displays an image of a keyboard on a touch-screen device. The screen functions as the actual input device, which is why the keyboard is considered virtual.

Virtual machine: A software implementation of a computer that executes programs like a physical computer.

Virtual memory: Feature of an operating system that increases the amount of memory available to run programs. With large programs, parts are stored on a secondary device like your hard disk. Then each part is read in RAM only when needed.

Virtual private network (VPN): Creates a secure private connection between a remote user and an organization's internal network. Special VPN protocols create the equivalent of a dedicated line between a user's home or laptop computer and a company server.

Virtual reality (VR): Interactive sensory equipment (headgear and gloves) allowing users to experience alternative realities generated in 3-D by a computer, thus imitating the physical world.

Virtualization: A process that allows a single physical computer to support multiple operating systems that operate independently.

Virtualization software: Software that creates virtual machines.

Virus: Hidden instructions that migrate through networks and operating systems and become embedded in different programs. They may be designed to destroy data or simply to display messages.

Voice over IP (VoIP): Transmission of telephone calls over networks. *See also* Telephony.

Voice recognition system: Using a microphone, sound card, and specialty software, the user can operate a computer and create documents using voice commands.

Voiceband: Bandwidth of a standard telephone line. Also known as low bandwidth.

VR: *See* Virtual reality.

W

WAN: *See* Wide area network.

Wand reader: Special-purpose handheld device used to read OCR characters.

Warm boot: Restarting your computer while the computer is already on and the power is not turned off.

Web: Introduced in 1992, and prior to the web the Internet was all text. The web made it possible to provide a multimedia interface that includes graphics, animations, sound, and video.

Web 1.0: The first generation of the web, which focused on linking existing information.

Web 2.0: The second generation of the web, which evolved to support more dynamic content creation and social interaction.

Web 3.0: The third generation of the web, which focuses on computer-generated information requiring less human interaction to locate and to integrate information.

Web auction: Similar to traditional auctions except that all transactions occur over the web; buyers and sellers seldom meet face to face.

Web authoring: Creating a website.

Web authoring program: Word processing program for generating web pages. Also called HTML editor or web page editor. Widely used web authoring programs include Adobe Dreamweaver and Microsoft FrontPage.

Web-based e-mail system: An e-mail system that does not require an e-mail program to be installed on your computer.

Web-based file transfer services: A type of file transfer service that uses a web browser to upload and download files, allowing you to copy files to and from your computer across the Internet.

Web bug: Program hidden in the HTML code for a web page or e-mail message as a graphical image. Web bugs can migrate whenever a user visits a website containing a web bug or opens infected e-mail. They collect information on the users and report back to a predefined server.

Web log: A type of personal website where articles are regularly posted.

Web page: Browsers interpret HTML documents to display web pages.

Web page editor: *See* Web authoring program.

Web suffix: Identifies type of organization in a URL.

Web utilities: Specialized utility programs making the Internet and the web easier and safer. Some examples are plug-ins that operate as part of a browser and filters that block access and monitor use of selected websites.

Webcam: Specialized digital video camera for capturing images and broadcasting to the Internet.

Webcast: An Internet delivery medium that uses streaming technology, in which audio and video files are continuously downloaded to a computer while the user is listening to and/or viewing the file content.

Webmail: E-mail that uses a webmail client.

Webmail client: A special program that runs on an e-mail provider's computer that supports webmail.

Webmaster: Develops and maintains websites and web resources.

Wheel button: Some mice have a wheel button that can be rotated to scroll through information displayed on the monitor.

Wide area network (WAN): Countrywide and worldwide networks that use microwave relays and satellites to reach users over long distances.

Wi-Fi (wireless fidelity): Wireless standard also known as 802.11, used to connect computers to each other and to the Internet.

Wiki: A website that allows people to fill in missing information or correct inaccuracies on it by directly editing the pages.

Wikipedia: An online encyclopedia, written and edited by anyone who wants to contribute.

WiMax (Worldwide Interoperability for Microwave Access): Technology that extends Wi-Fi networks to operate over greater distances.

Window: A rectangular area containing a document or message.

Windows: An operating environment extending the capability of DOS.

Windows 7: OS from 2009 that has a traditional user interface similar to previous versions of Windows. It provides enhanced features including improved handwriting recognition and advanced searching capabilities for finding files and other content on your computer.

Windows 8: OS from 2012 that is designed to better integrate Microsoft's desktop OS with its mobile OS. It provides support for gestures, cloud integration, and apps.

Windows Phone 8: Introduced in 2012 by Microsoft to support a variety of mobile devices including smartphones. It

has the ability to run many powerful programs designed for desktop and laptop computers.

Windows RT: A version of Windows 8 designed to run with tablets using a particular microprocessor from ARM.

Windows Update: A utility provided in the Windows platform that allows you to update the device drivers on your computer.

Wireless access point: Or base station. The receiver interprets incoming radio frequencies from a wireless LAN and routes communications to the appropriate devices, which could be separate computers, a shared printer, or a modem.

Wireless LAN (WLAN): Uses radio frequencies to connect computers and other devices. All communications pass through the network's centrally located wireless receiver or base station and are routed to the appropriate devices.

Wireless modem: Typically a small plug-in USB or ExpressCard device that provides very portable high-speed connectivity from virtually anywhere.

Wireless mouse: *See* Cordless mouse.

Wireless network card: Allows computers to be connected without cables.

Wireless network encryption: Restricts access to authorized users on wireless networks.

Wireless revolution: A revolution that is expected to dramatically affect the way we communicate and use computer technology.

Wireless wide area network (WWAN) modem: *See* Wireless modem.

Word: The number of bits (such as 16, 32, or 64) that can be accessed at one time by the CPU.

Word processor: The computer and the program allow you to create, edit, save, and print documents composed of text.

Worksheet file: Created by electronic spreadsheets to analyze things like budgets and to predict sales.

Worm: Virus that doesn't attach itself to programs and databases but fills a computer system with self-replicating information, clogging the system so that its operations are slowed or stopped.

WPA2 (Wi-Fi Protected Access): A secure encryption protocol.

WYSIWYG (what you see is what you get) editors: Web authoring programs that build a page without requiring direct interaction with the HTML code and then preview the page described by the HTML code.

Z

Zombie: A computer infected by a virus, worm, or Trojan horse that allows it to be remotely controlled for malicious purposes.

Photo Credits

Chapter 1

Opener: © Norbert Suto/age fotostock RF; page 3, 17: Ingram Publishing RF; p. 4, 16, 20: Inti St. Clair/Taxi/Getty Images; figure 1-1a, p. 18 (left): Clerkenwell/Getty Images RF; 1-1b, 1-1f, 1-5, p. 19: Used with permission from Microsoft; 1-1d: Chad Baker/Getty Images RF; 1-1e, 1-9, p. 19 (right): Courtesy of Dell Inc.; 1-2, p. 18 (right): Patrick Heagney/Getty Images RF; p. 10: Copyright © AVG Technologies UK Limited. Used with permission; 1-8: Courtesy of Lawrence Livermore National Laboratory; 1-10: Courtesy of Hewlett-Packard; 1-11: Oleksiy Maksymenko/Getty Images; 1-12: Courtesy of Apple Inc.; 1-13, 1-14: © Willis Technology; 1-16a: Copyright © 2013 Research In Motion Limited; 1-16b: Courtesy of Samsung USA; 1-16c-d: © IanDagnall Computing/Alamy.

Chapter 2

Opener: liangpv/iStock Vectors/Getty Images RF; page 27, 49: Steve Jurvetson/Flickr/CC2.0; p. 28, 53: © Photosindia/Alamy; figures 2-1, 2-14, 2-25, p. 50: Google and the Google logo are registered trademarks of Google Inc., used with permission; p. 30 (top): Reproduced by permission of Netflix, Inc. Copyright © 2010 Netflix, Inc. All rights reserved; p. 30 (bottom): Copyright © Hulu. Used with permission; p. 31 (top): The NBA and individual member team identifications reproduced herein are used with permission from NBA Properties, Inc. © 2014 NBA Properties, Inc. All rights reserved; p. 31 (bottom): Copyright © Roku. Used with permission; 2-5: © Allison Rocks! Photography; 2-8: Copyright © 2012 ContentWatch, Inc.; 2-11: Copyright © 2012 McAfee, Inc. Used with permission.

Chapter 3

Opener: © Blend Images/Corbis; page 59, 78: Image Source/Getty Images RF; p. 60, 76, 81 (bottom): Comstock Images/Getty Images RF; figures 3-1, 3-2, 3-19: Used with permission from Microsoft; 3-11, 3-15: Copyright © 2014 Adobe Systems Incorporated. All rights reserved; p. 77: Google and the Google logo are registered trademarks of Google Inc., used with permission.

Chapter 4

Opener: © Sean Gladwell/Alamy RF; page 87, 104: © Vince Clements/Alamy RF; p. 88, 103: Thomas Barwick/Getty Images RF; figure 4-1a: Clerkenwell/Getty Images RF; 4-1b, 4-6, 4-7, 4-10, 4-11, 4-12, 4-14, 4-16, p. 105 (top), p. 107: Used with permission from Microsoft; 4-1c, 4-4: Courtesy of Dell Inc.; 4-3: © pumkinpie/Alamy; 4-5, p. 106: © Stanca Sanda/Alamy; 4-15: Copyright © Symantec Corporation.

Chapter 5

Opener: Patrick Koslo/Brand X Pictures/Getty Images RF; page 113, 129: Cusp/SuperStock; p. 114, 128: © Jetta Productions/Dana Neely/Blend Images/Corbis RF; figure 5-1: Courtesy of Dell Inc.; 5-2, 5-3, 5-4, p. 130 (left): Courtesy of Apple Inc.; 5-5a, 5-6a-b, 5-8, 5-11, 5-14, 5-15, 5-16, 5-18, 5-19, 5-20, 5-21, 5-22, p. 130 (right, bottom), 131, 132 (both): © Willis Technology; 5-5b: © Tim Jones/Alamy; 5-5c: Miro Djuric/iFixit; 5-5d: Reproduced with permission Bill Detweiler/TechRepublic; 5-7: Lucidio Studio Inc/Getty Images RF; 5-17: Courtesy of USB-IF; p. 125 (top): Courtesy of AVerMedia; p. 125 (bottom): Used with permission from Microsoft.

Chapter 6

Opener: Colin Anderson/Getty Images RF; page 139, 160: Colin Anderson/Photographer's Choice/Getty Images; p. 140, 159: Buero Monaco/The Image Bank/Getty Images; figure 6-1: © Willis Technology; 6-2a, p. 161 (left): Nick Koudis/Getty Images RF; 6-2b: Justin Sullivan/Getty Images; 6-2c, 6-18: Bloomberg via Getty Images; 6-3: © Stock Connection/SuperStock RF; 6-4: LAMB/Alamy RF; 6-5, p. 161 (right): Ferran Traite Soler/Getty Images RF; 6-6a: © 2013 Logitech, Inc. All rights reserved; 6-6b: © 2013 www.mayflash.com. All rights reserved; 6-6c: Used with permission from Microsoft; 6-6d: Evan-amos/Public Domain; 6-7: Jose Luis Pelaez, Inc/Blend Images/Getty Images RF; 6-8: Courtesy of Ricoh Electronics, Inc. - USA; 6-9, p. 162 (left): © Jochen Tack/Alamy; 6-10: PAUL J. RICHARDS/AFP/Getty Images/Newscom; 6-11: Junior Gonzales/Getty Images RF; 6-12, 6-22, p. 163 (right): Courtesy of Canon-Europe; 6-13: JGI/Blend Images/Getty Images RF; 6-14: Used by permission of Sony Electronics Inc.; 6-15: © Maria Gritsai/Alamy RF; 6-17, p. 163 (left): Courtesy of Samsung USA; p. 150 (both): Kindle, Kindle Fire, Amazon, and the Amazon Kindle logo are trademarks of Amazon.com, Inc. or its affiliates; 6-19: Gerald Martineau/The Washington Post/Getty Images; 6-20: Courtesy of LG Electronics, Inc.; 6-23: Courtesy of Konica Minolta Holdings, Inc.; 6-24: MakerBot®; 6-25, p. 164 (left): 2013 Somic Industrial Co., Ltd. All rights reserved; 6-26: Courtesy of Royal Philips; p. 155, 156: Copyright © Skype/Microsoft. Used with permission; 6-27: Chris Salvo/Getty Images; 6-29, p. 164 (right): Courtesy of Fellowes; p. 162 (right): Travelpix Ltd/Photographer's Choice/Getty Images.

Chapter 7

Opener: © Sanford/Agliolo/Corbis; page 171, 185: Vladimir Pcholkin/age fotostock/Getty Images; p. 172, 184: ColorBlind Images/Getty Images RF; figure 7-1, p. 186: Nick Koudis/Photodisc/Getty Images RF; 7-5:

©2013 Seagate Technology LLC; 7-6, p. 187 (left): Courtesy of CalDigit, Inc.; 7-8, p. 187 (right): PhotoDisc/Getty Images RF; 7-9: Tetra Images/Corbis RF; 7-11: MacFormat Magazine/Contributor/Getty Images; 7-12, p. 188 (top): David Kilpatrick/Alamy; 7-13, p. 179: Courtesy of Kingston Technology Company, Inc.; 7-14: Copyright © Google, Inc. Used with permission.

Chapter 8

Opener: © Coston Stock/Alamy; page 195, 214: Agliolo M/Photo Researchers/Getty Images; p. 196, 213: Thomas Northcut/Digital Vision/Getty Images RF; figure 8-1, p. 215 (left): Fuse/Getty Images RF; 8-3: © Spectral/Alamy RF; 8-4, 8-5, 8-11a-d, p. 216 (all): © Willis Technology; 8-7, p. 215 (right): Stuart Gregory/Photodisc/Getty Images RF; 8-8: © Oleksiy Maksymenko/Alamy; p. 203 (all): © 2013 AT&T Intellectual Property. All rights reserved; 8-15: Courtesy of Shenzhen Ogemray Technology Co., Ltd.

Chapter 9

Opener: © Science Photo Library/Alamy RF; page 223, 244: Chad Baker/Ryan McVay/Getty Images RF; p. 224, 243: Peter M. Fisher/Corbis; figure 9-1: Copyright © Spokeo People Search. Used with permission; 9-2: Copyright © Google, Inc. Used with permission; 9-3, 9-4, 9-5, p. 239: Used with permission from Microsoft; 9-6: Copyright

© Lavasoft. All rights reserved; 9-8: Copyright © Symantec Corporation; 9-11a: Siemens press picture; 9-11b, p. 246: Varie/Alt/Corbis; 9-12: Copyright © Mozilla. Used with permission; p. 239: Copyright © Carbonite. Used with permission; 9-16: Courtesy of www.turnitin.com.

Appendix

Page 252 (top-left, top-right), 1951 (left), 1953, 1959 (top), 1964 (top and bottom), 1981: IBM Corporate Archives; p. 252 (bottom-left), 1952, 1958, 1959 (bottom), 1965, 1970, 1975, 1989: Courtesy of the Computer History Museum; p. 252 (bottom-right): John Foxx/Stockbyte/Getty Images RF; 1951 (right): © Bettman/Corbis; 1977, 1984, 1992, 2001: Courtesy of Apple Inc.; 1980, 1995 (bottom), 1997, 1998, 2002 (middle): Used with permission from Microsoft; 1993, 1995 (top), 2008: Courtesy Intel; 1991: Paul Sakuma/AP Images; 1999: www.blogger. com; 2000: Courtesy Rhapsody International; 2002 (top): The Amazon.com logo is a registered trademark of Amazon.com, Inc. or its affiliates; 2004: Google and the Google logo are registered trademarks of Google Inc., used with permission; 2005: Wi-Fi Alliance; 2006 (top): Myspace LLC; 2006 (bottom): YouTube and the YouTube logo are registered trademarks of Google Inc., used with permission; 2007: Shaun Curry/AFP/ Getty Images; 2009: © 2013 Vodafone Group; 2010: Daniel Acker/Bloomberg via Getty Images; 2011: The "Android" name, the Android Robot logo, and other trademarks are property of Google Inc.; 2012: © 2013 Twitter, Inc.

copyright and digital rights
management, 241–242
defined, 241
electronic monitoring, 198
filtering and monitoring, 35
image editing, 71
overseas factories, working conditions,
114
plagiarism, 242
virus protection scams, 101
webcam, 146
working conditions, 114
Evolution of the computer age, 252–262
age of connectivity, 258–262
integrated circuit age, 255
microprocessor age, 256–257
overview, 252
transistor age, 254
vacuum tube age, 253
Excel, 65
Expansion bus, 123
Expansion slots and cards, 121–122
ExpressCard, 122
External hard disk, 174
External serial advanced technology
attachment (eSATA), 124
Extranet, 211
Eyestrain, 157

f

Face recognition apps, 236
Facebook, 40, 260
Facebook Chat, 39
Facebook groups, 40
Facebook mobile app, 74
Facebook Pages, 40
Facebook privacy settings, 40
Facebook Profile, 40
Fake hotspot, 208
Family Educational Rights and Privacy Act
(FERPA), 231
FastAccess face recognition, 236
Favorites Bar, 32
FERPA, 231
Fiber-optic cable, 198–199
Fiber-optic service (FiOS), 201
Field, 69
File, 90, 91
File compression program, 95, 175
File decompression, 175
File encryption, 237
File History, 98
File recovery software, 175
File server, 184
File transfer protocol (FTP), 35
Filter, 34–35
findlaw.com, 44
Fingerprint scanner, 236
FiOS, 201
Firefox, 32
Firewall, 208, 212, 236
FireWire bus, 123
FireWire port, 123, 124
First-generation mobile telecommunications
(1G), 202
First-party cookie, 228
Flash, 72
Flash drive, 179
Flash memory, 121
Flash memory card, 179
Flash Player, 34
Flat-panel monitor, 148
Flatbed scanner, 144

Flickr Creative Commons, 71
Flora Photographs, 71
Flyer, 63
Folder, 90, 91
Font, 62, 63
Font size, 62, 63
Footer, 64
Footnote, 64
Foreground, 90
Form, 69
Formula, 65
FORTRAN, 253
Fourth-generation mobile
telecommunications (4G), 202
Fragmentation, 100
Freedom of Information Act, 227
Friend, 39
FTP, 35
Function, 65
Function keys, 141
Future technologies
anonymity, end of, 244
augmented reality displays, 160
brain implant, 129
car dashboard, 49
next-generation storage, 185
self-healing computer, 104
telepresence, 214
user interface, 78

g

Galaxy Tab, 149
Galleries, 62
Game controller, 142–143
Gamepad, 143
Gates, Bill, 257
GB, 120
Gbps, 200
GE Global Research, 185
General-purpose applications, 62–68
database management system, 67
presentation graphics, 67
spreadsheet, 65–66
word processor, 62–64
Gesture control, 91
Gigabyte (GB), 120
GIMP, 70
Global positioning system (GPS), 199
Gloves, 157
Gmail, 38, 260
Google, 43
Google+, 40–41
Google Chrome, 32
Google Cloud Print, 153
Google Docs, 62, 76, 77
Google Drive Apps, 47
Google Drive Docs, 180
Google Now, 75
Google Play, 74, 75
Google Plus, 40–41
Google search engine, 259
Google Street View, 226
Google Talk, 39
Google Translate, 147
.gov, 33
GPS, 199
GPU, 119
Gramm-Leach-Bliley Act, 231
Grammar checker, 63
Graphic artists, 68
Graphical site map, 72
Graphical user interface (GUI), 60, 61
Graphics, 68–71

Graphics card, 121
Graphics coprocessor, 119
Graphics processing unit (GPU), 119
Grayscale, 151
Group, 61
Guest operating system, 95
GUI, 60, 61

h

Hacker, 231
HAMR, 185
Handheld computer, 12, 116
Handheld wand reader, 145
Handwriting recognition software, 143
Hangout, 41
Hard copy, 151
Hard disk, 173–175
HD 720, 148
HD 1080, 148
HDMI port, 124
HDTV, 149
Head crash, 174
Headache, 157
Header, 64
Headgear, 157
Headset, 153
Health Insurance Portability and
Accountability Act (HIPAA), 231
Heat-assisted magnetic recording
(HAMR), 185
Help, 91
Hex, 127
Hexadecimal system, 127
hi def, 177
Hierarchical network, 210
High definition multimedia interface
(HDMI) port, 124
High-definition television (HDTV), 149
High-speed Internet wireless technology, 197
HIPAA, 231
Historical overview. *See* Evolution of the
computer age
History file, 228
historynet.com, 44
Hits, 43
Hoff, Ted, 256
Holography, 214
Home network, 207
Hopper, Grace, 253
Host, 206
Host operating system, 95
Hotmail, 38
Hotspot, 208
HTML, 33
HTML coding, 73
HTML editor, 72
http, 204, 238
https, 204, 238
Hulu Plus, 30
Hyper-V, 95
Hyperlink, 33
Hypertext Markup Language (HTML), 33
Hypertext transfer protocol (http), 204, 238
Hypertext transfer protocol secure (https),
204, 238

i

i7, 119
IBM PC, 257
IBM's Watson, 262
Icon, 60, 90

Identity theft, 234
IDS, 212
Illusion of anonymity, 228
Illustration program, 70
IM, 39
Image capturing devices, 146
Image editors, 70
Image galleries, 70–71
Immersive experience, 157
iMovie, 91
Incremental backup, 238
InDesign, 68
Information broker, 225
Information reseller, 225
Infrared, 200
Inkjet printer, 151, 152
Inkscape, 70
InPrivate Browsing, 229
Input, 140
Input devices. *See also* Output devices
    audio-input devices, 146–147
    defined, 140
    image capturing devices, 146
    keyboard entry, 140–141
    pointing devices, 142–143
    scanning devices, 144–145
Instagram app, 74
Instant messaging (IM), 39
Intego Personal Antispam, 38
Integrated circuit, 117
Integrated circuit age (1964–1969), 255
Intel 486, 257
Intelsat, 199
Interactive whiteboard, 149
Internal hard disk, 174
International Telecommunications Satellite
    Consortium, 199
Internet, 15–16
    anonymity, 244
    browsers, 32–33
    communication, 37–42
    e-commerce, 44–46
    historical overview, 28
    privacy concerns, 227–230
    providers, 32
    search tools, 43–44
    uses, 29
    web utilities, 34–36
Internet 2, 260
Internet access, 32–33
Internet communication. *See* Electronic
    communication
Internet Explorer, 32
Internet Explorer 4.0, 259
Internet protocol address (IP address), 204
Internet scams, 234
Internet security suite, 36
Internet service provider (ISP), 32
Internet technologies, 211
Internet telephone, 154
Internet telephony, 154
Intranet, 211
Intrusion detection system (IDS), 212
Intuit QuickBooks, 72
iOS, 92, 265
IP address, 204
iPad, 149, 261, 263
iPhone, 261
iPhone OS, 92
Iris scanner, 236
ISP, 32
iStockphoto, 71
IT security analyst, 243
iTunes, 260
iTunes Music Store, 242

j

Jacquard, Joseph Marie, 252
JavaScript, 33
Jobs, Steve, 256
Joystick, 143

k

Keyboard, 140–141
Keyboard shortcuts, 32
Keystroke logger, 230
Kindle, 148
Kinect, 78

l

LAN, 206–207
Land, 176
Language translator, 88
Laptop computer, 11–12, 114–115
    buyer's guide, 263, 264–265
    ergonomics, 159
    system unit components (figure), 116
Laptop keyboard, 141
Large databases, 225–226
Large-scale integration (LSI), 256
Laser printer, 152
LCD, 148
LED, 148
Light-emitting diode (LED), 148
Link, 33
LinkedIn, 41
Linux, 91, 94
Liquid crystal display (LCD), 148
Local area network (LAN), 206–207
Logical operations, 118
Long Term Evolution (LTE), 199
Low bandwidth, 202
LSI, 256
LTE, 199

m

Mac OS, 93–94
Mac OS X, 260
Mac OS X Mavericks, 94
Macintosh Computer, 257
Magnetic card reader, 144
Magnetic-ink character recognition
    (MICR), 145
Mail, 38
Mainboard, 117
Mainframe computer, 11
Making IT work for you
    cloud-based backup, 239–240
    cloud storage, 181–182
    e-book, 150
    free antivirus program, 10
    Google Docs, 77
    mobile Internet, 203
    online entertainment, 30–31
    Skype, 155–156
    TV tuner, 125
    Windows Task Manager, 96–97
Malicious programs, 232–233
Malware, 232
MAN, 208
Mass storage, 183
Mass storage devices, 183–184
Mauchly, John W., 253
Mavericks, 94

MaxiCode, 145
MB, 120
Mbps, 200
McAfee security suite, 36
mDP, 124
Media, 173
Media Player, 34
Medium band, 202
Megabits per second (Mbps), 200
Megabyte (MB), 120
Memory, 120–121
Memory capacity, 120
Menu, 60, 91
Menu bar, 60, 61
Mesh network, 210
Metallofullerenes, 185
Metropolitan area network (MAN), 208
MFD, 154
MICR, 145
Microblog, 42
Microphone, 146
Microprocessor, 118–119
Microprocessor age (1970–1990),
    256–257
Microprocessor chip, 119
Microsecond, 119
Microsoft Access, 68
Microsoft Excel, 65
Microsoft Expression Web, 72
Microsoft Internet Explorer, 32
Microsoft Office, 75
Microsoft Office Web Apps, 76
Microsoft PowerPoint, 67
Microsoft Project, 72
Microsoft Publisher, 68
Microsoft Security Essentials, 233
Microsoft Word, 62
Microwave, 199
Microwave dish, 199
MIDI port, 124
Midrange computer, 11
.mil, 33
Mini DisplayPort, 124
Mini notebook, 115
Mini tablet, 115
MiniDP, 124
Mistaken identity, 227
Mobile applications (apps), 74
Mobile browser, 33
Mobile device, 12, 116
Mobile hotspot device, 203
Mobile Internet, 203
Mobile operating system, 92
Mobile OS, 92
Modem, 200–201
Modulation, 200
Monitor, 147–149
Monitor features, 147–148
Monitor resolution, 147–148
Mosaic, 258
Motherboard, 117
Motion-sensing device, 143
Mountain Lion, 94
Mouse, 142
Mozilla Firefox, 32
MS-DOS, 257
MS Office clip art, 71
Multicore processor, 119
Multifunctional device (MFD), 154
Multitasking, 90
Multitouch screen, 142
Musical instrumental digital interface
    (MIDI) port, 124
MyFord Touch, 49
MySpace.com, 261

TIPS Index